Journal Gems

Journal Gems

✦

How to Keep a Daily Diary

Robert T. Uda, MBA, MS, BS^2

iUniverse, Inc.

New York Lincoln Shanghai

Journal Gems
How to Keep a Daily Diary

iUniverse books may be ordered through booksellers or by contacting:

iUniverse
2021 Pine Lake Road, Suite 100
Lincoln, NE 68512
www.iuniverse.com
1-800-Authors (1-800-288-4677)

ISBN-13: 978-0-595-37118-1 (pbk)
ISBN-13: 978-0-595-81518-0 (ebk)
ISBN-10: 0-595-37118-3 (pbk)
ISBN-10: 0-595-81518-9 (ebk)

Printed in the United States of America

I dedicate this book to all people of the world who write daily in their journals. They are the ones who think about those who follow them by leaving them with a personal history to read, enjoy, and remember.

Contents

Preface

Journal Gems is about keeping a daily diary or journal. I have been writing in my journal for over 30 years now and have prepared daily entries for 26 of those 30 years. Obviously, I possess a great passion for journaling. Indeed, I write a journal for fun, therapy, and profit. You can do likewise. Just start today and get going on a daily journal that will be a keepsake for your descendents.

All writings and opinions in this book are solely those of the author and not of any organization shown within the body of this book. Any errors would be my errors only. If you find errors, please bring them to my attention. I will correct them in subsequent editions of this book.

Robert T. Uda
San Marcos, California
bobuda@adelphia.net
September 2005

PART I

How to Prepare Your Journal or Diary

1

Journaling for Fun, Therapy, and Profit

We believe that journal writing is one of the great tools for listening to your heart.[1]

—Writing the Journal
Online Journal Writing Workshop

One thing I know for sure: *I am good at personal journaling.* How do I know that? Because it is one of my great passions, and I have been writing in my journal for over 30 years now. Furthermore, I have been writing daily in it for over 26 of those 30 years. Obviously, I possess a firm testimony of journal writing.

Thus far, I completed 32 journal volumes and have almost completed my 33rd volume. Each volume is about 200 pages in length. Hence, I have written over 6,500 journal pages. I will continue to do so until the day I die, which will be in about 37 years from now when I reach 100 years old. My dad lived until he was 89 years old, and my mom lived to 85 years old. Hence, it is possible and highly probable that I will make 100 years of age. By that time, I should have completed about 75 volumes. I plan to donate those volumes to the Church Family History Library of the Church of Jesus Christ of Latter-day Saints for safekeeping and preservation. That will be my legacy to my posterity who will be able to use it for research purposes.

---

1. Crow Communications Company of Phoenix, Arizona, quote extracted from http://www.writingthejournal.com/.

Janet Peterson said, "*President Spencer W. Kimball has urged all members of the Church to keep a personal journal. He himself has rows of journal notebooks on his bookshelf, journals that he has kept for most of his life. When called in 1973 to be president of the Church, he had filled 33 black binders.*"[2]

Dean C. Jessee wrote, "*Although a man of the land, without formal education, Wilford Woodruff nevertheless became one of the premier record keepers of the 19th Century. For him, record keeping was more than a casual activity; it was a religious service.... He not only kept a diary and collected family records but also carried on an extensive correspondence....At the heart of the Woodruff literary legacy is his daily journal....President Wilford Woodruff's day books and journals, comprising 31 handwritten volumes, cover almost the entire span of the Church's 19th Century history.*"[3]

Of all of the people I know, Ray and Elizabeth DeSpain are the most thorough, meticulous statistics keepers. When they reported on their missionary service in Canada to the stake high council upon their return, they read off the statistics of the people they visited, baptisms they participated in, meetings they attended, and on and on went the statistics of their mission. I was highly impressed.

That brought back memories to me. I remember when I had served the first time as bishop (of a traditional family ward), I too kept detailed, meticulous statistics of the various actions as shown in the table below.

Note the 22 different categories of actions for which I had kept statistics. I do want to point out, however, that I was human in that I did not have the statistics included for 1994. During that year, I was extremely busy seeking work (Rockwell International Corporation had laid me off), starting a new company (Bob Uda and Associates), working on proposal consulting gigs, and simultaneously serving as bishop. I maintained the statistics but never got around to transferring the data to my matrix at the end of 1994. After my released as bishop in February 1995, I lost the data sheets containing my 1994 data Hence, I have this six-year matrix with the sixth year of statistics missing. Naughty me.

---

2.   Janet Peterson, "Your Own Journal," *Friend*, January 1982, page 20.
3.   Dean C. Jessee, "Wilford Woodruff: A Man of Record," *Ensign*, July 1993, page 28.

Assuming I conservatively had over 500 actions during 1994 (the annual totals ranged from 642 to 751, so over 500 actions would be very conservative indeed), then the overall total for the six years of service as bishop would have come to over 4,000 actions. As bishop of a young single adult (YSA) ward, I currently do not perform half as many actions per year as I did while serving over a traditional family ward.

Total Actions Performed By Bishop Uda Each Year

Seq.	Actions	1989	1990	1991	1992	1993	1994	Tot.
1	Admins/Blessings Performed	40	23	26	20	28		137
2	All Baptisms Conducted/Attended	26	14	11	11	8		70
3	Baptism Interviews (8-yr-olds)	12	7	7	8	2		36
4	Calls Extended	59	32	34	71	31		227
5	Counseling Sessions Held	61	64	52	69	67		313
6	Homes Visited	14	14	40	42	7		117
7	Hospital Visits	68	46	97	59	67		337
8	Patriarchal Blessing Recom. Interv.	18	7	2	11	6		44
9	Personal Priesthood Interviews	147	104	59	122	117		549
10	Priesthood Advancement Interviews	30	22	18	17	31		118
11	Settings Apart Performed	34	52	78	71	108		343
12	Ordinations Performed/Assisted	15	15	20	14	26		90
13	Social/Employment Svcs Referrals	9	10	8	6	17		50
14	Temple Rec. Intviews (Incl. Youth)	101	112	68	112	77		470
15	Temple Sealings/Marriages Attend.	4	2	1	3	1		11
16	Civil Marriages Performed	1	1	0	0	2		4
17	Funerals Performed/Attended	1	2	1	3	4		11
18	Temple Endowments Attended	3	8	3	2	4		20
19	Tithing Settlement Interviews	55	57	62	48	47		269
20	Mission Interviews	5	8	3	3	5		24
21	Youth Annual/SA Interviews	48	38	51	55	50		242
22	Weddings/Receptions Attended	0	4	1	3	4		12
	TOTAL ACTIONS PERFORMED	751	642	642	750	709		3494

Journaling Defined

So, what is *journaling*? Journaling is the act of writing daily entries in a journal book (with either lined or blank pages) as a history to be read, studied, and cherished by the journalist's children, grandchildren, and posterity or descendents of all future generations.

President Spencer W. Kimball said, "*Your journal is your autobiography, so it should be kept carefully. You are unique, and there may be incidents in your experience that are more noble and praiseworthy in their way than those recorded in any other life. There may be a flash of illumination here and a story of faithfulness there; you should truthfully record your real self and not what other people may see in you.*"[4]

Uda Family History

Eric Coplen, Ashley Anderson, and Colin Anderson, did you know you were part of the Uda Family history? In my Monday, June 27, 2005, entry of my personal journal, I wrote the following: "*In the evening, I attended the joint ward Family Home Evening (FHE) with the Mount Woodson Ward. Eric Coplen did a super job giving the lesson. Ashley Anderson did a great job with the refreshments. I served milk. Colin Anderson is doing an excellent job as the FHE Council chair.*"

Eric, Ashley, and Colin, will you remember this event 5 years, 10 years, or 20 years from now? I will! Why? Because I wrote about it in my journal. So, do you see the importance of writing it down, documenting it, and saving it for your posterity? I have a firm testimony of journaling.

Who knows? A 100 years from now, 500 years from now, or a 1,000 years from now, these (holding up one of my small journal volumes) may be known as the Small Plates of Uda, and these (holding up one of my large journal volumes) may be known as the Large Plates of Uda!

In the 1977 October General Conference, President Spencer W. Kimball said, "*A word about personal journals and records: We urge every person in the Church to keep a diary or a journal from youth up, all through his life.*"[5]

---

4.   Spencer W. Kimball, "The Angels May Quote from It," *New Era*, February 2003, page 32.
5.   Spencer W. Kimball, "The Foundations of Righteousness," *Ensign*, Nov. 1977, page 4.

Benefits of Keeping a Journal

Doreene Clement in her *The 5-Year Journal* tool, says that some benefits of keeping a journal include the following:

- Reduces stress
- Sets goals
- Organizes
- Helps focus
- Improves well-being
- Makes time for you
- Creates a personal reminder
- Can be used for business or personal
- Becomes a treasured keepsake[6]

For me, the benefits of keeping a journal include the following:

- **Stress Reduction**–Relaxes me before going to bed and before reading a chapter of my scriptures and saying a nightly prayer
- **A Record**–Keeps a record of the day's events and some thoughts on whatever was discussed
- **Accomplishment**–Gives me a feeling of accomplishment as I complete my 33rd volume of my journal in 30 years
- **Keepsake**–Provides a keepsake for my future generations of descendents
- **Book Matter**–Provides me with the materials for books that I want to write starting with this one
- **Source of Facts**–Helps people when they call and ask me for their baptism date or other such important date that they cannot remember

---

6. Doreene Clement, *The 5-Year Journal*, http://www.the5yearjournal.com/index2.html.

- **Talks**–Helps me in preparing and giving my "Journal Talk" in church that has become something people remember and bring up to me from time to time as a memorable talk

So, start your journal today. It is a great pastime. It is a great hobby. It is fun. It is a duty and responsibility we have to our posterity. Don't put it off. Start today. Do it now!

Record Keeper

I admit it. I am a severe, obsessive, compulsive record keeper. I prefer to call it a passion. Further, I prefer writing to talking. Hence, I document everything. For example, I document facts, figures, and everything else in the following kinds of documents:

- **Journals** of work, church, and life happenings
- **Journal of creative and innovative ideas** that come to me in inspirations, dreams, brainstorms, and "light bulb moments"
- **Steno pads** of daily entries at work of meetings attended, action items accomplished, important discussions held, and major decisions made
- **Bound notebooks** of sketches, notes taken at meetings, discussions held, and telephone conversations
- **Calendars** of meetings, events, and other important occasions for both work and church activities
- **Photo albums** of photographs and certificates
- **Scrapbooks** of certificates, lists, business cards, old temple recommends, tickets, flyers, brochures, programs, and other important documents
- **Computer electronic files** of everything I write including emails
- **White papers** on topics of interest and answers to questions from students in my classes
- **Newsletters** written for the family and my businesses

- **Books** that I have written and published as well as unpublished manuscripts of other books

As can be seen from this list, I am a real packrat of data, information, and documents that I have created. If it were not for an accident/fire and my wife, Karen, continually getting after me to throw out my junk (sometimes she does it herself; ouch!), I would still have every originally written page from my high school days until now.

When I throw anything out, I experience severe withdrawal symptoms and excruciating pain. Furthermore, it never fails that, whenever I throw anything out, within two weeks, I have a need for whatever I threw out. Go figure! That is Murphy's Law in operation. *Whatever you throw out is what you are going to need within two weeks.* Hence, this statement is a corollary to Murphy's Law.

I do not suggest that you be as weird, strange, fanatical, and crazy as I am regarding keeping all of your written information. However, you should maintain some level of reasonableness and sanity.

Personal Journal Examples

For edification, I included in Part II of this book some of the interesting things that appear in my personal journal. I call them "journal gems." Hence, we have the name of this book. Just to give you an idea of the kind of passages you can write in your journal, I present to you a passage I had written some time in the spring of 1976 (almost three decades ago!):

Prayer of Blessing on Daddy's Butt	Ca. Spring 1976	Tonight, our home teacher, Brother Joseph Rogers, came to visit. At the close of his visit, he asked if we wanted to have a prayer. Karen was not home at the time, so Brother Rogers had visited only Atom and me. Brother Rogers asked me, as the head of the household, to call upon someone to give the prayer. Therefore, I called upon Atom.
		He is so cute. In the middle of his prayer, he asked Heavenly Father to "bless daddy's butt." I had been suffering from an anal condition at the time and for weeks had been applying medication. I almost broke out laughing during the prayer, and Brother Rogers probably wondered what in the world to which Atom was referring.
		I explained the situation to Brother Rogers so that he did not go away confused about what Atom had said. When I explained it to Brother Rogers, he broke out laughing. Atom, of course, had innocently blessed my lower anatomy and not realizing that we ask for such blessings only in our private family prayers.
		Therefore, I had to counsel with him in the most tactful, fatherly, loving way that he should only bless daddy's butt in our private prayers, not when guests are with us. Atom took the counsel in the proper spirit, and we have not had to deal again with a similar situation. *Our young, innocent children provide these choice incidents for all of our posterity to remember and enjoy.*

Here is a passage I wrote on January 22, 1979:

Dump the Bowl Into the Toilet	22 Jun 1979	This morning, Atom woke up sick to his stomach. Karen said to him, "Go get a bowl to throw up into in case you have to vomit." Then, she told him to go back to bed.
		About 20 minutes later, Atom started vomiting in the bowl. Then, he went into the bathroom to finish vomiting into the toilet, and he set the bowl on the basin countertop.
		Then, Karen said to him, "Dump the bowl into the toilet." He asked, "This bowl?" Karen naturally responded, "Yes!" After which he proceeded to throw the whole bowl (vomit included) into the already vomit-filled toilet.
		Then, Karen and I started laughing. Moreover, Karen said, "No, Atom, I meant the contents of the bowl, not the whole bowl!"

Here is another passage I wrote on January 23, 1984:

Heavenly Father Bald?	23 Jan 1984	Today, Heather said that Heavenly Father was bald. My amazement of her saying that caused her to cry. She felt so bad that she had said that that she cried several times. I asked her how she knew that Heavenly Father was bald, and she said that she saw that he was bald when she was in Heaven before she came to earth. I told her not to feel bad about saying it, because, who knows?...He may really be bald. There's nothing wrong with being bald. Heather asked me not to tell mommy because she would get mad at her for saying that Heavenly Father was bald. I told Karen about it anyway when she got home from work. Karen told me to write it down in my journal, for it was quite funny that Heather had said that. In addition, she said that she is not upset at Heather for saying it.

Do you get the idea of the great stories you can relay to your posterity? These are true stories…things that actually happened with our kids. Some of the funniest things will occur with your children while they are young. Never fail to capture everything that they say or do that were hilarious at the time. I do believe that even your posterity will find them funny and memorable.

2

Journal Writing

A journal is a continued series of writings made by a person in response to their life experiences and events. Diaries contain a description of daily events. A journal may include those descriptions, but it also contains reflections on what took place and expresses emotions and understandings about them. It doesn't matter what you call your writing, either a diary or journal, as long as you see the distinction between these two ways of writing.[1]

—Annette Lamb and Larry Johnson

*A*lways write in your journal every night or morning. *Write the things which ye have seen and heard, save it be those which are forbidden.* (3 Nephi 27:23) Keep good notes in your journal of all of the great doctrine and principles you learn and the life stories you experience. You too, some day, could use these notes to write a book.

Daily Journal Writing

Write daily in your journal. Learn a life-long lesson on this statement: *The faintest ink is better than the strongest memory* (Anonymous). Writing things down can bring back nostalgic memories when you reread your writings years and decades from now.

So, are you writing in your journal on a daily basis? Do as Abraham did when he said, "*I shall endeavor to write some of these things upon this record, for the benefit of my posterity that shall come after me.*" (Abraham 1:31) I hope you will write in your journal diligently every day…without miss.

---

1. Annette Lamb and Larry Johnson, "Journal Writing," http://www.42explore.com/journl.htm.

Write the things which thou hast seen, and the things which are, and the things which shall be hereafter. (Revelation 1:19)

In 1980, President Spencer W. Kimball said, "*Those who keep a personal journal are more likely to keep the Lord in remembrance in their daily lives.*"[2]

Publish a Book

You could retype all of your letters, journal writings, talks, and lessons; merge them as separate parts of a book; print up a couple dozen copies; and hard bind them for future reference for your family, children, and posterity. It could become your first published book.

I save all of my writings for future books. I try to write every day to complete the 55 books I want to write and publish in the next 25 years.

If you teach as a profession, you must live by the academician's motto, i.e., "publish or perish." So, think now of all the books and publications you need to write in the years ahead. Also, learn about proper punctuation, spelling, grammar, diction, and syntax. They will come in handy in the future.

Falling Behind On Journal Writing

Falling behind on your journal writing is a minor problem that can be easily remedied. When I am too busy, too tired, and too sleepy, I write only one sentence in my entry for the day. For example, you could write the following daily entries whenever you are too busy, too tired, or don't have the time:

1. I am too tired tonight to write anything in my journal.

2. It was a good day today.

3. This was a day off, so I wrote five letters to family and friends.

4. We attended all of our Church meetings today.

5. We had dinner at the Joneses this evening.

---

2.   Spencer W. Kimball, "President Kimball Speaks Out on Personal Journals," *New Era*, December 1980, p. 27.

6. I had a job interview today.

Do you get the picture? When too busy or too tired, it takes no more than 30 seconds to write a one-liner entry in your journal. In this way, you maintain an unbroken string of entries in your journal throughout your life without feeling guilty about missed days. Can you understand the logic in doing this? You remain consistent, dedicated, and accomplished. Then, when you do have the time, you can catch up by writing several pages.

Your posterity will appreciate it. *And upon these I write the things of my soul, and many of the scriptures which are engraven upon the plates of brass. For my soul delighteth in the scriptures, and my heart pondereth them, and writeth them for the learning and the profit of my children.* (2 Nephi 4:15)

In February 1979, I began writing daily in my journal. There were times when I was either too tired or too busy to write. To meet my self-imposed daily requirement, I write one sentence and close my journal. That way, I am able to say that I have written daily in my journal for the past 26 years.

Record Keeping

Be an organized record keeper. If you maintain that throughout your life, you will have everything you possess at your fingertips and readily retrievable. It comes in handy when you prepare talks and speeches, when you develop lessons and presentations, when you study for examinations, when you write reports, and when you conduct research.

By not spending endless amounts of time searching for information and other things, you are able to perform tasks more quickly. It even contributes to your ability to manage and lead better, to remember more things, and to accomplish more.

Save all letters, photographs, and tapes you receive from friends and all copies of newsletters you prepare. Maintain statistics and good record-keeping practices. Make lists, prepare statistics, measure how well you are doing against your goals, write in your journal daily, keep logs, document everything, make and keep copies of every original document you write (e.g., letters, papers, reports, themes, theses, proposals, articles, and poems). *But they taught them that they should keep their record, and that they might write one to another.* (Mosiah 24:6)

I recently saw a video in a high priest group meeting about one of our early prophets (I think it was President Wilford Woodruff), who kept meticulous records. He even kept records of the number of bricks that went into building one of our church buildings. I was amazed. Many people have poked fun at my meticulous record keeping and statistics keeping. When I saw what this prophet had done, I said, "I felt vindicated." Everyone laughed. I figured that if it is good enough for one of our prophets of the Lord to do, then it is good enough for me to do. I have the last laugh.

Whatever you do, keep up what you are doing for the rest of your life. You will be glad you did. Your posterity will be glad you did. The Lord will be glad you did. The angels will rejoice. We receive many blessings by doing what the Lord wants us to do. He wants us to keep records, family histories, books of remembrance, journals, and scrapbooks. So, do it and maintain it all days of your life.

I saved or got family members to save every important personal document received or prepared. I constantly kept after everyone in the family to save their original writings, certificates, report cards, thank you letters and cards, letters of congratulations, awards, ribbons, diplomas, transcripts, tickets, and printed programs. All of these items go into their books of remembrance.

I know it is hard to think about things to write about because you do the same things every day. I do the same things every day also. For example, when I worked at Sterling Software in Northern California, I left for Northern California every Sunday evening. I worked every day for 12–16 hours. I returned to my apartment around midnight. I went to sleep. I rose every morning and took a shower, shaved, and dressed. Then I returned to work. On Friday evenings, I returned to Southern California. I wrote my missionary son a letter on Saturday and finished it on Sunday. On Sunday, we attended our Church meetings. Then on Sunday evening, I returned to Northern California.

As you can see, I did the same thing just about every day and every week. Hence, you are right. It's difficult to think about things to write about. I guess that is why I feel my letters to my missionary son were boring. It's the same old thing every day.

Ecclesiastes 1:9 goes as such: *The thing that hath been, it is that which shall be; and that which is done is that which shall be done: and there is no new thing under the sun.* History repeats itself. What goes before comes again. Nothing new either occurs or exists. Journal writing is no different.

I need a more exciting life. For example, I could get a job in Washington, DC, and be close to the political happenings in our nation's Capitol. I could get a job that requires me to travel all over the world. Then I would be able to learn about other countries, peoples, customs, monetary exchange rates, and languages. I could visit the Seven Wonders of the World. I like to dream a lot. It is said that great accomplishments start with wild dreams.

Getting Into the Habit of Writing

To be successful at journaling, you must get into some good journaling habits. Susan Romney gives the following ideas that helped her family to become a family of journal keepers:

- **Get Started**–give each family member a folder in a file drawer where they can keep their special items

- **Write Journal Entries**–get children started as soon as they can write

- **Measure the Cost**–use spiral-bound notebooks and loose-leaf binders instead of the more expensive bound journals

- **Develop a Habit**–make journal writing part of your bedtime routine along with scripture reading and family prayer

- **Give Encouragement**–whenever something of consequence occurs, comment on what a nice journal entry it will make. Reward consistency

- **Teach the Gospel**–teach the importance of record keeping in family home evenings

- **Use Your Entries**–refer to your journals to improve your life, measure progress on problems, and answer questions

Susan has found that the more extensive and detailed their entries, the more often they looked to their journals for temporal and spiritual guidance.[3]

---

3.   Susan Romney, "The Write Habit," *Ensign*, September 1998, page 71.

3

What Should Be Written

Your Journal is the repository of your experiences. It becomes a guide, a mirror…a confidant and friend. It is important to have a Journal that is a statement of who you are.[1]

—Gerry Starnes

What should you write about in your journal? Just about anything and everything. Write about what was, what is, and what is to come. Write about the past. Write about the present. Write about the future. Write your personal history. Write about what happened yesterday and today. Write about your goals for the future. Write about your aspirations. Make predictions. Write about your feelings, biases, prejudices, likes, dislikes, perceptions, challenges, shortcomings, problems, sadness, illnesses, accidents, deaths, marriages, births, divorces, miracles, and aches and pains. You name it. You can write about anything and everything.

Whatever you write, someone in the future may be interested in what you have written. No matter how boring you may feel what you have written is, someone in the future (your children, relatives, and posterity decades and even centuries down the line) will be fascinated about your times in the 20th and 21st Centuries.

---

1.   Gerry Starnes has more than 30 years' experience in Journal writing. He holds a master's degree in education, psychology, and special education. He is the founder and CEO of The Life Dance Institute, Inc. This quote was taken from his website at http://www.journal-writing.com/. You may contact Gerry directly by email at g. starnes@journal-writing.com.

Hence, every new year's eve, write your new year's resolution for the coming year. Write about how much a gallon of gasoline costs from time to time. Write about the cost of your haircut from year to year. Write about the cost of a gallon of milk, pound of butter, head of lettuce, and a loaf of bread. Write about the cost of your new home and the increase in equity it experiences from year to year. As the prices of these items change throughout the years, your posterity will be amazed to see how much inflation has affected our lives.

Write about the movies you have seen and about the tourist sites you have visited. Write about political elections. Write about the schools you've attended and friends you've made. Write about your children's funny sayings. Write about the accidents you've experienced. In California, I can write about the earthquakes we have survived, traffic congestion, wildfires, mudslides, smog, and committed crimes.

I remember writing about Shuttle launches, the Watts riots, OJ Simpson, Rodney King, and the meetings I've attended. I wrote about the classes attended and degrees received. I wrote about service projects, church service, and work experiences including my lousy bosses. I also wrote about births, deaths, funerals, marriages, and other such events.

So, as you can see, you can certainly write about anything and everything. Write your goals, aspirations, and accomplishments. Write about your thoughts, dreams, feelings, trials, and tribulations. Even if you may think a subject or topic is boring, write about it anyway. Later on in life, you may find it interesting and nostalgic to reminisce about over what you went through a quarter century before.

President Spencer W. Kimball said, "*Get a notebook, my young folks, a journal that will last through all time, and maybe the angels may quote from it for eternity. Begin today and write in it your goings and comings, your deepest thoughts, your achievements and your failures, your associations and your triumphs, your impressions and your testimonies. Remember, the Savior chastised those who failed to record important events.*"[2]

---

2.   Spencer W. Kimball, "The Angels May Quote from It," *New Era*, October 1975, page 4.

Cautions

Here are some cautions, though. Try hard to refrain from writing the following kinds of things:

- Lies, falsehoods, and untruths
- Slanderous things about people
- Vulgarity, filthy language, and cuss words
- Explicit sexual behaviors, offensive sex acts, and torrid scenes (leave those things to the romance novelists)
- Purposeful violence, mayhem, and gore. Leave out the blood and guts
- Anything offensive, insulting, demeaning, threatening, and racist
- Very private or highly confidential or sensitive matters that should not be shared with others
- Government classified information

Keep your writing honest, uplifting, and truthful. Don't exaggerate the facts. Write what actually happened. Describe things in acceptable language. Do not "let it all hang out." But do describe, to the best of your ability, exactly what occurred. Write about your thoughts and feelings. Write about your opinions about things and issues. Let people know of what you are made.

Means of Storing Data/Information Used for Writing

Write from memory. If you write in your journal on a daily basis as I do, you would write about what occurred during the current or previous day. However, you may expand your writing by using previously written words or ideas obtained from various sources. For example, you can save all of your materials from the following sources:

- Applications prepared (employment, award, patent, security clearance, internships, etc.)

- Appraisals (performance) prepared and received
- Autobiography written
- Bios prepared
- Brochures, flyers, and handouts prepared
- Calendars marked
- Card catalog of notes accumulated
- Certificates received
- Complaints written/filed
- Computer folders of electronic files
- Course/class papers submitted
- Designs (creative) and inventions prepared
- Diaries written
- Documents/manuals prepared
- Dossier prepared
- Emails and replies written
- Essays written
- Eulogies written
- Family history/genealogical information
- Files (manila folders in file boxes, file cabinets, and credenzas) of saved hard copy information
- Goals/resolutions prepared
- Graphic artwork (tables, graphs, charts, flows, matrices, scenarios, etc.) prepared
- Ideas journal/notebook
- Instructions prepared
- Journal/magazine articles written

- Journal volumes completed
- Lessons learned written
- Lessons (Church, Sunday school, classes, etc.) prepared
- Letters (recommendation, nomination, introduction, and reference) prepared
- Letters to the Editor written
- Letters/correspondence written and received
- Lists (action items, achievements, awards, "to do," SWOT, accomplishments, etc.) prepared
- Manuscripts of books written
- Master's thesis prepared
- Minutes of meetings prepared
- News articles written
- News clippings
- Newsletters prepared
- Notebooks full of notes taken at meetings
- Papers prepared
- Patent applications prepared
- Personal history written
- Photo albums prepared
- Plans (business, annual, strategic, sales, marketing, test, etc.) prepared
- Poems/poetry written
- Policies and procedures written
- Presentations (PowerPoint) prepared
- Press/news releases prepared
- Proposals written

- Reports (assessment, trip, project, research, annual, historical, test & evaluation, etc.) written
- Resumes prepared
- Scrapbooks prepared
- Scripts written
- Self-evaluations prepared
- Speeches/talks prepared
- Steno notepads of things accomplished during the day
- Themes written
- White papers prepared

Face it; I am a packrat. I keep everything that I originally write. I save all of the certificates, letters, and other documents I receive. Because of these saved documents, I find it easy to prepare other written materials, applications, articles, books, and anything else for that matter. That is how I have written eight books thus far in 2–1/2 years with two more in the mill. You too can do likewise.

What Kind of Journals to Use

Thus far, I have used only the lined, book-bound journals. I have used five of the smaller-size journals (6"x8" and 6.5"x8") and 28 of the large-size journals (8.5"x11"). The small and large size journal books have come in handy when I give my "Journal Talk" and talk about the small plates of Uda and the large plates of Uda.

4

Where Should You Write

Good descriptive writing depends heavily on observing and recollecting vivid moments. As you observe an event, jot down everything that you observed. Push yourself to remember as many details as you can. It may help to close your eyes and bring yourself back to that earlier moment.[1]

—Virginia Hamilton

Where should you write in your journal? Any place, any time, anywhere. Write in your journal at your desk, while in bed just before turning in, or at the dinner table. It does not matter so much as to where you write in your journal, but it does matter that you do capture all of the important things that fleetingly come to mind at any day, time, or place.

Business Trip

When you are on a business trip or on vacation, pack your journal in your suitcase or your briefcase so you will maintain a continuously unbroken string of writings. Should you ever forget to pack your journal, write your daily passages on sheets of paper. When you arrive home, you can either transcribe the writing to your journal or, easier still, just glue, paste, or tape in the sheets of paper onto the appropriate journal pages.

1.　"Descriptive Writing with Virginia Hamilton" was written in 2001. Scholastic regrets to inform users that Ms. Hamilton died on February 19, 2002. This quote was extracted from her website at the following URL: http://teacher.scholastic.com/writewit/diary/.

Quiet Place

It is always best to write in a quiet, private place like your den (if you have one). However, you can write in hotel rooms (when away on trips), while flying on an airplane, while a passenger in a motor vehicle or train, while on a sea cruise, or when you rest on the side of a mountain if you are on an overnight hike or campout. You can also write in your tent, sitting in your parked car, or at a picnic table at a rest stop.

Janet Brigham said, "*I began setting aside time to write. I wrote in the same place—sitting on the sofa, by the lamp.*"[2] Find a place that suits you...anywhere...just so you sit down and write in your journal.

Keep Your Pages Dry–Like Keeping Your Powder Dry

You can write at a table on your patio, while sitting on your living room sofa, or while sitting on the throne in your bathroom. However, don't ever write while you are taking a shower, walking in the rain, or swimming in your backyard pool. Those are no-no places to write. You want to be sure that you don't get your journal pages wet!

Where to Store Your Journals

I keep the journal I am working on next to my nightstand to have it available when I need it every night when I write in it. I store my completed journals on a bookshelf in my den. Make sure your journals are in a location that is free from water or rain. Keeping your journals dry will keep it in good condition for a much longer time than otherwise.

---

2.   Janet Brigham, "A Notebook by Any Other Name," *Tambuli*, April 1981, page 33.

5

Who Should Write and Who Should Be Written About

Daily or weekly journal entries become a diary of our lives. A written record of who we are, what we have done, our hopes, dreams, and a time capsule for moments in the past. A sense of accomplishment, not of a single day, but of an entire life can be seen in the pages of such a journal.[1]

—Echoing Whispers
Journal Writing Resources

Who should write in a journal? You, me, and everyone else should write in our own personal journal. Writing a journal should be a chronological, daily history of your life. Set the example for the rest of your family members by writing in a journal every day of your life. Let them see you writing in your journal. Once you get into the habit of doing it daily, it becomes easier to do with passing time.

If you are hospitalized, ill, or somewhat temporarily disabled, your spouse should write in your journal for you until you can return to writing. It usually is only for a few days or weeks at most. It is very important that your spouse write about your condition, pain, recovery, and your attitudes during your incapacitation and recuperation periods.

1.　This quote was extracted on 7/27/05 from the Journal Writing Resources website located at <u>http://journal-writing.webdjinni.net/</u>.

Whom Should You Write About

Whom should you write about in your journal? Everybody and everything. Write about yourself. Write about your spouse. Write about your children. Write about your parents. Write about your siblings. Write about your neighbors. Write about your extended family members. Write about your friends. Write about your boss and coworkers. Write about your dogs, cats, and other domestic animals. Write about your home, your job, your hobbies, your clubs, your church, your activities…everything.

Write about people, places, and things. Write about people you like, people you dislike, and people you don't even know. Write about places you live, work, and dine. Write about places you visit, places you want to visit, and in places in your imagination. Write about your inventions/patents, innovations, creations, and discoveries. Write about your parties, vacations, and other happenings. Write about Saddam Hussein, Osama bin Laden, and George W. Bush. Write about the Democrats and Republicans and about liberals and conservatives.

Who Should Have Access to Your Journals

Only close family members (spouse and children) should have access to your journals. When I donate my journals to the Church Family History Library, then everyone will have access to these journals. Of course, that will be after I kick the bucket. So, at that time, it will be okay for people to read about the many private things I have written in my journal. When I am dead, I will not be around to complain.

6

How Should You Write

Everyone has a story. Your experiences, your feelings, ideas, thoughts, and dreams all combine to form your life and your journey, which is your story. A great way to keep a relative reflection of all those things that have happened in your life is to keep a journal. A daily journal, a weekly journal, a month-end summary journal, any or all these are ways you can keep track and record your experiences, your story.[1]

—Doreene Clement

*H*ow should you write? Verrry carefully! Actually, write in any way you can or desire. You may write in the following ways:

1. In longhand on hard copy pages of a journal

2. Electronically on your desktop or laptop computer and saving the material on floppy disks or CDs

3. Recording your verbal journal on a tape recorder

No matter what medium you use, the most important thing is to get it down so that you can refer back to it in the future. Your children and your posterity will honor and praise you for doing it.

---

1. Doreene Clement, "Your Journal, Your Journey, Your Story," Doreene Clement is the creator of, *The 5 Year Journal*, a journal where you can journal your life in one book for 5 years. You can tour the book at the following URL: http://www.the5yearjournal.com. Contact Doreene by email at aboutjournaling@aol.com or call her at 480-423-8095. This quote was extracted from the Memoir Writers website located at the following URL: http://www.memoirwriters.com/.

Don't be so concerned with your spelling, punctuation, and grammar, but do be concerned with the content and with just getting it down in writing or recorded.

It is preferable to write in complete sentences. However, you can write in short phrases, lists, drawings, sketches, and in uninterrupted sentences and paragraphs. The main thing is to get it down on paper, disk, or recording medium.

Write to express, not to impress. Write from the heart. Write whatever comes to mind at the moment. Write things from which people can learn. Write in any way you can, with whatever medium you have available, and in any manner that grabs people's attention. Write poetry. Write songs. Write essays. Write anything and everything.

Write about things with a moral to them. Write messages to your future relatives and friends. Leave them something about which they can learn. Leave them your knowledge, genius, and wisdom. Write about things that benefits your posterity. Write your testimony to your descendents.

President Spencer W. Kimball said, *"Your journal should contain your true self rather than a picture of you when you are 'made up' for a public performance.... The truth should be told, but we should not emphasize the negative."*[2]

21 of the Best Journal Writing Techniques

In her e-book, *21 Ways to Write a Journal*, Tami Marple discusses 21 of the best journal writing techniques as follows:

1. Unsent letters

2. Conversations

3. Lists

4. Ask yourself a question

5. Grief

---

2.   Spencer W. Kimball, "The Angels May Quote from It," *New Era*, October 1975, page 5.

6. Topics and themes

7. Here and now

8. Best day, worst day

9. Pictures

10. Reality check

11. Dreams for yourself

12. Goals

13. Objectives

14. Before and after

15. Monitor and track

16. Stories

17. Memories

18. Fears

19. Mirror

20. See yourself

21. Writing happy[3]

Important Things About Daily Entries

The most important thing about daily entries is to date each entry. I go to the extreme by writing the day of the week, date, and time of writing. For example, this is how I start my daily entry:

Thursday, July 29, 2005, 9:50 PM

However, whenever I make an entry after midnight, I do not put down the time.

---

3. Tami Marple, "A-Woman's-Life" website, http://www.woman-living-single.com/journal3.htm.

The other things you should do are to:

- Number each of the pages of your journal. I place the number at the bottom center of each page

- Identify the title page of your journal with the following:

  - Your full name

  - The journal volume number

  - The date of the first entry on the first page of the volume and the date of the last entry on the last page of the volume

- Highlight with a Magic Marker those important passages (I call them gems) that you know you would use in a book should you write one

How to Get Started

Wendy Fisher of Canberra, Australia, said, "…*a seminary teacher in our branch challenged me to write in my journal every day for 20 days. She said if I did, it would become a habit. I decided to try it.…I received my 20-day challenge five years ago. I'm still writing in my journal every night. I get it out before I go to bed. I read my scriptures; then I write in my journal. Now it's automatic, and I plan to keep writing in it throughout my life.*"[4]

How to Write Things of Value to You and Future Readers

Jeffrey S. McClellan asks the question, "So how do you write a journal that will have value for people in the future as well as for you today? Here are some thoughts that may help:

- **Set a time to write**–Pick a regular time that works for you, and then do it.

- **Pick an audience**–Write as you talk; be casual. Don't worry about trying to impress anyone. Be yourself.

---

4. Wendy Fisher, "The 20-Day Challenge," *Liahona*, August 1995, page 8.

- **Write about you**–Here are some ideas to help you get started:
  - Describe people and places.
  - Talk about your feelings.
  - Try to see yourself from a distance.
  - Make lists.
  - Write letters in your journal.
  - Be a historian.
  - Include selected keepsakes.

7

When Should You Write

I occasionally receive e-mails asking for advice on how to start journal writing. The best advice I can give you is to just find a journal and pen that feel comfortable and start writing. Other than making sure that you date your entries, there are no rules to keeping a journal.[1]

—Carol Martzinek

When should you write in your journal? Any time, all the time, and whenever something significant occurs or is said. However, the best way to do it is at the same time of the day, i.e., either in the evening before you go to bed or in the morning when you rise. The main thing is this: We should get ourselves into the habit of writing daily in our journals.

President Spencer W. Kimball said, "*I promise you that if you will keep your journals and records, they will indeed be a source of great inspiration to your families, to your children, your grandchildren, and others, on through the generations…rich passages…will be quoted by your posterity.*"[2]

From the Mouth of Babes

"From the mouth of babes" comes some of the most profound and funny things ever said. Whenever your child or children say or ask something that is really funny, write it down immediately. If you don't do that, it will

---

1. Carol Martzinek, "How Do I Start Keeping a Journal?," extracted from URL http://www.suite101.com/article.cfm/journal_writing/53081, published on November 29, 2000.
2. Spencer W. Kimball, "President Kimball Speaks Out on Personal Journals," *New Era*, December 1980, page 26.

be a passing thing that is quickly forgotten and lost for your posterity to enjoy. So, I repeat, whenever your children say something funny, write it down immediately. What they have said decades before becomes great reading years from now.

Fleeting Inspirational Thoughts

Whenever you receive an inspiration, idea, or original thought. Write it down! Do it immediately. These great ideas and inspirational thoughts are fleeting. If you don't capture it in writing immediately, five minutes later you'll forget the ingenious thought or idea. All you'll remember is that you had this great idea, but you cannot remember exactly what it was! So, write it down as it comes up.

President Kimball said, "*Your story should be written now while it is fresh and while the true details are available.*"[3]

Capture the Moment

If you don't have your journal with you, write it on an envelope, napkin, or piece of scrap paper. You can then transcribe it later into your journal. Capture the moment by writing things down as they occur. That is the best way to document all of the wonderful ideas and inspirations that you are sure to have throughout your life.

Dreams

If you have an interesting dream, write it down immediately after you wake up. Dreams also are fleeting. Write down your dreams. The documented description could come in handy in the future. Even if your dreams are nightmares. Write them down too. You might be able to find a dream analyst to analyze your dream. Do you remember when Joseph had interpreted Pharaoh's dream? None of the magicians and wise men could interpret the dream. But Joseph did. He made a name for himself and was then favored of Pharaoh.

---

3.   Spencer W. Kimball, "The Angels May Quote from It," *New Era*, February 2003, page 32.

Write about the other kind of dreams. You know? The daydreaming type of dreams. Things you wish you had. Things you wish you were. Things you wish you did. Things you wish you could do. I dream about being a famous concert conductor of something like the Philadelphia Philharmonic Orchestra. Dream on, Bob!

24 Ways to Find Time for a Journal

Mary Lynn Hutchinson of Fairfax, Virginia, provides us with a list of 24 ways to find time for a journal. Here is an abbreviation of her list:

1. Keep a pen clipped to the cover of your journal.

2. Get up half an hour earlier than usual to spend 15 minutes studying the scriptures and 15 minutes writing in your journal.

3. Keep your journal under your pillow and take a few minutes before or after your evening prayer to record your daily thoughts.

4. Write while you wait in the dentist's office, launderette, or soccer practices.

5. Write while you commute by bus, train, [or carpool] to work.

6. Pack your journal in your lunchbox and write while you eat.

7. Write while the baby takes a nap.

8. After the children leave for school, take a few minutes to make an entry in your journal before you start your day's work.

9. Write while your children do their homework.

10. Set aside half an hour each Sunday for "family journal time."

11. Make "family journal time" a regular part of family home evening.

12. Arrange with your spouse to read to the children while you write or offer to play a game with them while your spouse writes.

13. Jot a few ideas or key phrases on the calendar daily or weekly to bring your journal up to date.

14. If you use a card filing system to help schedule your day, add a card with "Write in Journal" to your file.

15. Use a cassette tape recorder to keep an oral journal.

16. Use a word processor or home computer to keep your journal on disk and keep a back-up file on CDs or print out a hard copy.

17. Write while the bread rises, the soup simmers, or the cake bakes.

18. Keep copies of the letters you write to family and friends in a loose-leaf binder.

19. Turn off the television and write in your journal.

20. Keep a list of ideas inside the front cover of your journal for those days when you "really don't have anything to say."

21. Post a "Have you written in your journal yet today?" reminder on your refrigerator door and bathroom mirror.

22. Use the time you would otherwise spend in meal preparation and eating on Fast Sunday to write.

23. Begin writing your personal history.

24. Persevere as it takes about three weeks of daily effort to acquire a new habit.

You can make time to write, no matter how busy you are. If you try one of these suggestions and it doesn't work, try another. Above all, don't give up! Your posterity will thank you, and you will learn a great deal about yourself by writing about both your failures and your triumphs.[4]

---

4. Mary Lynn Hutchison, "24 Ways to Find Time for a Journal," *Ensign*, July 1986, pages 64–65.

8

Why Should You Write

So why write a journal anyway?

- *To become happier!*
- *Repeat your past successes!*
- *Create what you want to get out of life!*
- *Avoid future failures!*

—Tami Marple[1]
Also Known as Ms. Independent

Why should we write in a journal? In the 1977 October General Conference, President Spencer W. Kimball said, "*A word about personal journals and records: We urge every person in the Church to keep a diary or a journal from youth on up, all through his life.*"[2]

We should write in a journal to keep records. We should keep a record of important events of our lives. These journal records comprise part of our family history, which is a record for our future generations to read. We can refer back to our journal entries later for use in talks, lessons, or magazine articles. Ultimately, it will be for our children, grandchildren, and posterity or descendents to read and enjoy. Who knows. It could become scripture millenniums from now.

---

1. Tami Marple, "A-Woman's-Life" website, http://www.woman-living-single.com/journal3.htm.
2. Spencer W. Kimball, "The Foundations of Righteousness," *Ensign*, November 1977, page 4.

Purpose of Writing a Journal

Devin Durrant gives his purpose of why he writes a journal. It is a good purpose. Devin says, *"One purpose of my journal is that it serves as a blessing counter. As I write down my experiences, happy and sad, and my feelings about them, I am able to see better the blessings that each day brings."*[3]

Purpose of Keeping Good Records

The good thing about keeping good records is that they may be used for the following purposes:

1. **Reference.** To refer to them later to remember what was done, what was said, what decisions and commitments were made, things seen, and things heard.

2. **Legal.** To use as written proof when needed in court or other proceedings. Everything you write, date, and sign your name to is considered legal documents. If you do not place your signature on either a typed or a handwritten document, it serves better as evidence if it is in your handwriting rather than as a typed, unsigned document. This is because a handwriting analyst could verify your handwriting. On the other hand, a typed piece could have been typed by anybody. However, a trained writing expert could establish your writing style even when typed.

3. **Posterity.** For your children and other posterity to read and see what you did in your lifetime.

4. **Record.** To use as a journal and family history record. This may also be used to record both genealogical and book of remembrance items. Further...*and a book of remembrance was written before him for them that feared the Lord, and that thought upon his name.* (Malachi 3:16)

---

3.   Devin Durrant, "The Blessing Counter," *New Era*, November 1981, page 42.

5. **Events.** To record important events such as births, deaths, blessings, baptisms, callings, priesthood advancements and ordinations, graduations, marriages, and other significant life events.

6. **Proof.** To prove points to people whenever they deny saying that they had said something or deny writing something they had actually written. You have the written proof because you quoted them or documented what they said or wrote.

Value of Journal Writing

We may think that what we write may be boring. This fact may be so for most of what we write. However, there exists those few little "gems" that we, from time to time, write about that make it worth the effort. These gems are those little true stories that make interesting reading. Some interesting gems are shown in Part II of this book.

President Kimball said further, "*I promise you that if you will keep your journals and records, they will indeed be a source of great inspiration to your families, to your children, your grandchildren, and others, on through the generations.... Rich passages...will be quoted by your posterity.*"

Why Write a Journal?

By writing a journal, Tami Marple says that you will be better able to:

- Communicate with yourself and others
- Ask for what you want
- Retain clear thinking
- Articulate thoughts
- Express yourself clearly
- Express your feelings
- Translate your thoughts to paper
- Get your point across
- Become a better listener

- Increase your negotiation skills
- Offer constructive criticism
- Open your heart and mind
- Create and chase your dreams
- Become well-spoken[4]

There's Magic in Journal Writing

John and Patrice Robson said that journaling is one of the most powerful tools for self-growth. Simple but effective, journaling can help you:

1. Release pain, frustration, and negative emotions like anger and fear
2. Clear confusion and make good decisions more easily
3. Grasp valuable insights that clear blocks and move you forward
4. Spark your innate creativity
5. Uncover and nurture a bigger picture for your life
6. Reach new heights in self empowerment[5]

Important Reasons for Writing in a Journal

Janet Peterson gives four important reasons why young people should keep a journal. These are her reasons:

- The prophet has asked all of us to do so.
- By recording our feelings, thoughts, and events as they occur, you can have an accurate record of your youth to read later.

---

4. Tami Marple, "A-Woman's-Life" website, http://www.woman-living-single.com/journal3.htm.
5. John and Patrice Robson, Journaling Tools for Self Empowerment, Higher Awareness Inc., 111 Kulawy Drive North, Edmonton, AB, Canada T6L 6T9, Phone 780-462-2167 Mountain (GMT-7), Email: John Robson, http://www.journalingtools.com/.

- It helps us to understand ourselves.
- To record your spiritual growth.[6]

These are sound reasons for writing in a journal. Start today. Do it now!

Why Write It?

I remember when I had resigned my regular commission and exited the USAF in 1974, we moved from Southern California to Central Florida for a job on the Space Shuttle Ground Systems Design Contract with Planning Research Corporation at the Kennedy Space Center. The semi-tractor-trailer Mayflower moving van held the household goods of five families, and we were one of those families.

There was a brush fire in the middle of Texas. The smoke from the brush fire blew across and covered the freeway. As the moving van entered the smoke (apparently there was zero visibility), it became part of a massive 15-vehicle accident with one vehicle piling upon another as each entered the smoke. Unfortunately, the van caught fire and everything burned to ashes. We lost everything we had in the moving truck!

Fortunately, this was about a year before I started writing in a personal journal, so I didn't lose any journals. However, we lost all of our priceless photo albums, certificates, trophies/plaques, important papers, books, and other valuables. Our little family of three had driven across country in our little Honda Civic and didn't have much room to haul anything across country. We just had our luggage and a few of our belongings. We lost almost everything.

Brad Wilcox relates a similar but more interesting story. He relates, "When my in-laws were moving to Colorado, a tragic moving-van fire destroyed all their belongings, including family photograph albums and personal journals. One well-meaning friend lamented, 'All that work for nothing!'

"My wise mother-in-law responded: 'The process we went through writing our journals can never be burned. Every hour we spent on those books helped to make us the people we have become.'

---

6.   Janet Peterson, "Your Own Journal," *Friend*, January 1982, page 20.

"Like my mother-in-law, I have found my personal journal an ideal environment in which to 'become.' It is a perfect place for me to think, feel, discover, expand, remember, and dream. Let us look at each of those areas in more detail:

- **Think**–thoughts are created in the act of writing
- **Feel**–journal writing helps us find words for hard-to-express feelings
- **Expand**–writing such experiences make us become more aware of them in our lives
- **Remember**–writing down experiences help us remember them longer and with greater accuracy
- **Dream**–a journal is a protected place, an invitation to open up

"My personal journal is helping me become more like Jesus Christ and reach my highest potential. That is why I will continue to keep my journal–whether my grandchildren ever read it or not."[7]

Benefits of Journal Keeping

Gawain and Gayle J. Wells provide some good benefits of keeping a journal. These benefits include the following:

- The best way to keep our personal history current.
- A map of our past, present, and future.
- Can bring peace of mind and greater tolerance to present stresses.
- Also important…is the recording of both our failures and successes.
- To better understand ourselves and recognize the responsibility we must take for our actions.
- Become less worrisome and…less fearful….
- Our…own books of personal revelation.

---

7.   Brad Wilcox, "Why Write It?" *Ensign*, September 1999, page 56.

- Chronicle the milestones we pass....

- To record our feelings as we witness important periods...in our life-time.

- A much needed reference point...[to] see and evaluate how our lives are going, both temporally and spiritually.

- We are...a history-keeping people.[8]

---

8.   Gawain and Gayle J. Wells, "Hidden Benefits of Keeping a History," *Ensign*, July 1986, page 47.

PART II

Gold Nuggets and Pearls
from My Daily Journal
(1975–1984)

9

Funny Things

$\mathcal{S}$ome of the funniest things will occur in your lifetime. Whenever these incidents occur, write them down immediately. If you don't have your journal handy, write it down on any piece of paper you can find. You can transfer it to your journal later. If you don't capture the incident in writing, you will miss many laughs and funny times in the future. In this chapter, I show entries of some of the hilarious occurrences in our life thus far. Enjoy!

Absent-mindedness	31 Mar 1979	I went to work this Saturday morning about 10:00 A.M. and put in about 6–1/2 hours of work. Karen made me a sack lunch, but somehow it never got into the car. Off I went to Capistrano Test Site without my lunch.
Apricot, the Dog	24 Apr 1983	I got up at 5:00 A.M. to get ready to drive to Utah. I was about ready to leave at 6:20 A.M. when I found that I had stepped in Apricot's doodoo, which she made in Atom's room during the night. I went into Atom's room to kiss him goodbye; he was asleep. Of all the square footage of available floor space, I *had* to step in Apricot's dump. I could have missed it by an inch. However, no, it seems I always step in it when I'm in a rush to "hit the road." I was so mad. Hence, I finally left at 6:30 after Karen washed my left shoe and I changed my pants. Yes, I rubbed some of it from my shoe onto my pant leg when I was getting into the car. I even got some on the car's carpet, which I had to clean.
Atom the Angel	7 Mar 1982	I taught the…Blazer B class in Primary. There were four 11-year-old boys in the class. Atom was the only angel. I guess it was because his dad was the instructor.

Awful Wedded Wife	7 Jan 1984	Heather asked me today, "Daddy, do you take this woman (meaning mommy) to be your *awful* wedded wife?" I split a gut. I then asked her where she learned that. She said, "On TV." I told her to tell her mom what she said.
Baby Sitting	4 Dec 1983	We went home about 8:15 P.M. and found Atom and Marc sleeping, but Heather was still up. Thirteen-year-old Atom was supposed to be baby-sitting! Instead, it looks like four-year-old Heather was baby-sitting them!
Bad Day	1 Jun 1984	This was a bad day for me. First, I missed going over to the Stake Center at 6:00 A.M. to serve at the Seminary Breakfast. I slept right through the whole thing! Then, in the afternoon, I was supposed to have picked up Heather and Julie Riddle from pre-school at 2:30 P.M. Somehow, I got it in my mind that I was supposed to be there at 3:30 P.M. I got there at 3:20 thinking I was 10 minutes early. Instead, I was 50 minutes late! Boy, was Karen irate at me for being so irresponsible. As I said, it was a really bad day for me.
Barf	27 Aug 1980	Karen went to Linda Bradford's home to do some Primary work with her. I babysat the kids. While Karen was out, Marc got sick and vomited on the kitchen floor. Thank goodness he didn't barf on the carpet. It stunk so badly that Atom called Karen home. We absolutely could not survive without mommy. She's the only experienced one in the family when it comes to wiping up barf!
Bird Drop-pings	6 Oct 1980	Marc got some bird droppings in his hair today. Since this doesn't happen to anyone every day, I thought this event was significant enough to write about it in this journal.
Bicycle Accident	5 Oct 1983	Marc crashed his bicycle into the tile wall out front today and terribly scratched the side of his face. I told him that he wouldn't need a mask now for Halloween if he went dressed as Franken-stein. ☺
Burnt Pound Cake Wasn't Half-Bad!	18 Feb 1979	After we came home, Karen made us some minute steak sand-wiches. Later she made a pound cake, which burned after 40 minutes (It should have been in the oven for 60 minutes.) because the oven was not working right. So, after she took it out of the oven, she dug the good part out of the center of the burned mass and served it to us with butter and milk. It didn't taste half-bad!

Daddies Marry Mommies	24 Nov 1982	Today, at the breakfast table, Marc exclaimed, "I'm going to marry mommy!" Heather retorted, "I'm going to marry Atom." I expressed to them both that "you can't marry mommies or brothers and sisters!" Heather then exclaimed very profoundly, "Daddies marry mommies!" We all laughed! (input from Karen)
Death of Suzie, the Male Hamster	27 Jan 1979	Suzie, Atom's hamster, which he obtained about three years ago, died today. Suzie, a male hamster, got that female name because we initially thought it was a girl when we bought it from a pet shop while living in Titusville, Florida. We had a short burial service in our back yard with Karen giving a prayer. Atom and Karen cried. I dug a small hole in the area near our back yard tile wall. Suzie was put in a small cardboard box. We hope to get Atom another hamster soon. Atom called grandma Rowland to tell her about Suzie's passing.
Diarrhea Galore	7 Apr 1979	Marc had some really bad diarrhea today. Because Karen wasn't feeling up to it, I had to clean it up. Marc didn't make it to the toilet in time, so I ended up wiping it off the floor, his shoes, his legs and butt, his fingers, the bathroom rug, his underpants, trousers, etc. It was bad news! I then just put him in the bathtub, gave him a shower, and washed him clean.
Does Your Face Stink Too?	26 Jul 1983	Daddy was in the bathroom putting on some underarm deodorant. Heather comes in and asks, "Why are you putting that thing on?" Daddy says, "Because my underarm stinks." Then daddy starts putting on after-shave cologne on his face. Heather then asks, "Why are you putting that on? Does your face stink too?"
Dump the Bowl Into the Toilet	22 Jun 1979	This morning Atom woke up sick to his stomach. Karen said to him, "Go get a bowl to throw up into in case you have to vomit." Then she told him to go back to bed. About 20 minutes later, he started vomiting in the bowl. Then he went into the bathroom to finish vomiting into the toilet, and he set the bowl on the basin countertop. Then Karen said to him, "Dump the bowl into the toilet." Then he asked, "This bowl?" Karen naturally responded, "Yes!" After which he proceeded to throw the whole bowl (vomit included) into the already vomit-filled toilet. Then Karen and I started laughing. And Karen said, "No, Atom, I meant the contents of the bowl, not the whole bowl!"

Elder Swallows Marble	10 Oct 1982	After church, I took Elders Roper and Avgikos to their apartment. At 5:00 P.M., Marc and I went to pick up the two elders to bring them over to our home for dinner. We had an enjoyable time, especially when we found out that Elder Roper had accidentally swallowed a marble while playing around with it in his mouth. Karen gave him a couple of spoons full of Castrol to assist him in passing it, hopefully, in the next 24 hours. At 8:15 P.M., the three kids and I drove the elders back to their apartment.
Father's Day	14 Jun 1981	Karen had thought that today was Father's Day (it really is next Sunday) and had prepared a delicious *sukiyaki* dinner. I enjoyed it anyway, even if it was a week early.
Feeding the Missionaries and Then Some	9 Aug 1981	In the evening, we had Elders Pearce and Pine over for dinner. Karen cooked a delicious baked ham dinner with mashed potatoes, tossed salad, corn, sliced bread and butter, and lemonade. For dessert, we had ice cream. The three kids really enjoyed playing with the missionaries. While talking to the missionaries in the living room, we heard a loud thump in the kitchen. We didn't think much of it until Atom went into the kitchen and found that our dog, Princess, had jumped up and pulled the leftover leg of ham off the countertop and was devouring it on the kitchen floor! I had hopes of chopping up the leftover ham and cooking it with some Navy beans. Now, we won't be able to eat the delicious leftover ham. However, Princess sure had a great dinner tonight!
Game of Life	5 Oct 1980	In the evening, we played the game of "Life," which Marc won. I don't like this game too much because we always end up screaming and hollering at each other.
Haircut	7 Apr 1979	I gave Atom a haircut. I was doing really well until Karen started helping with the electric clippers. Her first contact with Atom's hair caused a big "rat bite." In trying to fix the rat bite, I had to cut Atom's hair rather close to his scalp in the back portions of his head. I was going to let Karen cut my hair also, but, after that, I thought I'd go see the barber next week instead.

Heavenly Father Bald?	23 Jan 1984	Today, Heather said that Heavenly Father was bald. My amazement of her saying that caused her to cry. She felt so bad that she had said that that she cried several times. I asked her how she knew that Heavenly Father was bald, and she said that she saw that he was bald when she was in Heaven before she came to earth. I told her not to feel bad about saying it, because, who knows?…He may really be bald. There's nothing wrong with being bald! Heather asked me not to tell mommy because she would get mad at her for saying that Heavenly Father was bald. I told Karen about it anyway when she got home from work. Karen told me to write it down in my journal, for it was quite funny that Heather had said that. And she said that she is not upset at Heather for saying it.
Icing the Cake	19 Aug 1979	After we came home from sacrament meeting, Karen had baked a cake, and so we let Atom and Marc spread on the chocolate icing. They did a fairly decent job, but with one exception. Marc and Atom were licking the knives with which they were spreading on the frosting, and they were licking the knife as they went along! How gross! At any rate, the cake still tasted pretty good as long as you didn't think too much about how the icing was put on.
Illness	29 Mar 1979	For lunch, I had a huge Pepper Burger. It was filled with chopped up green onions with an attendant large slice of raw round onion. *I ate the whole thing.* Unfortunately, onions do not agree with my stomach. I had diarrhea, stomachache, fever, headache, and overall bad feelings. It wiped me out for the rest of the day and night. I vomited whatever I could out of my mouth. The rest came out of the other end of me. I simply was miserable all night. It felt like I had a bad case of the flu.
Love	31 Jul 1983	While we were driving in the car, Marc said, "I used to have a girlfriend (Alisa Sutherland), but she grew too tall for me." It seems like love at that age is inversely proportional to growth rate!
Love Note	3 Feb 1982	Karen did a sweet thing today. She put a note in my sack lunch, which said, "Sweetheart, I love you because you are so special. You're very patient with me. Yours forever–Karen." That made my whole day. I was as happy as a flea on a dog's belly.

Marc's Talents	24 Aug 1982	Karen found out in a telephone call from Marc's teacher that he would be recognized for scholarship in school. Marc really loves school and is eager to learn. He does talk a lot in class, though. Obviously, he gets that talent from his mother. And he gets his desire to study and learn from his father.
My Son, the Idiot	26 Mar 1982	A funny thing happened at work today. Jim Sorbo had told me that someone in A&T (Assembly and Test) had spilled 25 HPUM (Hydraulic Power Unit Midsection) bottles down the ramp and scratched up, nicked, and damaged the $60,000 worth of accumulator bottles. While I was at Blaise Revay's office, I had mentioned to him aloud, "Some idiot had dropped 25 HPUM bottles down the loading ramp." By chance, Carol Frazier was sitting at her desk outside of Blaise Revay's door. She said to me, "Bob, that idiot you are referring to happens to be my son." Oh, was I embarrassed! I said that I was going to have to watch what I said because you'd never know who was related to whom at APCO. She took it good naturedly, and everyone around the immediate area had a good laugh. She said that she thought it would be best to tell me then, than for me to find out later that it was Dave Frazier, and then I would feel even more embarrassed after realizing that I had said what I did while standing next to her desk. Now I know how an idiot feels!

No Film In the Cam- era!	10 Aug 1979	All nine of us except Karen (because of her pregnant condition) went to Disneyland. Those that went included Betty Rowland, Richard Rausch, Winnie Rausch, Darcy Dick, Jessi Dick, Tracy Rausch, Atom Uda, Marc Uda, and me. It was an exhausting day for me, as Marc insisted that I carry him whenever he wasn't in the stroller.
		We experienced and enjoyed such rides and attractions as the Matterhorn, Pirates of the Caribbean, Haunted House, Country Bear Jamboree, It's a Small World, People Mover, Autopia, America the Beautiful, America Sings, and Peter Pan. We also saw the Disney Characters Parade. We had lunch there, the cost of which was exorbitantly atrocious.
		A funny thing that happened was Richard's taking of photo- graphs of a 36-shot roll of film only to find out later that there was no film in the camera! Boy was Winnie mad at him for this mistake.
		Grandma Rowland and I pooped out at about 6:00 P.M., so we left for home with Marc and Traci, while the other five people in our group stayed until about 10:00 P.M.
		Another funny thing that happened was Grandma Rowland failed to leave the car keys in Winnie's purse. And, so, she and Karen had to go back to Disneland to take them the keys.
Obscene Phone Call	2 Apr 1982	Marc received an obscene phone call this evening from a weirdo. Marc (at almost six years of age), of course, didn't know what an obscene phone call was. He came into my den to explain this strange caller. Marc said that this person was breathing as if he was doing push-ups.
		Even though it was a serious matter, it was difficult for me to keep a straight face and listen attentively. I explained to Marc what kind of call he got and how he should respond if he should get another such call. I had to chuckle to myself at the way he explained the matter to me. He is really a cute kid.
Oppor- tunity Cost	28 Dec 1979	I spent much of the day baby-sitting Heather while Karen painted the outside of the house. I'm glad she likes to do those things. Because, if I had to do the painting, I would hire a pro- fessional painter. My basic rationalization is *opportunity cost*. Karen calls it laziness.

Passing of Suzie I	4 Mar 1980	Our hamster, Suzie I, died. We buried it today. Atom was a little upset since it was his hamster. But what was really cute was after we dug the hole, we put the hamster in the ground, and I started to cover it up with dirt when Marc said, "Don't cover him up, he can't breathe; he'll die." I tried to explain to Marc *again* that he was already dead. He just looked very puzzled and said, "Oh." Then we covered him up, and Atom said a little prayer for her.
Pleasures of Raising Children	23 Aug 1980	Heather must really get relaxed when Karen is gone, and I am baby-sitting her. It seems that every time I am baby-sitting Heather, she dumps in her pants. She did that twice in the hour-and-a-half while Karen was gone. She could dump her pants before Karen leaves or immediately after she returns, but no! She always dumps when Karen is not here, and I have the distinct (or stink) pleasure of changing her whiffy diapers. Oh well, such is life! These are some of the pleasures of raising children.
Potty Training Applying Pavlov's Law	24 Aug 1981	Heather has been getting potty trained. She is doing very well going in our adult toilet. We had to put her baby portable toilet away because she didn't like using it. Every time she goes potty in the toilet, she gets some M&M candy, which helps in motivating her to always go in the toilet instead of in her pants.

Prayer of Blessing on Daddy's Butt	Ca. Spring 1976	Tonight, our home teacher, Brother Joseph Rogers, came to visit. At the close of his visit, he asked if we wanted to have a prayer. Karen wasn't home at the time, so Brother Rogers visited only Atom and me. Brother Rogers asked me, as the head of the household, to call upon someone to give the prayer. So, I called upon Atom. He is so cute. In the middle of his prayer, he asked Heavenly Father to bless daddy's butt. I had been suffering from an anal condition at the time and for weeks had been applying medication. I almost broke out laughing during the prayer, and Brother Rogers probably wondered what in the world to which Atom was referring. Needless to say, I found it necessary to explain the situation to Brother Rogers so that he didn't go away being confused about what Atom had said. When I explained it to Brother Rogers, he broke out laughing. Atom, of course, had innocently blessed my lower anatomy not realizing that such blessings should be only for our private family prayers. So, I had to counsel with him in the most tactful, fatherly, loving way that he should only bless daddy's butt in our private prayers, not when guests are with us. Atom took the counsel in the proper spirit, and we have not had to deal again with a similar situation. *Our young, innocent children provide these choice incidents for our posterity to remember and enjoy.*
Pronunciation	11 May 1984	Karen wrote down these funny pronunciations of our three kids during their childhood: *Atom*–"Di doo" = Thank you, "You wa doo" = You're welcome, "Tear" me = Carry me *Marc*–"Gecause" = Because, "Feeder Fadder" = Heavenly Father, "Hangerber" = Hamburger, "Header" = Heather *Heather*–"Fruck" = Truck, "Mazagine" = Magazine, "Hangerber" = Hamburger, "Aom" = Atom, "Scripers" = Scriptures, "Basketti" = Spaghetti
Sleepy Heads	5 Jan 1980	After a spaghetti dinner, we went to a drive-in movie at 6:30 P.M. in Fountain Valley. We saw a sequel to the "Poseidon Adventure" and "Star Trek." Atom and Marc slept through the second movie, Star Trek, which was the one we went to the drive-in to see!

Stinkers	9 Jan 1980	The beans I ate for dinner last night really reacted with my system such that I laid stinkers all day. I was so embarrassed when one of our secretaries walked into my office at two different occasions only 10 minutes apart immediately after I had let go of the stink gas.
Swimming Lessons	9 Jul 1979	Both Atom and Marc started their two weeks of swimming lessons today. Atom made it several times across the width of the pool. We are investing $7.00 for Atom and $8.00 for Marc for the two weeks of lessons. Marc was initially frightened to go into the water, but after he did go in with the cute instructor (this is according to Karen), he didn't even cry.
Swimming Lessons	11 Jul 1979	Marc seems to be coming along really fine and shortly should be swimming on his own, so says his swimming instructor, whom he really likes. Karen tells me she is a little cutie with long, blond hair and is really thin. Karen said she didn't know how Marc could tell when a girl is really cute. I told her that he is just a "chip off the old block." He knows how to pick 'em just like his old man does.
Tooth Fairy	23 Mar 1981	A funny thing happened. Atom lost a tooth yesterday and put his tooth under his pillow last night. However, the stupid tooth fairy forgot to switch the tooth with some money. So, tonight, the tooth fairy wised up and put a dollar under Atom's pillow.
Tooth Fairy	6 Dec 1982	Marc's first tooth came out today. He put it under his pillow for the tooth fairy. I think he will be getting a dollar for it.
Two Lunches	5 Mar 1982	I brought a sack lunch to work that Karen had prepared, but when lunchtime arrived, I forgot that I already had my lunch. So, I bought some lunch from the lunch wagon that comes to our plant every day. After I finished eating my purchased lunch, I saw my sack lunch sitting on my file cabinet. So, I had two lunches today, as I also ate the sack lunch.

10

Church and Gospel Things

*F*ace it. Our church is a huge part of our lives. In fact, it is a way of life for us. Every aspect of our lives either influences or is influenced by the church. Hence, I cannot write anything without including our activities in the church. Thus, this chapter includes all of the significant church and gospel things in our lives.

Administering to the Sick and Afflicted	13 Aug 1981	Scott Bucher got into a bicycle-car accident this evening. His home teacher, Brother Scott McClellan, and I went to the hospital to administer to him. Brother McClellan did the anointing, and I did the sealing of the anointing.
Administering to the Sick and Afflicted	18 Feb 1982	Late this evening, we found that Farrah Billimoria was in Holy Cross Hospital with a high fever and asthmatic condition. After talking with Billy Billimoria at about 11:30 P.M., I felt prompted to go to the hospital to give Farrah a blessing. I got there about midnight. By the time I got home, it was 1:00 A.M. I feel Farrah will be well tomorrow.
Administering to the Sick and Afflicted	24 Sep 1983	In the evening, Karen, Rich Nichols, and I went to Henry Mayo Hospital where Rich and I administered to Chris Wycoff. Sister Vivian Wycoff was there. Chris had her wisdom teeth removed today. While in the dentist's office, she stopped breathing because of the combination of anesthetics she was given. The paramedics rushed down there to revive her and then took her to Henry Mayo Hospital. Bro. Nichols anointed, and I blessed her. I felt that she would fully recover soon and blessed her to that effect. After we dropped off Bro. Nichols at his home, we went to Sav-On Drug to copy a letter.

Administering to the Sick and Afflicted	25 Sep 1983	Bishop McKeon and I drove to Henry Mayo Hospital to visit Chris Wycoff, who had complications last night after we had left her upon administering to her. She was okay when we saw her.
Administering to the Sick and Afflicted	25 Nov 1984	After a short period in the Stake Melchizedek Priesthood Committee meeting, I was informed that Sister Virginia Davis, a widowed sister that Atom and I home teach, had a stroke the night before, and that she was in Holy Cross Hospital. So, I took off for the hospital. I met Brother and Sister Wallace and Grandma Wallace there. After a 1–1/2-hour wait, because they had taken Sister Davis to a lower floor for X-rays, Brother Jim Wallace and I administered to Sister Davis. Jim anointed and I pronounced the blessing.
Baptism, Marc	3 Jun 1984	Atom and I got the primary room ready for Marc's baptism and filled the font. Marc's baptism was held from 6:00–6:30 PM. It was brief. Many people attended including our next-door neighbors (the Illeras and Moodys) and the Billimorias. Atom gave the talk, and Heather sang a solo. They both did excellently. I baptized Marc and later confirmed him a member of the Church. After the baptism, almost everyone came over to our house for refreshments. It was really great. This has been an exhausting weekend.
Bishop Monte McKeon	24 Mar 1984	In the evening, Karen and I attended the Ward Social, which was "An Evening to Honor Bishop Monte McKeon." It was a super evening, which ended in a roast of the Bishop. It was a lot of fun. Bishop McKeon was a great bishop of the Canyon Country Ward for 52 months. His wife, Kathy, has been a real fitting bishop's wife. We are going to miss them when they move to the Solemint Ward.
Bishop Monte McKeon	20 Aug 1984	I almost forgot to mention that I received a really nice congratulations and thank you note from Bishop Monte McKeon. He expressed his appreciation for my serving with him in the bishopric when he was bishop of the Canyon Country Ward and his congratulations for my being called to the stake high council. I will be serving with him as a fellow high counselor.

BYU Educa-tion Week	7 July 1979	About 2:00 P.M., Karen went to the three afternoon sessions of the BYU Education Week. Marc was put down to bed. I stayed home to baby-sit the boys. At 6:30 P.M., I attended the next three classes in the BYU Education Week program. What was really great was that I had learned a little about music and on conducting music. This, to me, was quite a milestone as I have several times led the singing in priesthood meeting without really knowing what I was doing.
Calling	21 Aug 1983	We attended Stake Conference today. All of the speakers were excellent. I received a call this afternoon from Ed Banks, stake executive secretary, who scheduled me for an interview with the stake president (Larkins) for 6:30 P.M., Tuesday, August 23. I wonder what this could be. I'm sure I will be called to some position. Bro. Dale Sutherland was released as 1st counselor in the bishopric and called as an alternate high councilor. Bro. Bill Thompson was released from the Stake High Council. Because I am currently unemployed, trying to get a job, and also trying to get my business going, I hope that Bro. Thompson will be called to the bishopric and I am called to a cushier position. I don't know if I can handle the extra burden and stress at this crucial time. However, whatever the Lord sees fit to call me to, I will gladly accept. He certainly knows what's best for my family and me at this time of need.
Calling	23 Aug 1983	In the evening, Karen and I went for an interview with Presidents Larkins and McKeon. I was called to serve as second counselor in the bishopric of the Canyon Country Ward. Brother Bill Thompson was called as first counselor, and Brother Glen Singley was called as ward executive secretary. We will be sustained and set apart this coming Sunday. From 8:00–10:30 P.M., Bishop Monte McKeon met with Brother Thompson and me at the chapel to give us an orientation. This should be an exciting experience in an exciting moment in our lives.

Calling	28 Aug 1983	We attended our Church meetings today. Heather sang the "Genealogy" song beautifully today in sacrament meeting. I was sustained and set apart as the second counselor in the bishopric of the Canyon Country Ward, Los Angeles–Santa Clarita Stake. It was a beautiful day today. I am very thankful to Heavenly Father for having me called to the bishopric. Brother Bill Thompson was called to serve as first counselor in the bishopric. Brother Glen Singley was called as ward executive secretary. Brother Steve Schaerrer continues as ward clerk.
Calling	23 Oct 1983	Then, I started conducting sacrament meeting. However, at 1:00 P.M., I had to leave the stand to meet with Karen and President Larkins for an interview. Karen was called as homemaking counselor of the stake relief society. She was really shocked about that calling.
Calling	9 Feb 1984	In the evening, Karen attended a Stake Relief Society Board meeting. Simultaneously, I attended the bishoprics meeting with the stake presidency. At 9:00 P.M., we attended an interview with the stake presidency, where I was called as first counselor in the new bishopric. Brother Bill Thompson was called as the new bishop of the Canyon Country Ward. Because we saw the Singleys and Schaerrers in the halls, I assume that Glenn Singley is going to be called as second counselor and Steve Schaerrer is going to be called as executive secretary. Atom baby-sat Marc and Heather while we were away.
Calling	12 Feb 1984	Today, the entire bishopric of our ward was officially released. Then, Bill Thompson was called as bishop, I was called as 1st counselor, Glenn Singley was called as 2nd counselor, and Steve Schaerrer was recalled as ward clerk (this was the one I guessed incorrectly). The executive secretary was not sustained today because the candidate was out of town.
Calling	21 Jun 1984	In the evening, we went to the Thompsons' for dinner with the bishopric. Unfortunately, Sis. Klein fell ill, and so the Kleins didn't make it. However, we enjoyed the evening with the Thompsons, Singleys, and Myrvangs. Atom babysat Marc and Heather.

Calling	1 Aug 1984	While I was away at the girls' camp tonight, Karen had received a telephone call from Bro. Brian George (stake executive secretary) who said that the Stake President (President Gary Larkins) wanted to see both of us at 6:00 PM this Friday. So, anxiety will set in over the next two days. Either Karen or I will be released from our callings, or we will be called to new callings. I don't know what it is, but I make a promise to the Lord that I will never reject a calling as long as I live. I will do the best I can at whatever I am called to do.
Calling	3 Aug 1984	Wonders and blessings never seem to fail. Karen and I went in for an interview at 6:00 PM with Stake President Gary Larkins and President Tim McKeon. To our shock, we found that the Canyon Country Ward was being split in two as Canyon Country Ward I and Canyon Country Ward II. We will be in Canyon Country II and will have a new bishop. Bishop Thompson will head Canyon Country I and will have portions of Mint Canyon and Solemint Wards moved into their ward. What a shock!
		Then, I was called to serve on the stake high council. And I feared all the while that I was going to be called as a seminary teacher. I thank the Lord that I didn't have that decision to make. Now, the speculation begins as to who will be called to what offices. My guess is that Bro. Dale Sutherland will be called as the new bishop of the new Canyon Country II Ward. Karen feels the same. So, this Sunday should be interesting, as the stake presidency will be calling a special 5:00 PM meeting for members of all three wards using the stake center as a meetinghouse.
		I will be released as 1st counselor this Sunday and will have to wait for two weeks until stake conference before I will be sustained as a stake high counselor. This certainly has been an unusual day for Karen and me.
Calling	12 Aug 1984	This was our first Sunday in our new ward–Canyon Country II. Bishop Dale Sutherland and his counselors did an excellent job their first week together. In sacrament meeting, I was the first speaker. We had about 10 people that spoke today because of the incoming and outgoing people. Our church services went from 3:00–6:00 PM.

Calling	19 Aug 1984	At 7:00 PM, I met with Bishop DeVon Tufts of the Mint Canyon Ward who gave me an orientation of the education material he was responsible for when he was on the stake high council. I was overwhelmed with the stuff I need to do in the next three to four weeks. Getting the Seminary Program off and rolling will be my biggest task.
		I also must take care of the "Know Your Religion" series and the "Education Week/Days" program. In addition, I am chairman of the Library Committee along with serving as the Stake Education Committee chairman. I don't know how I am going to do all of this work. However, with the Lord's help, I know I will be able to do it.
		I am also assigned to oversee the Elders Quorums of the Canyon Country I, Mint Canyon, and Solemint Wards. I must attend two elders' quorum meetings per ward per month. I also must hold monthly personal priesthood interviews (PPIs) with each elder's quorum presidency. Additionally, I must speak once a month in one of the nine wards in the stake. I am also assigned as the stake representative to my home ward, Canyon Country II. Furthermore, I must attend two Stake Priesthood Executive Committee meetings at 7:30 PM on the first and third Thursdays of each month.
		This is going to be a challenge for me. At this time, I am overwhelmed at the magnitude of the calling.
Calling	9 Sep 1984	My day went from 7:00 AM to 11:30 PM. Needless to say, I am exhausted. Tomorrow morning, I will be rising at around 5:00 o'clock to get ready to visit all three buildings and six classes in seminary.
		This new high council calling has really kept me hopping. I hardly have any time to work my real job. Things should simmer down in a couple of months when I get into a set routine. Life is really hectic, but I'm having an awful lot of fun.
Calling	10 Sep 1984	I got up early this morning and visited the three buildings in our stake–this being the first day of seminary. As expected, things were pretty chaotic today. Atom started in seminary this year as a freshman. Atom is also attending Canyon High School.

Canning	6 Aug 1980	Karen went to Orange County to pick up five cases of tomatoes at $1.50 per case. She will be doing some canning in the next few days.
Church Attendance	31 Aug 1980	Atom received a Book of Mormon for having 100 percent attendance, and Marc received a colored photograph of the Los Angeles Temple for 99 percent attendance. Atom and Marc also both received certificates for their good attendance.
Church News	21 Feb 1979	I came home from class about 9:40 P.M. and read my mail, which included the *Church News*. I really enjoy reading the *Church News*. It gives us an opportunity to know what's happening in the Church throughout the world.
Church Welfare Farm	30 May 1981	I rose at 5:30 this morning to work on the Church peach farm out by Palmdale. We thinned down the peaches on the peach trees. Eleven of us from the Canyon Country Ward attended along with about 100 others from other wards and stakes. We got home at about 11:30 A.M. We had one mishap. Brother Jan Smith fell off his ladder and broke his hand. I am sore all over from working in the hot sun all morning. After I got home, I doze off for a while. Then I took a shower.
Church Welfare Farm	2 Sep 1981	Karen got up at 5:30 A.M. to go to the Church farm out by the Lancaster/Palmdale area with a bunch of Relief Society sisters to pick pears and peaches. We got Margie Groff to baby sit. Karen worked a half-day out there and was quite scratched up from the branches, not to mention being very exhausted. In the morning, Atom was a great help to me feeding everyone and dressing Heather. I wouldn't be able to survive without Atom's assistance. As a matter of fact, he did everything, while I just supervised. He's a really good kid.
Conducting Church	27 Jun 1982	I was informed by the bishop that next Sunday everyone in the bishopric would be away on either vacation or business. Also, the ward executive secretary, ward mission leader, and elders' quorum president will be gone. So, as high priests group leader, I will be conducting the priesthood and sacrament meetings. Only the ward clerk will be there to assist me. To top it off, next Sunday is fast Sunday, so we will have fast and testimony meeting. It should be a very short meeting.

Conducting Church	4 Jul 1982	Today was Independence Day. I went to the chapel at 8:30 A.M. to prepare the agenda for the priesthood meeting. Every member of the priesthood executive committee was either out of town or absent. The only exception was me, the high priests group leader. So, I presided and conducted the priesthood meeting. After priesthood meeting, I went to the bishop's office to prepare the agenda for the fast and testimony meeting. I had Brother Stig Dahlstrom (ward clerk) and Brother Glen Singley (young men's president) accompany me on the stand. It was a unique experience presiding and conducting the fast and testimony meeting. The meeting was very spiritual. Everything went well. I was very pleased with the proceedings of the day.
Date Night	14 Aug 1981	This evening, Karen and I went to see "Victory" at the Mann 6 Theater. Sylvester Stallone starred in the movie, which was about World War II prisoners in a German prisoner camp and their efforts to escape. The plot was centered on a soccer game played between the German Nationalist team and the Allied prisoner team. We saw the Davis' there. They were sitting in the two seats in front of us. After the movie, we all went to Baskin-Robbins to get some ice cream. We got home at about 10:15 P.M. Becky Moody babysat the kids for us.

Deacon, Atom	14 Nov 1982	I attended the WCC (Ward Correlation Council) meeting from 9:00–10:30 A.M. The Sniders came from Orange County to attend church with us and to witness the ordination of Atom to the office of deacon. We attended our Sunday meetings. Karen was called on by surprise during sacrament meeting to bear her testimony on how she prepared Atom for receiving the priesthood and did a splendid job. After sacrament meeting, we all met in the bishop's office, where I conferred the Aaronic priesthood on Atom and ordained him to the office of deacon. Those standing in the circle included Bishop Monte McKeon, Brother Dale Sutherland (1st counselor), Brother Dave Bradford (2nd counselor), Brother Jack Gratrix (our home teacher), Brother Dave Collings (Atom's scoutmaster), Emerson Snider, and myself. After that, we came to our house for dinner. Karen fixed a delicious meal of roast chicken, baked potatoes, corn, spinach, Jell-O, and milk. For dessert, we had apple and cherry pies.
Emergency Communications	5 Nov 1983	I attended a stake emergency communications test this morning from 7:30–8:05 A.M. at Brother Lowell Tobin's home. He and people from most of the other wards in the stake communicated over their ham radios. It was quite interesting. I spoke over the airwaves too. I was impressed to see how advanced our stake is over many of the other organizations in this valley. President Larkins gave us a message over the ham radio system.
Family Home Evening	8 Feb 1979	Because I had a class at Golden West College on Monday evening, we held our Family Home Evening tonight. The lesson was on love. Atom was in charge of leading us in the lesson. I helped him prepare it. He did a super job. I think Atom is a really special spirit. He will someday do a great work in the Gospel of Jesus Christ.

Family Home Evening	9 Apr 1979	Then, we had Family Home Evening (FHE). Atom was in charge tonight and gave the lesson out of the manual. It was on receiving the gift of the Holy Ghost. Atom did a wonderful job. We started FHE off with singing "Give Said the Little Stream." Mommy gave the opening prayer. Then, Atom gave the lesson. For the closing song, we sang "Book of Mormon Stories." I gave the closing prayer. Then, mother made some chocolate pudding for dessert.
Family Home Evening	27 Oct 1980	For Family Home Evening, we made some baked bread dough figures for Christmas tree decorations. We had a great time rolling the dough and punching out the various figures with Karen's cookie cutters.
Family Home Evening	10 Nov 1980	After dinner, we danced to some Ernie and Bert records as our Family Home Evening activity.
Family Home Evening	1 Dec 1980	After work, I came home and had tacos for dinner with the family. After that, we had Family Home Evening. Darcy Kay Dick conducted the FHE and gave the lesson. She did an outstanding job. I am really proud of her. After FHE, we had ice cream sundaes.
Family Home Evening	16 Feb 1981	For FHE tonight, we had a treasure hunt, which ended in us eating some chocolate pop sickles.
Family Home Evening	11 Oct 1982	We had leftovers for dinner. After dinner, we had family home evening. We practiced fire drills in the home in case of a fire. Then Karen made some caramel-covered apples for dessert.
Family Home Evening	18 Oct 1982	After work, our family went to the Sierra Vista Junior High School playgrounds to play flag football as our FHE activity. After that, we came home to a rock lobster and red snapper seafood dinner. The rock lobster was delicious! After dinner, Karen and the kids played the piano, and we sang some songs.
Family Home Evening	15 Nov 1982	For family home evening, we mixed some batter for making a gingerbread house. After that, we went to Winchell's to buy some donuts and cheesecake. I had the cheesecake, and the kids had donuts.

Family Home Evening	6 Dec 1982	For family home evening, each one of us made a house of graham crackers and candy. Except Karen, who made a graham cracker and candy train. Karen fixed the train and four houses in a town scene and put it on the stereo.
Family Home Evening	29 Aug 1983	We had Family Home Evening tonight and made up a bulletin board, which showed who would be responsible for music, opening prayer, lesson, closing prayer, and refreshments for future FHEs. The assignment is rotated from week to week.
Family Home Evening	9 Jul 1984	In the evening, I went home for a delicious ham dinner, which Karen had prepared. After dinner, we held Family Home Evening. I conducted. What I did was have a family testimony meeting, where each member of the family bore his testimony. After that, each member of the family stood and spoke about a few of the outstanding character traits of other members of the family. It went really well. After that, the kids went for a swim in the pool, and I went back to the office to do some more work in preparation for tomorrow's meetings.
Family Home Evening	20 Aug 1984	Karen bought a fried chicken dinner from the deli at Von's Supermarket. It was really good. For FHE, we went up to visit Sister Brockbank. Atom has been watering her yard for the past couple of weeks, and she paid him $15.00 tonight. It was really too much, but she wouldn't take back the $5.00 that Atom tried to return. So, we agreed that Atom would water the yard for another week without any additional pay. After that, we came home, sang a song, Marc gave the prayer, and we all had ice cream sticks. Then, I returned to my office to catch up on some work.

Family Home Evening	3 Sep 1984	I left work at 6:00 PM to go home to eat and get ready for the Barneys who were coming over. Karen cooked up some delicious barbeque beef ribs on the charcoal stove. They were really great. The Barneys came over a little after 6:30 PM and stayed until after 8:30 PM. Karen had invited them over for FHE and to celebrate Sister Barney's 31st birthday with some pie, cake, and ice cream. Karen made some delicious peach pies. We had an enjoyable two hours of discussion. After the Barneys left, I went back to the office to do some more work.
Fasting	6 Jan 1980	After the fast and testimony meeting, we returned home at about 2:45 P.M. Since this was Fast Sunday and we were fasting since 5:00 P.M. yesterday, we had to wait out the afternoon before we could eat dinner. The boys were feeding their faces all day, which made it quite difficult for those of us who were fasting.
Fasting	3 Jul 1983	Karen and Atom (for the first time) fasted today. I thought they both did well with Karen and her migraines and this being Atom's first time. Because of my ulcers, Karen won't let me fast.
Fast Offerings	2 Jan 1983	Atom went out with Brother Lowell Tobin for the first time in gathering fast offering. It was a good experience for him.
Feeding the Missionaries	20 May 1979	The kids took their naps while Karen prepared for the elders who were coming over for dinner at 4:00 P.M. For dinner, we had beef tomato, fried corn and lima beans, steamed rice, bread and butter, milk, and (for dessert) lemon cake. Karen thought she had bought vanilla cake, and so we had lemon cake with chocolate frosting. She thought she had prepared vanilla cake with chocolate frosting. Even though the combination was weird, it didn't taste bad at all. The cake was soft and moist. Karen had decorated the frosting with the inscription that said, "Farewell and Good Luck Elder Hill."

Five Points to Guarantee a Safe Home	18 Feb 1979	Since Karen wasn't feeling too well and Marc had a slight fever because another of his back teeth was breaking through the gums, only Atom and I went to sacrament meeting. It was a pretty good meeting. President Bawden, 1st counselor in the stake presidency, was the concluding speaker. He spoke on safeguarding the home. He listed five points we can do to guarantee a safe home. They are:

1. Hold weekly family home evenings.

2. Hold daily private and family prayers morning and night.

3. Read the scriptures as a family on a daily basis.

4. Hold interviews periodically with your children.

5. Husbands and wives should have a date at least once a week–without the children.

Food Storage	9 Jun 1979	This evening, I also went over to Brother Wilden Haws' house to pick up four plastic containers and covers for our food storage program. Brother Haws showed Marc and I his food storage program and backyard.

Forming a New Ward	5 Aug 1984	Today was a historic day in the Los Angeles-California Santa Clarita Stake. Three wards (Canyon Country, Mint Canyon, and Solemint) were reorganized and divided into four wards. Canyon Country was divided into Canyon Country I and Canyon Country II. Bishop Bill Thompson was recalled to serve as bishop of Canyon Country I. We are in Canyon Country II. Bro. Dale Sutherland was called to be bishop of our ward. His counselors are Bro. Sam Davis (1st counselor) and Bro. Dave Orme (2nd counselor). Bro. Ollie Myrvang was recalled as ward executive secretary and Bro. Scott McClellan was called as ward clerk.

I now get a two-week vacation before stake conference where I'll be sustained as a stake high counselor. It is really exciting to see the plan for growth in this part of the stake. I foresee, at the stake conference following the one coming up in two weeks, Saugus I and Saugus II wards being divided into three wards. The stake should be divided into two stakes in about three years.

The stake president also announced the plan for a new ward meetinghouse in about 18 months for the Mint Canyon and Solemint wards. Then, only Canyon Country I and Canyon Country II will be sharing the stake center.

I am so thankful to our Heavenly Father for the opportunity of serving as 2nd counselor in the Canyon Country Ward bishopric from August 1983–January 1984 and as 1st counselor in the bishopric from January–August 1984. I am also very thankful for the opportunity now of serving as a member of the stake high council starting in two weeks.

I have to start really becoming organized and becoming a better husband, father, patriarch of the home, and priesthood holder. I hope and pray that the Lord will forgive me of my shortcomings and transgressions and will give me the strength necessary to overcome the temptations of Satan. I want very much to do what's right and good. But I constantly need the Lord's help. There is no way I can do it alone.

I love my wife, Karen, very much as I do our three children (Atom, Marc, and Heather). I hope I can really get my business going strong in the next 11 months so that I can give more of my time to my family and my church calling instead of spending most of it in building my business. The Lord willing, the business will grow and flourish so that I can hire people to do the work and contribute more of my time, talents, and money into the building of my family and His Kingdom.

Wonders never fail to cease. In the 5–1/2 years since I have been writing daily in my journal, today has just been

Forming a New Ward	1 Dec 1984	Tomorrow is going to be an eventful day for the Saugus Wards. At a specially called 5:00 PM meeting, it will be announced that the two wards will be divided into three. Brother Randy Favero, currently 1st counselor in the Saugus 2nd Ward, will become the new bishop of the Saugus 3rd Ward. I think he is a good man who will do an excellent job.
Forming a New Ward	2 Dec 1984	I headed for the Saugus Chapel where I attended a special meeting of the Saugus 1st and 2nd Wards at 5:00 PM. Both wards were realigned, and Saugus 3rd Ward was formed. Brother Randy Favero was called as the new bishop. It was a good meeting, which lasted for an hour.
Garden	10 Mar 1979	Atom and I turned some of the sand-dirt in our back yard in preparation for a garden. The Prophet, President Spencer W. Kimball, has counseled us to grow gardens in our yard, so this is what we are doing. Every week for the next month, I will be turning more ground to prepare it for seeding. We are doing the entire plant area that follow our side fences and back tile wall in our back yard. We plan to plant about a dozen different kinds of vegetables. I really burned a lot of calories doing the digging. Plus that, it was pretty warm this afternoon and that added to the extensive perspiring I had experienced.
Garden	31 Mar 1979	Karen and the kids planted some vegetables in our garden today. They planted lettuce, cabbage, cauliflower, chili peppers, tomatoes, corn, carrots, eggplant, and leeks. We have yet to plant the rest of our lettuce, cantaloupes, cucumbers, bell peppers, green beans, and peas. If it doesn't rain next Saturday, we might plant the rest of these vegetables. Growing a garden is in keeping with the counsel we received from President Spencer W. Kimball.
Garden	28 Jun 1979	After work, I came home and watered the garden. The garden is coming along beautifully. I picked a large head of leaf lettuce of which Karen made us large chef salads.
Garden	5 Jul 1979	I came home, watered the garden, and cooked myself some of the beans I had picked from our string bean vines in our garden. I love to half-cook the beans in butter. Then, with salt and pepper on it, yummy!

Garden	7 Jul 1979	I picked another head of cabbage and the last head of red leaf lettuce from our garden. I chopped up some of the cabbage and half-cooked it in butter, salt, and pepper in a frying pan. That's what I had for lunch along with a glass of milk. It wasn't bad at all!
Genealogy	23 Feb 1979	Upon coming home, Karen and I watched another episode of "Roots II," the sequel to the original "Roots." It is a movie based on books written by Alex Haley concerning the genealogy of his family, which went back to Africa. Alex Haley has done more to further the cause of genealogy work than any other person in recent times. Genealogy is now a hobby second only to coin and stamp collecting. I'm really going to have to get going on my genealogy work. Karen has done a lot, relative to me, on her side of the family. My younger brother, Carl, has done a lot of work on our side of the family. Since I'm the high priest group leader in our ward, I'm going to have to get with it and set a better example. After all, genealogy and temple work are the major responsibilities of the high priest group leader along with home teaching and missionary work.
High Council Assignment	24 Aug 1984	I worked in my office for most of the day on my high council calling. It is an overwhelming task to organize the material that was handed to me. Seminary enrollment and Know Your Religion will be taking most of my time in the next few weeks. It is a real task, but with the Lord's help, we will make it.

High Council Assignment	26 Aug 1984	This morning, I distributed some educational material to the wards in the Saugus and Newhall buildings. After that, I returned to my office and worked on my talk, which I gave at the Valencia 2nd Ward at their sacrament meeting. The talk was on "Education–An Eternal Pursuit." From the feedback I received, I think it went pretty well. After that, I went home for a while. Then, we went to the stake center where I was set apart by President Gary Larkins. Then, I attended the Canyon Country 2nd Ward (our home ward) priesthood, Sunday school, and sacrament meetings. After church, Atom, Marc, and I went home teaching to two of our four newly assigned families–the McIntoshes and Ellerns. We will be visiting the other two families (the Martins and Sis. Davis) this coming week. I then spent the rest of the evening at home with the family.
Home Teaching	17 Nov 1980	After dinner tonight, we made sugar cookies in the shape of turkeys and pumpkins for my home teaching families.
Home Teaching	14 Dec 1980	I took Ambrose Hosteenez with me to home teach the Logans, one of my newly assigned families. After that, I took the family with me to visit the Gratrixes and Neils and to give them some fudge that Karen had made. Since I am no longer assigned to those families on home teaching, I thought it would be nice to take them some of Karen's fudge…this being the Christmas season.
Home Teaching	26 Aug 1981	After work, Atom and I home taught the Weavers, Brockbanks, and Means. Atom gave the spiritual message in all three cases.
Home Teaching	20 Apr 1982	After coming home, Atom and I home taught the Fretzes and Brockbanks. Atom helped me present the spiritual message and gave the prayers. He does such a great job. I am really proud of him and look forward to the day when he becomes a deacon and my home teaching junior companion.
Home Teaching	26 Sep 1982	Atom and I went over to home teach the Fretzes. Atom gave the spiritual message on "Noah and the Ark."
Home Teaching	26 Aug 1984	I am also very proud of Atom for taking the responsibility of setting up our home teaching appointments with our assigned families. He is doing an excellent job in this area.

Home Teach-ing	5 Sep 1984	After I got home around 7:30 PM, I took a shower and got ready to go with the family to visit Sister Brockbank who is moving to Utah tomorrow. We picked Atom up from his Scout meeting at around 8:55 PM and went to Sister Brockbank's around 9:00 PM. We visited with her, her son, Bill, and Paul and Delight Penrod (her sister and husband) till around 9:30 PM before we left for home. We are really going to miss Sister Brockbank whom (along with her husband, Bob, who passed away on April 1, 1984) we served as their home teachers for about three years ago.
Home Teach-ing	28 Oct 1984	After church, Atom and I visited the Ellerns on a home teaching visit. We dropped off a loaf of pumpkin bread, which Karen had baked.
Home Teach-ing	30 Nov 1984	Jack Gratrix came over about 6:25 PM and stayed for about 10 minutes to home teach us. He had just come home from work where he was putting in a new telephone system at Michael Jackson's (the rock star) house.
Incentive Motivation	2 Dec 1979	I taught course 12 again today in Sunday school. Karen made some pound cake cupcakes for the kids in the class. We had eight kids in attendance today, and Karen had made 16 cupcakes. So, each student had two cupcakes each. The criterion for getting the cupcakes was that they were supposed to tell me of two things they learned from the lesson at the end of the class period. Needless to say, the kids were quite attentive today. It's amazing what a little incentive motivation will do.
Incentive Motivation	30 Dec 1979	It was pretty good teaching my course 12 class today. I had the students look up scriptures on Adam and Eve and answer questions. I held a contest to see who could get the most correct answers. Again, I bribed the students by bringing in a plate of cookies. The criterion for receiving the cookies was that either all or none of them would receive the cookies depending on whether they were quiet and attentive or not. Those that got the most correct answers would get the extra cookies. The kids really went after it.

Incentive Motivation	6 Jan 1980	After we separated for classes, I taught the course 12 class. I had a little contest today by having the kids answer questions from Genesis. Eric Pederson won the prize for getting the most correct answers. Karen had made up a ribbon with a roll of Life Savers attached to it as the prize. It had an inscription on the center of the ribbon, and the prize was neatly wrapped in a small box.
Journal Writing	1 Mar 1979	I've been doing pretty good thus far keeping up on making a daily entry in this journal. Like everything else, if you can get into a habit or ritual, you can keep up on doing anything indefinitely. I think it is just a matter of making up your mind that you are going to do it, setting a goal, doing it, and then sticking to it. Stick-to-it-iveness, perseverance, determination, persistence, will power, and desire–these are the key words to sustaining any endeavor.
Journal Writing	25 May 1980	Atom read parts of this journal and really enjoyed reading about himself. It makes it all worthwhile to write in this journal daily when someone enjoys reading about what was written.
Journal Writing	22 Mar 1981	This is the end of this volume of my personal journal. Tomorrow I will start on a new volume. It is my hope that I will be able to continue writing in my journal for the rest of my life.
Journal Writing	9 Jan 1983	Atom has been writing in his journal, which is really neat. I hope he will keep it up all of his life.
Journal Writing	24 Dec 1983	How the years fly by. It has been nearly five years since I started writing in my journal on a daily basis. I already have filled about a half dozen volumes. I hope I can keep this up for the rest of my life. Now, all I have to do is to go back and write my history from birth till about my 36th year. Then, I'll have a complete history of my life.

Journal Writing	13 Nov 1984	I have been writing daily in my journal for five years and nine months now. This is my ninth volume. I heard some passages read by Brother Richard Soto and Mike Creel this Sunday from their journals. What they read seemed really interesting to me. In comparison, my journal seems boring to me. Mine is more of a chronological listing of what transpired each day. Oh, I also heard passages read by Brother Gordon Risser, Jr., from his journal. They too were quite interesting. I wish I were able to write in a more interesting manner.
Know Your Religion	9 Oct 1981	After work, I came home about 6:30 P.M., had dinner with the family, and attended the Know Your Religion meeting. Brother Reed Benson, son of President Ezra Taft Benson, gave an outstanding talk on "How to Know the Will of the Lord for You."
Know Your Religion	19 Oct 1984	I worked in my office all day getting prepared for the Know Your Religion lecture series, which starts tonight. We had 165 people show up for the lecture. It came off really well.
Lambaste from a Bishop	14 Nov 1984	Today, I received a very negative letter from a certain bishop in our stake lambasting a statistical study I did on the seminary absences and tardies. The letter was so full of untruths and distortions that I had to answer it point by point. I hope I did the right thing because he sent copies of his letter to the stake presidency and another bishop in the stake. It just did not seem right to let it go unanswered. I hope things work out alright. I spent six hours all evening drafting and typing the five-page response plus six attachments. I hope this all blows over.
Lambaste from a Bishop	15 Nov 1984	The stake presidency talked to me this evening and expressed their support for me and stated that the bishop who had written me that nasty letter (of which they all received copies) was way out of line in doing so. It's really too bad. I feel sorry for that bishop and am disappointed in him. A bishop should be above that kind of behavior. President Larkins said that he would be having a talk with that bishop in question. As far as I'm concerned, the case is closed.

Lambaste from a Bishop	17 Nov 1984	The bishop in question that I discussed a couple of journal entries ago called me tonight. He didn't really apologize for his nasty letter to me, but he did say he appreciated my letter responding to his letter, and that he loved me and felt I was a good high councilor doing a good job. I told him, as far as I was concerned, it was water under the bridge, and we'll just go from here. He agreed. He did sound like he was in a better spiritual tune. I'm sure President Larkins spoke to him and straightened him out. But, I'm glad this thing is finished. I don't need this kind of hassle in my life. I thought I left it when I departed the corporate jungle and started my own business.
Missionary Work	8 Mar 1979	Missionary work is not one of the best areas that I excel in, but I hope some day that Karen and I will be able to serve on a full time mission. I would also like for us to be called, someday, as full-time temple workers. I think both of these full-time callings would be exciting and rewarding. When both Atom and Marc come of age, I hope and pray very much that they both will go on full-time missions and after that be married in the temple. Even though I was born and raised in the Church, I "missed the boat" on both of these goals. I'm sure that if I did these things I would have been much more spiritually advanced than I presently am today. I have so much lost time to make up. In addition, I'm trying my best to make up that lost time.
Missionary Work	11 Mar 1979	At Priesthood meeting, our 70's group leader and ward mission leader who also is one of the seven presidents of the Stake 70's Quorum, Brother Alex Patterson, presented Brother Merle Jager and me with Books of Mormon. We are to place these books with someone during the ensuing week and report our experiences at our next meeting. My intention is to place my copy with Billy Billimoria. I pasted a colored photograph of our family on the backside of the front cover. Then I wrote in my testimony of the truthfulness of the Gospel and my desire to share it with him. I hope this Book of Mormon will have a positive affect on Billy and motivate him to join the Church.

Missionary Work	2 Apr 1979	I got a call at work from Billy Billimoria. I invited him over for dinner on Friday evening. This will be my opportunity to present him with the personalized copy of the Book of Mormon that I have been meaning to present to him for the last couple of weeks. I hope it works in convincing him of the truthfulness of the gospel. It would surely be great to baptize him into the Church.
Missionary Work	6 Apr 1979	Billy Billimoria came over for dinner tonight. We cooked T-bone steaks on our barbecue grill outside. Karen prepared a fantastic dinner, which included (in addition to the steak) corn, baked potatoes with margarine and/or sour cream and chives, hot rolls, and milk. Prior to dinner, Karen had prepared a *hors d'oeuvres* platter, which included potato chips, sour cream cheese dip, carrot sticks, celery sticks, and radishes.
		After dinner, I presented Billy with a specially prepared, personalized, marked copy of the Book of Mormon with a photograph of our family and my testimony in it. I hope this book will spark him into gaining a testimony of the gospel. It would be a great honor and pleasure for me to baptize him into the Church.
Missionary Work	21 Aug 1979	I have decided to send gift subscriptions of the *Church News* and the *Ensign* magazine to Billy Billimoria. I hope it works in teaching him more of the gospel and converting him to it to the extent that he makes the commitment to enter the waters of baptism.
Mormon Pioneer History	1 Jul 1979	From about 8:00 to 10:00 P.M., we watched "Donner Pass" on TV, which was a movie on the ill-fated Reed-Donner Party mentioned briefly in Mormon history. The story was about a band of travelers in 1864–65 that became stranded in the Sierras in the middle of winter, while they were on their way to California.
		It showed how many of the travelers starved to death and how the survivors turned to cannibalism when they began to eat their dead. It was a sickening movie, but I decided to watch it only because I briefly read about it while reading about the history of our Church.

Mutual	26 Jun 1979	Then I went off to Mutual....The Priests showed a silent film on the "Creature from the Black Lagoon" with a dubbed in sound made by several Priests on a tape recorder. It really was hilarious.
Mutual	30 Aug 1983	This evening, I attended the Mutual combined activity, which was a swim party and dinner at the McKeon's mansion in Sand Canyon. There were about 30 of the youth and about 15 adults there. It was an excellent event, which everyone enjoyed. Atom enjoyed swimming and eating.
New Sunday Meetings Program	2 Mar 1980	Today we attended our new ward, the Canyon Country Ward, for the first time. It was Fast Sunday. Since this was the first Sunday the new Sunday Meetings Program was put into effect, there was some confusion. However, I am sure, as we all get used to this new meeting schedule, things will settle down to a routine. We attended Priesthood, Relief Society, Mutual, Primary, Sunday School (without any opening exercises), and Sacrament (Fast and Testimony today) meetings during a three-hour block between 11:30 A.M. and 2:30 P.M. today. I can see this time block is a little difficult for the young children, as it was quite noisy during the F&T (fast and testimony) meeting. Seems like it would probably be easier on the young ones if we had the Sacrament Meeting first followed by the classroom type meetings. Then the young kids could expend their extra energies in the classrooms as smaller groups than as one large group in the chapel. The morning three-hour block is probably the easiest/best followed by the late afternoon three-hour block. Starting this new program off with the most difficult three-hour block will make us appreciate the other blocks more when we rotate to them in the next couple of years. At any rate, I like this three-hour block approach because it gives me more time for other things during the day. For one thing, I get to sleep in late on Sunday mornings. Then I have time for preparation in the late morning. Church is over by 2:30 P.M., so I then have the entire rest of the day for other things like studying, for instance.

Newsletter	31 Aug 1979	After I came home from work, I spent the entire evening and into the wee hours of the morning (1:30 A.M.) preparing the September issue of the YMYW monthly newsletter, which I have dubbed the "Mutual Nuz."
Patriarchal Blessing	13 Nov 1984	I read my patriarchal blessing tonight for the first time in a long while. Three things really stood out that I must do before I pass on. They are: (1) genealogy work, (2) temple work on my ancestors that I dig up in my genealogy work, and (3) missionary work. I hope some day after I get my company really going good to go on a full-time mission to Japan with Karen. It would be a good opportunity for me to learn how to read, write, speak, and understand Japanese and to do some genealogy work in Japan. I also hope some day to be a temple worker with my wife, Karen.
Potential Emergency	28 Aug 1984	Around 3:00 AM, Brother Lane Martin called me from the Airport Holiday Inn in San Francisco. I had gone to bed around 1:00 AM, so I was fast asleep. He tried to call his wife all night but wasn't able to get her, and so he was quite worried. As it turned out, the phone wasn't working too well, and so they never connected. I dressed and drove over and got her out of bed just as the phone rang. Guess what? It was Lane who had finally gotten through. Therefore, by the time I went back to bed, it was 3:30 AM.
PPI	6 Jan 1984	I had a real good hour-and-a-half PPI this evening with Atom. We just had a real good talk, which I ended up agreeing on playing an hour of basketball with him every Saturday.
Prepared-ness Fair	26 Jul 1981	After we got home, I took a shower, dressed, and went to the chapel with the family to work on the Career Development booth and to view all the other displays. Karen won first place (blue ribbon) on her chocolate mint candy and third place (white ribbon) on her canned tomatoes. After tearing down the display at about 4:00 P.M., we came home, and the kids and I went for a swim in the pool.

Priesthood Awards	13 May 1983	In the evening, Atom and I attended the Stake Fathers and Sons Banquet at the Saugus Chapel from about 7:00 P.M. to 9:15 P.M. Karen did most of the work preparing the salad for 225 people. The dinner was delicious. Atom received the Nephi Award for his first year of effort in the Aaronic Priesthood.
Primary	2 Jan 1983	We attended our Sunday meetings today from 11:00 A.M. to 2:00 P.M. This was Heather's first day in her Sunbeam class. She received her graduation certificate from the Nursery class.
Primary	13 Nov 1982	We all attended the Canyon Country Ward Primary Country Fair. The kids had a good time. Marc played the piano in the talent show. He also received a yellow ribbon for a crayon drawing he made and entered in the arts and crafts competition.
Primary	25 Sep 1983	The sacrament program was a presentation by the Primary. It as excellent. Heather was absolutely darling singing a duet with Amy Gratrix. Marc did excellently reciting a part in the program and also sang in a trio after Heather and Amy.
Road Show	30 Mar 1984	In the evening, we attended the Stake Road Show at the Stake Center. We took Chris Moody and sons, Don and Kenny, with us. It was an excellent show, which provided us with lots of laughs. Our Ward's entry did well. Our kids came a long way from last night's dress rehearsals. After the show, we went over to 7–11 for some refreshments. Atom went to a cast after-party at the Mitchells' home. He came home at about 12:00 midnight. I think Atom had an enjoyable time being in the Road Show. He initially didn't want to be in it. Karen had to force him, as she does in many things he initially doesn't want to get involved in. However, he always seems to enjoy it after trying it out for a while.
Rob Klein	1 Apr 1984	I had a nice chat with our Elders Quorum President Rob Klein. Rob is a real sharp guy–a very holy man. I can learn a lot from him.
Sacrament	21 Nov 1982	We watched Atom pass the sacrament for the first time. He was so cute. He was assigned to start things off first by going up the stand to pass the bread and water to the stake visitors and the bishopric.

Scouting	1 Sep 1982	At 7:30 P.M., I attended Atom's Boy Scout meeting to help plan the Scout Encampment we will be attending on 9/3/82–9/6/82 at Camp Pendleton, California.
Scouting	2 Sep 1982	For our Scout Encampment, Karen did some shopping for Atom and me. We will leave tomorrow afternoon. It should be quite an experience for me since I definitely am not the outdoorsman type.
Scouting	3 Sep 1982	I worked in the morning and left at 11:30 A.M. to go to the three-day Scout Encampment at Camp Pendleton. We got everything packed up and left for the Stake Center at 1:20 P.M. I had Atom and Marc with me. We took Marc to the Sniders to spend the night. We also took Danny Seegal and Scott Smith with us to Camp Pendleton. It was about 2:00 P.M. before we finally left and arrived at the camp area at 6:30 P.M. It was a long haul through heavy traffic. After we set up camp, cooked, and ate dinner, we were bushed. This is not what I would call luxurious living–this is roughing it.
Scouting	4 Sep 1982	It was a tough night sleeping last night on solid ground, which was quite uneven. Some of the boys were up until about 2:00 A.M. laughing and carrying on. Then, this gung-ho scoutmaster of another troop adjacent to ours started rousting his boys out of bed at 6:00 A.M. Official reveille wasn't until 6:30, so it was difficult maintaining my cool because of his yelling and screaming at his boys. We could have really used that extra half-hour of sleep. It was an extremely hot day (102 degrees F) today. We all were so hot that, in the afternoon, we all went to the beach for a swim for about three hours. We also viewed the museum of old landing craft, tanks, etc. The boys really enjoyed that. In the evening, we attended a show and program for the 10,000 scouts in attendance. We saw Lorne Greene, Beryl Ives, and President Ezra Taft Benson during the program.

Scouting	5 Sep 1982	We got up at six-thirty this morning and started the charcoal stove. I froze throughout the night because my sleeping bag's zipper was broken by someone who had previously borrowed our sleeping bag. Furthermore, the ground is so hard and uneven that it was uncomfortable all night. This is the kind of camp-out that builds character. It is difficult to keep a positive mental attitude under the circumstances.
		We cooked pancakes for breakfast. We also had hot chocolate and orange juice. After breakfast, we went to the rodeo area for Sunday services. It lasted two hours in about 100-degree F weather. There were over 10,000 scouts in attendance. We heard a talk by President Ezra Taft Benson. After the meeting, we came back to the campsite and had lunch.
		Then we spent the afternoon trading some cards of Zion's Camp (our camp) with nine other camps to get a complete set. This was an opportunity for us to meet others from other sub-camps.
		At about 5:15 P.M., we cooked dinner, which was *sautéed* squash and chili. In the evening, we attended a fireside with Elder Robert Backman. He gave a very interesting and motivational talk on "Desire."
		After that, we came back to the campsite, and some of the scouts and Brothers Collings and Van Horn played "Fox and the Hound." Atom went to bed early as he did the past two nights. The Tracys left this afternoon because Will Tracy said that he had a daughter that fell ill.
		The temperature has been the damper at this Scout Encampment. Yesterday, I found out, the temperature went as high as 110 degrees F. Some of the boys really wanted to go home early because they felt that they were having a miserable time. It all boils down to attitude. You only get out of anything whatever you put into it. If they wanted to have a good time, they could have a good time by just adjusting their attitudes.
Scouting	6 Sep 1982	Today is Labor Day. We got up at 6:00 A.M. to cook breakfast and pack up to leave for home. I slept in the car last night, which was warm and comfortable. We finally left for home at about 9:20 A.M. and arrived home at about 12:30 P.M. After that, we took baths, washed our clothes, and washed the car.

Scouting	24 Aug 1983	Atom went to his Boy Scout meeting this evening nicely dressed in his scout uniform. He has qualified for the rank of First Class. Next, he will work towards Star Scout, then Life, and, hopefully, Eagle.
Scouting	31 Aug 1983	In the evening, we attended the Scout Court of Honor for our troop (Troop 585) at the Stake Center. Atom walked away with his second-class and first-class ranks, three skill awards, and two merit badges. Not bad! He is well on his way to Eagle scout. Lately, he has again become really fired up about scouting.
Scouting	16 Dec 1983	Atom went on a Scout overnighter at Hart Park. They are now probably freezing their tushies.
Scouting	17 Dec 1983	Atom came home from the overnighter about 1:00 P.M. He didn't seem to have enjoyed it too much.
Scouting	8 Feb 1984	In the evening, Atom and I attended the Boy Scout meeting. Bro. Nichols, the new scoutmaster was sick and, hence, missed the meeting. The scouts played blackout football in rooms 7, 8, and 9. It was a riot. Atom got his nose smashed in, as did a couple of others. It is a dangerous game!
Scouting	31 Mar 1984	At 6:00 P.M., we attended Atom's Scout Court of Honor. About 24 scouts were in attendance. Atom was one of the four boys that received their Star rank. Atom also received about five merit badges. He should be making Life rank in June of this year and Eagle at the end of December. Marc is so fired up about Cub Scouts from watching Atom receive all of his scouting badges. I think Mark will go all the way through Webelos and Arrow of Light in cubs and Eagle in scouts. It is uplifting to see them so enthused in the scouting program. The entire bishopric wore the scout uniform to the Court of Honor tonight. Paul Lankes and Chris Nichols received the Life rank. Both boys should receive their Eagle rank by October 1984.

Scouting	2 Apr 1984	Marc, Heather, and I went to Howard & Phil's to buy Marc a Wolf Book for Cub Scouts. Marc is so excited about becoming a Cub Scout in two months that he wants to study up and meet all of the requirements for Bobcat on his first meeting date. I hope he keeps up that enthusiasm to become a Webelos and Arrow of Light in Cubs and an Eagle in Scouts. Heather also is getting fired up to become a Brownie Scout.
Scouting	6 Jun 1984	I went to a Boy Scout Father and Son softball game. We had an enjoyable time beating the scout troop. After the game, we went to the ward meetinghouse for refreshments.
Scouting	27 Jun 1984	Atom attended his Scout meeting in the evening. He is only one merit badge shy of meeting the requirements for the Life Scout rank.
Scouting	2 Jul 1984	Atom finished his last merit badge today, which qualifies him for the Life Scout rank, which he will receive at the Court of Honor this Saturday evening. I do believe that Atom is going to make Eagle. I hope he does it by the end of the year.
Scouting	7 Jul 1984	I left for home at about 5:10 PM to take a shower, eat, and go to Atom's Scout Court of Honor at 6:00 PM. Atom received four merit badges, the Life Scout rank, and the On My Honor medal. We are really proud of his accomplishments. He is well on his way to eagle scout by year's end. After the Court of Honor, I came back to the office to do more work.
Scouting	4 Aug 1984	Atom came home from camp this afternoon. He completed two merit badges while at camp, which is two more than he did at last year's camp. That's two more merit badges closer to receiving his Eagle scout rank.
Scouting	22 Sep 1984	After arriving in Canyon Country around 7:00 pm, I went directly to the Scout Court of Honor. Atom received a couple of merit badges and a camp patch. He is only five merit badges away from meeting the Eagle requirement for merit badges! He should make Eagle during the first quarter of 1985. I hope he makes it. He will be the first Uda to do so.
Scouting	18 Dec 1984	Atom went to the Scout meeting this evening. I hope he gets his Eagle before he totally loses interest in the Scouting program.

Scripture Reading	5 Dec 1982	Atom has really started reading the Book of Mormon and has shown great interest in catching up with all the other Aaronic Priesthood holders as shown on a bar chart in the lobby of the chapel. He should be up with the leaders by the first of the year.
Scripture Reading	26 Dec 1982	Atom is doing a lot of scripture reading lately, particularly in the Book of Mormon. Last week he said something uplifting to me when he said that he felt really good when he read the scriptures. I hope he keeps it up. He will make a good missionary and future leader in the Church. I see him as a future bishop and stake president.
Secret Santa	22 Dec 1983	At about 10:15 P.M., Karen, Marc, Heather, and I took three boxes full of presents and dropped them off on the _____ front porch. I rang the doorbell and ran off to the car. We backed the car (with headlights off) down the street and waited for a few minutes before driving by the _____ to see if they had taken the gifts into the house. They did! Marc and Heather were quite excited about secretly doing this. Atom was at home sound asleep. Karen got a bunch of friends to go along with us to donate gifts for this clandestine project. Others that contributed gifts included the McKeons, Davises, Pringles, Barneys, Wycoffs, and Moodys.
Seminary	16 Sep 1984	I sustained and set apart Judge Roger Boren of the Saugus 1st Ward as a seminary teacher. At 7:00 PM, I attended the Melchizedek Priesthood meeting and at 7:30 PM the Elders/High Priests meeting.
Seminary	21 Dec 1984	Atom and I got up at about 5:10 this morning and went to the Seminary Breakfast at the Newhall building. It was supposed to have started at 6:00 AM, but by the time enough people got there to start the meeting, it was 6:15. President Shaw presided, and I conducted the testimony meeting. Many of the youth got up to bear their testimonies including Atom. He bore a great testimony. After that (at 7:00 AM), we all went into the cultural hall for a delicious breakfast prepared by the Newhall Ward.

Service	13 Oct 1984	I helped the Martins between 8:30 AM and 12:30 PM load the moving truck/trailers with their household goods. They will be moving to Provo, Utah, on Monday (10/16/84). After that, I went home and took a shower. Then Karen and I went to the going-away party for the Martins at the Sutherlands' home. After that, I returned to my office to prepare some stuff for my Know Your Religion kick-off meeting to be held tomorrow at 6:30 PM.
Speaking Assignment	2 Dec 1979	Brother Emerson Snider, counselor in the bishopric, asked me this morning to be a speaker at next Sunday's sacrament meeting. Both Karen and I will be speaking on the subject of "Tithing." It seems as though our speaking assignments always come in lumps. They are seldom spread out over the year.
Stake Arts Fair	17 May 1984	Karen worked all day setting up the Stake Arts Fair. In the evening, Heather and I attended the Stake Arts Fair. I received a certificate for excellence in writing daily in a journal and reading the scriptures daily. Karen won three blue ribbons for her ceramic doll, brownies, and "Home Sweet Home" needlework on Victorian parchment paper.
Stake Conference	15 Nov 1980	At 7:00 P.M., Karen and I attended the Stake Conference session. Darcy baby-sat the kids. We heard Elder Howard W. Hunter (member of the Council of the Twelve Apostles) speak to the congregation. The theme for the evening was genealogy, journals, and temple work.
Stake Conference	16 Nov 1980	We attended the general session of Stake Conference from 9:00–11:00 A.M. Elder Howard W. Hunter was the concluding speaker, who spoke about the youth of the Church among other things. After Church, we came home and had lunch. Then Karen and I attended a 12:00 noon meeting on Missionary Work. It was an excellent meeting, which lasted for an hour-and-a-half. The best talk was by Mission President Hyrum Smith, who gave an interesting and enlightening talk on Missionary Work. The significant thing he said was that "character" *is the ability to carry out a decision after the emotion of making that decision has passed.*

Stake Confer-ence	6 Feb 1982	In the afternoon at 4:00 P.M., I attended the Priesthood Leadership session of Stake Conference. Elder George P. Lee of the First Quorum of the Seventy was the speaker. The meeting lasted till 6:00 P.M.
Stake Confer-ence	4 Feb 1984	After that, I went home for a half hour before returning to the Stake Center for the 4:00 P.M. Priesthood Leadership Session of Stake Conference. We are having a General Authority, Elder F. Burton Howard, with us this weekend. He gave an excellent session today. Then, I went home for about 20 minutes to have dinner with the kids. I returned to the chapel immediately to participate in choir practice before the 7:00 P.M. Adult Session of Conference started. Sis. Joan Miller of our ward gave a super talk followed by another excellent talk by Elder F. Burton Howard of the First Quorum of the Seventy. Karen helped with fixing dinner for the Stake Presidency and Brother Howard. They had roast chicken with gravy, rice pilaf, among other things.
Stake Confer-ence	5 Feb 1984	We had the Stake Conference General Session this morning from 10:00 A.M. to 12:00 noon. I sang in the choir. The shock of the day was the announcement that Bishop McKeon was called as a stake high councilor. Bro. John Houck was released from the stake high council. Karen was sustained as 1st counselor in the Stake Relief Society presidency, but she was a little bit puzzled because she was not informed about it beforehand. She got the Stake Relief Society president inquiring into it to see if there was an error made or whether it was an intentional change for her.
Stake Confer-ence	18 Aug 1984	Karen cooked and served dinner for the regional representative (Elder Robinson) and the stake presidency. We then attended the 7:00 PM session of stake conference. The theme was "self-reliance and service to others." It was an excellent meeting. After the meeting, we went with six other couples (Thompsons, Barneys, Sutherlands, Hathcocks, Singleys, and Howarths) for something to eat at Big Boy's Restaurant. By the time we got home, it was after 11:00 PM. Atom babysat Marc and Heather while we were away all evening.

Stake Conference	19 Aug 1984	We attended stake conference this morning from 10:00 AM to 12:00 noon. I was sustained as a stake high counselor in the Los Angeles California Santa Clarita Stake of Zion.
Talk	7 Aug 1983	We attended our Sunday church meetings today. Heather gave her first talk (on genealogy) today in Primary. I missed it because I was in the Priesthood opening exercises. However, from all the feedback I received, she did a super job giving her talk and then singing the genealogy song afterwards.
Talk	1 Jan 1984	Atom spoke in sacrament meeting today and did an excellent job. I'm very proud of him. He talked about setting goals and plans for a mission and preparing himself to achieve his goals.
Talk	23 Dec 1984	After that, I attended our ward's sacrament meeting. Karen was one of the speakers and gave an excellent talk. After sacrament meeting, we had Elders Blasko and Kearney over for dinner. Karen cooked a delicious prime rib dinner.
Temple Recommend	3 Dec 1980	After work, I went to Howard and Phil's for a temple recommend renewal interview with President Howard McKeon (who is now Congressman Howard P. McKeon).
Temple Work	8 Mar 1979	Every time I go to the temple, I learn something new. It brings me closer to our Heavenly Father, and it broadens my insight to the gospel. We have now been in the Washington Temple (that's where we were sealed on August 28, 1975) and the Los Angeles Temple. I hope, before we leave this good earth, that we will have been able to do work in every one of the 16 or so temples we have in existence to date.
Temple Work	14 Jun 1979	I left for the L.A. Temple at 4:15 P.M. to attend our Stake Temple Night. Karen went earlier with Sisters Bingham and Kidd. They did 15 initiatories each. I did 15 initiatories and one endowment. Because I get so hot and sweaty during the day, I took a shower at the temple prior to doing initiatories. It felt so good to smell clean before starting temple work. I think I'll do that every time I go to the temple directly from work.
Testimony	12 Apr 1981	Atom, Marc, and I bore our testimonies during the Fast and Testimony Meeting today. The two boys did really well.

Testimony	11 Mar 1984	I conducted the Fast and Testimony Meeting. Atom, Marc, and I all bore our testimonies today. Marc and Atom did outstandingly bearing their testimonies. Marc stood up before Atom, and Atom wasn't going to be outdone, so he stood up too.
Testimony	1 Jul 1984	Marc bore his testimony today and did a super job. His teacher, Tammie Hathcock, gave him a neat poster with candy bars on it for his birthday. Sister Hathcock made a really nice gesture.
Testimony	4 Nov 1984	Marc bore his testimony in Fast and Testimony meeting today. I am really proud of him for doing it on his own volition.
Tithing Fiasco	2 Dec 1984	In the evening, I received a phone call from Brother Dave Orme, 2nd counselor in the bishopric of our ward, who said that Brother _____ had given his daughter, _____, a tithing envelope on Sunday, 8/26/84, to give to a member of the bishopric. She claims that she gave the envelope to me. I wasn't even in the bishopric at that time having been released two weeks previous to that date. And the envelope had $650.00 in *cash* in it! How can anyone put that much cash in a tithing envelope instead of writing a check? Anyway, I found out from _____ in a telephone call to him that he had filled out the tithing slip on that Sunday, 8/26/84, but that he had mistakenly put down Saturday's date, 8/25/84, on the slip. Also, _____ said that she gave me the envelope in front of the bishop's office. When I asked which bishop's office, she said Bishop Thompson's office. I don't go over to the other side of the chapel anymore after sacrament meeting–there is no reason to. Bishop Sutherland's office is on the other side of the chapel. We always come out on Bishop Sutherland's side after sacrament meeting.

It appears like _____ was remembering the July donation when I was still in the bishopric under Bishop Thompson. Since I was released from the bishopric, I have never ever received any tithing envelops from anyone. If anyone had offered to give me an envelope, I certainly would have directed them to give it to a member of the bishopric.

I believe the Sunday of 8/26/84 was the weekend that Bishop Sutherland had to be out of town on business. And since Brother Sam Davis was in charge, being 1st counselor, he was in a spin. After being sustained and set apart on 8/12/84, the Stake Conference was held the following week on 8/19/84. Then, Bishop Sutherland left town for the following week on 8/26/84.

It is no wonder Brother Davis was in a spin. He had never served in a bishopric before, and now he was the first counselor and in charge without the bishop there. They also didn't have an assistant ward clerk–finance at that time. So, Brother Orme and Ward Clerk Rob Klein counted the money that Sunday. Either of them, also being new to the game, had never counted the money before.

At any rate, the Lord knows, I never took the money. It was either lost or misplaced. One of them might still have it stuck in a pocket, purse, book, or notebook. It might have been inadvertently discarded in the wastebasket when they were emptying the envelopes. Or it might have been left in a coat pocket–the coat having been sent to the dry cleaners. A happy worker might have found the envelope in the pocket. Or it might have dropped on the chapel floor, and someone might have picked it up. A hundred and one things could have happened to the money. But one thing I know for a surety; I did not take it. I sure hope they can find the error soon if there was one made.

Visiting Teaching	25 Jul 1982	Karen's visiting teachers, Sisters Joan Miller and Sherryle LaBass, came by at 3:30 P.M. Sister Miller made Karen some oatmeal cookies, which the kids and I promptly consumed.

Visiting the Sick	3 Dec 1983	After I got home, I received a call from Brother Brockbank who informed me that Sis. Brockbank had a seizure at 4:30 A.M. and that the paramedics took her to Henry Mayo Hospital. He asked me if I would administer to her. Therefore, I got hold of Bro. Rich Nichols, and we went to the hospital to administer to Sis. Brockbank.
Visiting the Sick	4 Dec 1983	At 4:45 P.M., Karen and I drove up to the Brockbank's to drop off the new Family Home Evening (FHE) Manual with Bro. Brockbank, but he wasn't there. We then went to choir practice at the chapel. We practiced for about 1 hour and 45 minutes. After that, we went to Henry Mayo Hospital to visit Sis. Brockbank. Then we drove to the Brockbanks' home to visit Bro. Brockbank to give him the FHE Manual. His brother and sister-in-law (Sis. Brockbank's sister) were there. We visited with them for about a half-hour.
Visiting the Sick	6 Dec 1983	In the evening, Atom and I visited Sis. Brockbank in the hospital. She didn't appear to be coherent in her speech. Atom was emotionally affected by her condition that he shed some tears on the way home and again after we arrived at home. Atom is a very sensitive boy. I think he is going to be a great bishop and/or stake president some day.
Visiting the Sick	10 Dec 1983	Bro. Brockbank called about 10:00 A.M. and said that Sis. Brockbank asked that I come to the hospital to give her another blessing. By the time I got there, it was 11:30 A.M. I had to take a shower, and I went to Alpha Beta to buy her a small evergreen plant. After I arrived at Henry Mayo Hospital, we talked for a while, and then I gave her a special blessing.
Visiting the Sick	11 Dec 1983	Karen and I then left at 7:30 P.M. to visit Sis. Brockbank in Henry Mayo Hospital. She is recuperating just fine and is scheduled to come home around noon on Wednesday.
Visiting the Sick	15 Dec 1983	In the evening, Atom and I visited the following people at Henry Mayo Hospital: Sis. Helene Flaim, Sis. Yvonne Brockbank, and Walter Gist. Then, we went to Valley Presbyterian Hospital in Van Nuys to visit Bro. Gordon Risser, Sr. It is odd that someone from each of our assigned home teaching families is in the hospital this month.

Visiting the Sick	9 Jan 1984	In the evening, our whole family went to visit Sis. Brockbank as our FHE activity. We had a good 45-minute visit with Yvonne. Bro. Bob Brockbank was not there. He had left earlier on a business appointment.
Ward Conference	10 Jan 1982	We had our Ward Conference today from 8:00–11:00 A.M.… After Priesthood Meeting, we attended a neat presentation on the three degrees of glory. We went into the breezeway, which had the chairs lined up like we were in a large commercial airliner. We were on flight 409 when it crashed. We then were taken through the telestial kingdom. After being notified that a mistake was made and that we should have gone to the terrestrial kingdom, we all went into the cultural hall to sit in a group of chairs. The announcer then described the terrestrial kingdom. Then a messenger came in and said that a mistake was made again and that we were supposed to have gone to the celestial kingdom. So, up we got and all filed into the chapel, which represented the celestial kingdom. The stake presidency and all helpers were dressed in white. The announcer then described the celestial kingdom. The presentation ended with some remarks by President Dwight Stevenson. After that, we all met in the chapel for sacrament meeting. The stake presidency administered the sacrament, which was neat to see.
Ward Overnighter	18 May 1984	I worked in the office all day. In the evening, we packed up, and, along with Jeremy Davis, the whole family went to the Ward Overnighter at Cottonwood Campgrounds, which is located past Lake Hughes about a 50-minute drive from here (i.e., Canyon Country).
Ward Overnighter	19 May 1984	We went to bed around 2:00 A.M. having played a silly trivia game until then. In the morning, we got up about 6:00 o'clock having frozen all night. The bishopric cooked breakfast for about 70 people in attendance at the campout. We left for home at 10:00 A.M. because Karen had to go to work at 12:00 noon. I was really exhausted. Karen and I are not much of campers, though the kids really enjoyed themselves.

Wedding Reception	27 Dec 1984	In the evening, our whole family went to Cheryl Houck's (now Richards) wedding reception at the stake center. They're in for a fun time tonight! Maurice is a really sharp person. She's a lucky girl. He's a lucky guy, too. Karen went to the sealing at the L.A. Temple early this morning.
Welfare Farm	26 Aug 1982	Karen drove Sister Sue Singley to work with her on the church peach farm in Little Rock, California, today. She left at about 6:10 A.M. and came home around noon. Along the way, she had a flat tire and had an enjoyable time changing it. There were others from the Canyon Country Ward, including the Thompsons and Wallaces, who worked there also.
Welfare Farm	27 Aug 1983	Atom and I got up at 5:30 this morning to get ready to go to the Church Pear Farm to pick peaches. Brother Lane Martin and son, Brandon, came by at 5:55 A.M. to pick up Atom and me. Then we drove over to the Nichols' and picked up Brother Rich Nichols and son, Chris. We drove to Little Rock and arrived at the farm at 6:50 A.M. By 7:00 A.M., we were out in the groves picking peaches. We picked peaches until 10:00 A.M., when it started to get really hot. We left the peach farm for home at about 10:20 A.M. and arrived home at about 11:10 A.M.
Writing Missionaries	11 Jun 1979	Before I went to my Statistics class to turn in my final exam, we held a Family Home Evening. For our activity, all four of us each wrote a letter to Elder Mike Fanoga who is on a full-time mission in South Dakota from our ward. He ought to get a kick out of Atom and Marc's letters.
Youth Baptisms	11 Oct 1983	Atom went for a temple recommend interview with Bishop McKeon tonight. He will be going to the Los Angeles Temple next Wednesday to do baptisms for the dead with some of the other youth of our ward. It should be a good experience for him.
Youth Baptisms	19 Oct 1983	Atom went to the Los Angeles Temple with other youth from our ward to do baptisms for the dead. He did 15 baptisms and really enjoyed the experience so much that the next time our ward has an assignment he wants to go again. I'm really glad he had a good experience.

11

Occupational and Professional Things

I spend at least half of my 24-hour-day on work and professional activities. Work is good for the soul. Hence, it is a huge part of my life and being. I find growth and satisfaction in my occupation. This chapter covers all of the occupational and professional things in my life during 1975-1984. It has been a tough career in the aerospace and defense industries, but it has been both rewarding and fulfilling.

Apollo Systems Technology, Inc.	8 Feb 1984	Don Knapp tells me that he is going to buy all 120,000 shares for $12,000 in Apollo Systems Technology, Inc.
Apollo Systems Technology, Inc.	1 Mar 1984	Good news! I found out today that General Dynamics-Convair in San Diego is interested in giving me a subcontract on the Small ICBM Program (also known as the Midgetman Missile Program). I hope we can get the contract finalized soon.
Apollo Systems Technology, Inc.	11 Jun 1984	This morning, Karen and I went out looking for office space to lease. We found a plush 530 sq ft office on the second floor of the Canyon Professional Center in Canyon Country. It will cost us $500 per month plus triple net. In other words, we will be paying our proportionate share (about 1/40) of the total expenses of the building (i.e., electricity, gas, water, trash, taxes, building and grounds upkeep, etc.). I hope that cost doesn't exceed $100 per month. At any rate, John Houck has agreed to pay about $150 of the $500 to use some of the space.

Apollo Systems Technology, Inc.	12 Jun 1984	Karen took a $1,000 check to the Canyon Medical Plaza and put the money down to hold the office we will be renting on Friday.
Apollo Systems Technology, Inc.	15 Jun 1984	I worked on the systems engineering management plan (SEMP) outline all day today. Karen got the typewriter "fixed," but now it doesn't even run! It cost us $78 for the guy to clean it, and now it doesn't work. I signed the commercial lease agreement today for the new office suite in the Canyon Professional Plaza. We will move in tomorrow.
Apollo Systems Technology, Inc.	16 Jun 1984	I spent the morning working on the SEMP outline. In the afternoon, Atom, Eric Foyt, Jaime Illera, Marc, Karen, Heather, John Houck, and Jonathan Houck moved a lot of furniture and equipment into our new office at the Canyon Professional Plaza, 27141 Hidaway Avenue, Suite 205, Canyon Country, California. We worked from around 1:30–6:30 PM. Thank goodness the Moodys loaned us their Isuzu truck to haul all of the furniture. We hauled a lot of furniture and equipment from John Houck's home and a drawing table and two desks from the Illeras.
Apollo Systems Technology, Inc.	17 Jun 1984	I did some work on the SEMP outline this morning. At this point, I am now in the panic state. Tomorrow evening around 7:00 PM, I leave for San Diego to spend the night and then meet with the General Dynamics Convair (GDC) people on Tuesday. I may be up most of the night tonight typing up the SEMP outline.
Apollo Systems Technology, Inc.	18 Jun 1984	I spent the morning in our new office typing up Part II of the SEMP outline. We received our brand new Toshiba BD-3301 copying machine today. It cost about $1,720. In the afternoon, I typed up the rest of the SEMP outline in our home office. It was a miserably hot day today. Karen took Heather with her to check into some office phones in SFV. At 7:00 PM, I left for San Diego for my meeting with GDC in the morning. It took me three hours to drive from Canyon Country to the College Travelodge Motel in San Diego near San Diego State University.

Apollo Systems Technology, Inc.	19 Jun 1984	I delivered the SEMP outline to the GDC people this morning and spent the rest of the morning reading some documentation on the Small Intercontinental Ballistic Missile (SICBM) Program. I left for home at a little after noon and arrived in Canyon Country a little after 3:00 PM. After I came home for about 45 minutes, I went over to the office and worked till about 5:50 PM.
Apollo Systems Technology, Inc.	20 Jun 1984	I worked in my new office all day today. It was another extremely hot day. We had the phones connected in our new office. I received my first paycheck from AST today.
Apollo Systems Technology, Inc.	9 Jul 1984	I spent the whole day preparing the handout packet for the 2nd Board of Directors Meeting and the 1st Annual Stockholders Meeting.
Apollo Systems Technology, Inc.	10 Jul 1984	I worked feverishly all day today preparing for the Annual Stockholders Meeting and the 2nd Board of Directors Meeting. The meetings were held from 7:00–9:00 PM. Those attending included myself, Karen, Don Knapp, Jay Barney, Peachy Thomas, John Houck, Emerson Snider (he became a director tonight), and Francis Illera.
Apollo Systems Technology, Inc.	24 Jul 1984	I went into GDC today to deliver my first SEMP draft and to talk to the Hard Mobile Launcher (HML) people. When I got home, I received the purchase order (PO) from GDC for risk assessment and analysis on the HML program. It is a subcontract for $23,875.00. I spent the evening working in my office.
Apollo Systems Technology, Inc.	13 Aug 1984	I met with Don Knapp who desired to stop functioning as V.P. Marketing of AST and to stop receiving 1,000 shares per week effective 8/11/84. So, Don will have earned 15,000 shares for his work between 4/30/84 and 8/11/84.
Apollo Systems Technology, Inc.	16 Aug 1984	At about 2:40 PM, I went to the Security Pacific National Bank to pick up the papers for the $14,000 line-of-credit we are receiving from them. This cash will come in handy during our "valleys."

Apollo Sys-tems Techno-logy, Inc.	3 Sep 1984	Today is Labor Day. However, I went into the office to work because, as usual, I am behind the eight ball again. It seems that everything I must accomplish each day is never totally finished. I'm always in the catch-up mode. John and Carol Houck came into the office to work today also.
Apollo Sys-tems Techno-logy, Inc.	5 Sep 1984	I went to bed at 2:30 AM having worked on my input to GDC until that time. Then, I rose at 4:30 AM to take a shower and get ready to leave for San Diego. I left at 5:23 AM arriving at GDC at around 9:00 AM. I spent the entire day until 4:30 PM working in an un-air-conditioned building. It felt like it was 100 degrees F in there with the humidity around 90 percent. It was miserably hot, and I was covered with perspiration all day. Needless to say, I stunk from body odor (BO) all day!
Apollo Sys-tems Techno-logy, Inc.	1 Oct 1984	I worked in my office all day. The Apollo Systems Technology, Inc., sign for my door was finally installed today. It really looks good. Now, all they need to do is to get me the marquee signs for the two entrances.
Apollo Sys-tems Techno-logy, Inc.	4 Oct 1984	I had the photographer from the signal come over to the office today to take a picture of Karen and me at the computer for an ad in this Sunday's edition of the "New in Town" page. The ad cost us $50.00.
Apollo Sys-tems Techno-logy, Inc.	6 Oct 1984	I purchased a six-shelf oak bookcase for my office today. It cost $158.03.
Apollo Sys-tems Techno-logy, Inc.	23 Oct 1984	I labored in the office all day today preparing for a trip tomorrow to GDC–San Diego. To focus needed attention on marketing, proposal preparation, and new business development, I must devise a way to avoid having to perform all contracts by myself. I need, very badly, to hire a full-time secretary so that I can relieve myself of all of the typing, copying, and running errands that I currently do. In addition, I need to get myself in a position to hire a couple of engineers so that I can delegate and off-load a lot of the technical work that I am now doing. If Apollo Systems Technology, Inc. is going to grow to a $5 million operation in four more years, these things absolutely must be done.

Apollo Systems Technology, Inc.	20 Nov 1984	Boy, the months just seem to fly by. I just can't believe I've been in business for over 16 months now. I need to get this business growing faster. Being in the trenches while trying to build an organization is just not the thing to do. I need to hire a full-time secretary and two full-time engineers next year so that I can relieve myself of this grunt-work burden and spend most of my time in marketing and preparing proposals. New business development has to be my game. Doing the contract work must be done by hired hands.
Apollo Systems Technology, Inc.	20 Nov 1984	I worked in my office all day and evening. Karen is so good; she brings me my lunch and dinner. I love that sweetheart of mine. There are two more significant things I'm hoping will happen with the business before the end of this year. First, I hope we receive an 8(a) certification. And secondly, I hope we receive our facility clearance so that we will be able to do classified work. I am also in the process of getting another $10,000 as an add-on to my SICBM SEMP subcontract with GDC–San Diego. I am quoting the additional $10,000 for system requirements analysis (SRA) work as an increase in scope to the contract for 250 hours. I am really in a panic to complete my contract deliverables before the end of December 1984.
Apollo Systems Technology, Inc.	23 Nov 1984	I worked all day in my office today preparing charts for the SBIR proposal that I am preparing on the "Definition and Assessment of Physical Security Threats to Small ICBM Basing Systems." This is one R&D contract that I'm going to win. I can taste the victory on this one.
Apollo Systems Technology, Inc.	27 Nov 1984	I worked on the SEMP all day in my office today. The Pitney Bowes EMS-1 Electronic Mail Scale came today and works fine. Now, I hope the Touchmatic Postage Meter comes tomorrow.

Apollo Systems Technology, Inc.	30 Nov 1984	I suffered from the cold all day today. The Pitney Bowes Touchmatic Postage Meter came today. I was notified by Ed Gronich from New Dawn Communications that the first rough draft of our brochure was completed. He will be sending me a copy of it to review. Today, I received a letter from the Los Angeles office of the Small Business Administration (SBA) that they had completed their review of our 8(a) application and that they were forwarding it to the San Francisco Regional Office. It has been only eight months so far since we first submitted our application. The Civil Service is really a big joke. They tell me that it'll be another five months before we get a final decision on it. What a joke!
Apollo Systems Technology, Inc.	4 Dec 1984	Dr. Ohn Tin took me on a wasted trip to the Ballistic Missile Office (BMO) at Norton AFB, San Bernardino, today. He gave me the impression last week that a contract was 99.9 percent sure from a friend he has there. But it was a bunch of horseradishes! I had a bad headache today. I guess it's because of the three hours of driving and the frustration of a wasted day that I could have spent more profitably working on the SEMP.
Apollo Systems Technology, Inc.	7 Dec 1984	From the amount of work I have to complete between now and the end of the year, I do not believe that we will be able to make it to Utah for the Christmas-New Year's break. I will probably be working all the way to January 2, 1985, to meet my SRA deadline submittal. I am just too busy. I need to get more help to delegate work to. It seems that I can't do everything myself. My stomach is beginning to hurt again. And I just ran out of Tagamet pills last night. I think the stress and pressure is beginning to show on me. I must to be able to relax and take it easy.
Apollo Systems Technology, Inc.	20 Dec 1984	I worked right through last night on the SEMP and finally finished it tonight just before 11:00 PM. It ended up being 231 pages long. Karen helped me reproduce five copies of it today. I went to New Dawn Communications this afternoon to proof the brochure that they are putting together for AST. I have to admit, it looks really good.

Apollo Systems Technology, Inc.	21 Dec 1984	I received a check from GDC today for around $7,200. I am still waiting for the purchase order change for about $10K of additional work.
Apollo Systems Technology, Inc.	31 Dec 1984	This is New Year's Eve. I worked in my office all day and evening and completed the Type B3 specs–all 43 of them. Now, I have to get started on the Form Bs. It doesn't look like I'm going to make it by Wednesday morning. Well, at midnight tonight, we ushered in the New Year–1985. I was at work feverishly working on the specs.
Associate Fellow of AIAA	31 May 1979	Karen and I attended the Orange County Section of the American Institute of Aeronautics and Astronautics (AIAA) Installation Banquet. The event was held at the University of California at Irvine. First, we attended a cocktail party (Karen and I had ginger ale, of course) in the Engineering Building. Then we went on a guided tour of the various engineering laboratories. After that, we went to the Commons Cafeteria, where we had a buffet dinner. After the dinner, awards were presented and the new officers were installed. I was honored to receive a pin and certificate upgrading my membership from Member to Associate Fellow. Since Karen wasn't feeling too well, we left early (about 10:00 P.M.). We got home about 10:20 P.M., and I drove the baby sitter (Darlene Pitchforth) home.
Astronaut Kathryn Sullivan	13 May 1981	I gave Dr. Kathryn Sullivan, female NASA Astronaut, a tour of the APCO plant today.... After work, I attended the Management Club dinner, where we heard Astronaut Sullivan speak. I found out that I was elected a director of the Management Club.
Awards	18 Dec 1980	Karen made some finger sandwiches for me to take to work today. I finally got the "Atta Boy" and "Atta Girl" awards from the Art Department today and handed out a few. It was a big hit with the recipients.

Bad Day	10 Jan 1980	I drove the Chevy Nova to work today because Carlton Baab was coming by the plant for a visit, and I had planned to take him out for lunch. However, would you ever guess that, while driving on I-405 and before reaching the Westminster off-ramp, I experienced a flat tire?
		Because I felt it unsafe to fix the tire on the shoulder of I-405 while all the traffic was zooming by, I drove with the flat for about a mile so that I could get off the freeway and onto a street that was not busy to change the tire. I had a difficult time changing the tire, but after much hassling, I finally got it changed. While all this was going on, I must have stepped on some dog dump because I had it on the bottom and sides of my right shoe when I got to the office.
		Somehow, I must have snagged my coat on some sharp edge because my coat's right shoulder had a bunch of thread that was bundled up. It looked like a woman's stocking with a runner in it. I hope we can find a tailor who can pull the threads back in and return the coat's appearance to its original look. The coat is one of the new ones I bought a little over two months ago just before starting work at HRT (HR Textron). So, I finally got to work a half-hour late, my hands all dirty from changing the tire, dog dump on my shoe, and my coat unraveled.
		Carlton Baab was waiting for me in the lobby for almost a half-hour. I spent about five hours with Carlton explaining to him about HRT, giving him a tour of our Valencia and Pacoima plants, and taking him to lunch at the golf course clubhouse. I left work for home at about 5:00 P.M. and got home at about 6:30 P.M. Karen made tacos for dinner.
		Generally, it was a pretty bad day for me. We are going to have to buy another tire as a spare because the tire that went flat today had worn down to the threads and was damaged beyond use. I'm extremely exhausted tonight.
Bonus	5 Mar 1982	I received my bonus today. It wasn't as large as I had hoped it would be. It was for $5,376.00. I got only about 71–72 percent of the possible $7,500.00. I was also moved from a group D to a group C on the incentive plan. I'll probably have a possibility of earning maybe $10,000 or more for this calendar year.

Congress-man Barry Goldwater, Jr.	16 Nov 1981	I attended a breakfast for Congressman Barry Goldwater, Jr., in the Valencia Main Plant Cafeteria this morning at 8:00 o'clock. He gave a very interesting speech.
Congress-woman Bobbi Fiedler	21 Apr 1981	Congresswoman Bobbi Fiedler visited our plant today. I gave her a tour of our APCO operations, and Steve Kaplan gave her a tour of the Filters operations.
FIGMO	8 Oct 1979	Now that I know that I will be submitting my resignation on Monday, 15 October 1979, I have no great desire to work at TRW. In the military, they call it FIGMO. It has a vulgar meaning, but I call it "Forget it, I Got My Orders." It's the great letdown feeling you get when the job you're doing has no more value or meaning to you anymore.
Golfing	2 Jul 1982	Today was a holiday for us, which was part of a four-day fourth of July weekend. Karen and I went nine holes of golf with Ray and Janet Marbach (some work-related friends) at the Valencia Golf Course. Karen performed the best with a score of 67. I had a 68. Ray had a 91, and Janet's score was too high of which to keep track. Atom baby-sat Marc and Heather.
Gunther Klaus	15 Sep 1981	After work, I attended the Management Club meeting at the Odyssey Restaurant. The featured speaker, Gunther Klaus, gave a very exciting speech on "Sell 'em–or How to Have Success in Marketing."
Hospital Visit	6 Aug 1981	It was a usual hectic day at work today. After work, I went to visit Anita Ohl at Henry Mayo Newhall Memorial Hospital. She is Bill Ohl's wife, who also works at HRT. Bill is the production control supervisor at APCO. Anita works up in the main plant in Contracts. Bill was there at the hospital tonight at 6:15 when I went by to visit. Anita had surgery for an internal infection. I stopped off at Alpha Beta to buy some flowers and a get-well card before going over to the hospital. Anita was feeling better and is recovering from her operation, which she had on Tuesday.

Job Offer, HR Textron	24 Sep 1979	Alan Roney of HR-T called and made me an offer for $34,996 (or $35K for all practical purposes) for a job as program manager working for Chuck Collins.
		Chuck Collins called about 9:15 P.M. to talk about the job offer. Since earlier in the day I had told Alan Roney that I would think about it and call him tomorrow, I'm sure Chuck was concerned as to why I didn't accept it on the spot. After Chuck explained his rationale for offering me $35K instead of the $36K I had asked for, I felt prompted to accept the offer verbally. He said that Alan Roney would have the official offer letter out by Wednesday.
		Chuck would call me again on Wednesday to discuss when I will be reporting for work. He wants me to report as soon as possible, since he wants to put me on his most pressing program—the large contract (about $25M backlog) HRT has with Boeing providing them with actuators for the 747 aircraft.
		I guess the ward members will be shocked when we break the news of our pending move, as will the people at TRW—I'm sure. Life must move on. I have to take the opportunities as they come. This job will be my biggest break in my career thus far. I have a feeling it will be the one that will either make or break me. And I'm surely not going to let it break me. So, I will be putting my all into it in the first few months.
Job Offer, HR Textron	25 Sep 1979	At about 9:30 A.M., I called Alan Roney to tell him that I spoke with Chuck Collins last night and that I had accepted the offer. Alan said that he would get the official offer letter sent to me today. I'll have to take a physical exam up at the Valencia plant before I should submit my resignation to TRW.
		Hydraulic Research-Textron wants me to start work fairly soon, I'm sure, and they are willing to pay me either 20 cents per mile to travel to and from Westminster for 30 days or put me up in a townhouse for a month. We will make that decision on Wednesday when Chuck calls me again.
Job Offer, HR Textron	26 Sep 1979	Chuck Collins of HRT called. We agreed on my reporting for work on Tuesday, 30 October 1979. I called Alan Roney about getting my physical exam scheduled. He told me to call Nancy Wright, the nurse at HRT, to set it up. Alan told me he sent out the formal letter of offer yesterday, and that I should receive it either today or tomorrow. I then called Nancy Wright and set up my physical exam for 10:00 A.M., Monday, 1 October 1979.... I did receive in the mail the offer letter from HRT.

Job Offer, HR Textron	1 Oct 1979	This morning I went to HRT in Valencia to get a pre-employment physical examination. I passed "with flying colors." So, now the offer of employment has been officially offered to me, which I am accepting. I plan to submit my written resignation to TRW DSSG on Monday, 15 October 1979. My last day of work at TRW will be 29 October 1979. I will start working at HRT on Tuesday, 30 Oct 1979. Chuck Collins took me out to lunch today. We had a good chat.
La Costa Long-Range Planning Meeting	27 Apr 1981	Karen's mom flew into LAX today. She will be watching our kids from Wednesday through Sunday this week while we are at the Long-Range Planning Meeting at La Costa.
La Costa Long-Range Planning Meeting	29 Apr 1981	I worked until 1:00 P.M. today. I then went home to pick Karen up to go to La Costa. We left at 2:30 P.M.… We arrived at La Costa at 6:30 P.M. At 7:00 P.M., we went to dinner in the Steak House. We then returned to our hotel room and watched TV and read for the rest of the evening.
La Costa Long-Range Planning Meeting	30 Apr 1981	We met in work sessions today between 8:00 A.M. and 1:00 P.M. Before I went to the workshop, however, Karen and I had breakfast delivered to our room. I made a presentation on "The Organization." What I did was take notes during our one-hour Group A session. I then prepared flip charts and presented them to the entire PC (President's Council). After our sessions broke up at 1:00 P.M., Karen and I went to lunch in the dining hall. After that, we came back to the room for a rest. I read my *Strategic Planning* book while Karen watched TV. After a while, we went shopping and sightseeing the homes in the area. In the evening, we attended the Mexican dinner in the Cantina Room. It was a real blast. At about 9:45 P.M., we got back to our room. I did more reading while Karen watched TV. I think I ate too much, as I've a tummy ache.

La Costa Long-Range Planning Meeting	1 May 1981	We met in session today from 8:00 A.M. to 1:00 P.M. After that, Karen and I had lunch together. Then we went back to the room to rest. I attempted to do some work on Chapter 1 of my thesis. At 6:15 P.M., everyone got on a chartered bus for dinner at Anthony's Restaurant in San Diego. We had all the seafood we could eat, which included crab, oyster, clam, shrimp, scampi, lobster, etc. Bert Smith won the oyster-eating contest by eating 51 oysters. Karen and I won the lobster-eating contest by eating nine half-lobsters between us. We got back to the hotel by 11:30 P.M.
La Costa Long-Range Planning Meeting	2 May 1981	We had a good meeting today between 8:00 A.M. and 12:00 noon, which covered life cycle and market share analysis. The wives/spouses came in at 12:00 noon for a brief review of the proceedings of our meetings. The plastic incentive checks were passed out. My check was for $7,500.00. If we met our objectives to Textron this year, I will be able to keep the $7,500.00 check. After the meeting, Karen and I went to lunch with Dr. Y.N. Chang and his wife, Jean. Dr. Chang was the consultant who worked with us on strategic planning over the last three days. I took about a 3–1/2-hour nap in the afternoon. At 7:00 P.M., we attended a dinner-dance with the rest of the HRT PC group. Since Karen wasn't feeling too well, we left about 10:15 P.M.
La Costa Long-Range Planning Meeting	3 May 1981	We slept until after 10:00 this morning. After having lunch, we checked out. Our bill came to about $550 for the four days. We left for home at about 12:45 P.M....We arrived home at about 3:40 P.M. and were too exhausted to make it to sacrament meeting.
Manufac-turer's Rep-resentative	26 Jul 1983	I met with Ellwood Jae, chairman of the board, and Jeffrey Jae, president, of Tavco, Inc. this morning and shook hands on STS serving as a manufacturer's rep for Tavco. Mr. Ellwood Jae will be preparing a memorandum of agreement on this contract. They will be paying us a $250/week retainer for 10 hours of work per week. We will be receiving a 5 percent commission on all new work acquired in Southern California (whether or not we did anything to capture the work). I will be starting on Monday, August 1st.

Merit Increase	5 Mar 1979	Good news! Today I received my merit review at work and was informed that I will be receiving a 7.5 percent raise, which will be reflected in my 15 March 1979 paycheck. The 7.5 percent comes to about $2,200 increase in salary per annum. Now I make $31,400 per year.
Merit Increase	22 Dec 1981	I received my annual review at work today and got a 10 percent merit increase. My salary is now $46,228 per year.
New Job Search	7 Sep 1982	I went to work today and found that there will be a reorganization next week, which would adversely affect my status and standing in the company. Consequently, I am actively starting to look for a new job....I spent the evening typing up some resume cover letters....
NAMC	1 Nov 1982	I failed to mention that last night I received a call from _____. He concurred to giving me $52K per year plus a bonus, which pays on a monthly basis. After he documents the bonus formula and sends it to me, I will evaluate it and make my final decision. But I have tentatively accepted to report for work at North American Manufacturing Corporation (NAMC) in Spanish Fork, Utah, on January 17, 1982. This will be an opportunity for me to become a vice president and general manager.

NAMC	3 Jan 1983	I submitted my resignation from HR Textron today to Dave Stewart. My resignation is effective on January 16; however, my last day of work will be on Friday, January 14. I start work at NAMC on Monday, January 17, 1983. I plan to leave for Utah on Friday, January 14 and arrive at my apartment in Springville, Utah, late Saturday, January 15, 1983.

This evening, we called my sisters, Diane and Sharon, and my brother, Carl, to let them know that I accepted the job with NAMC and that I will be coming to Utah on the 15th. We will be putting our house on the market in a couple of weeks and expect to sell it in three to six months. Our family should be moving to Utah by the beginning of summer.

I also received a phone call from _____ who was visiting Boeing in Seattle, Washington, on an equipment quality audit (EQA). He was checking with me to see if I had submitted my resignation. He said that he was getting me a better apartment in Springville and that he had already gotten me a car.

Karen is suffering from her fifth consecutive day of an extremely bad migraine headache. This is the cross she has borne over the past three years ever since we moved to the Santa Clarita Valley. I hope that our move to Utah will help in reducing her migraines.

Karen wants to move to either Orem or Provo, Utah. My brother, Carl, and his family live in Provo. My sister, Sharon, and her family live in Lindon, Utah. And my sister, Diane, and her family live in Ogden, Utah. Now, we will have four of the seven Uda kids living in Utah.

Lowell and his family live in Montana. Florence and Kelton and their families live in Hawaii. My parents also live in Hawaii, but they may also be moving to Utah.

It looks like the entire Uda clan is migrating to Zion or the Holy Land.

NAMC	17 Jan 1983	This was my first day at work at the NAMC. My alarm rang about 5:30 A.M., but I lay in bed for about 20 minutes before getting up to take a shower. Eric Duncan got up right away and took his shower. After he was through, I got up and took a shower. After getting dressed, I cooked up some bacon and eggs for breakfast. Eric didn't eat breakfast. Then we took off for work arriving there about 7:05 A.M.
		_____ arrived shortly thereafter and started to introduce us to those in the office area. After a short while, _____ called all the shop management/supervision together to introduce me to them. After a short introduction, _____ turned the floor over to me for a short speech, which I gave for about five minutes.
		Then Eric and I in-processed with Personnel. After _____ left with Jack McConnell to fly back to California, I met briefly with _____. During the lunch hour, I went to pick up the phones for our apartment in downtown Spanish Fork. I also stopped for lunch at a drive-in and went shopping for wall hooks and screwdrivers at Grand Central.
		In the afternoon, I spent some time talking with my administrative assistant, Joyce Robb, and to _____. I had a real good discussion with _____.
		We worked until after 5:00 P.M. Then I went to duplicate some keys. Eric Duncan drove a company van home because we were going to pick up a couch at his brother's apartment. After I got back to the apartment, we installed the phones. Then we cooked some hamburgers for dinner.
		After that, we drove to Provo and Orem to see if there were any cheap furniture stores open. This being Monday evening (FHE night), no furniture stores were open. Hence, we drove to Eric's brother's apartment.
		After talking with his brother and sister-in-law (Jeff and Shirlene) for about a half-hour, we decided to leave without the couch. We felt that they needed it more than we did, and that we probably wouldn't sit on it much in our living room without a TV. But mainly, Eric didn't want to lug it out to the van. So, we returned home at around 8:30 P.M.
		I sure do miss my wife, Karen, and our three kids: Atom, Marc, and Heather.

NAMC	18 Jan 1983	I really miss my family and hope our house sells fast. We get our phones turned on tomorrow, so I'll be able to call home tomorrow evening. Having to shop, cook, wash dishes, do the laundry, and run errands have really "cramped my style." Usually, Karen would do all these things for me. Doing them myself would take a lot of my time and effort. This obviously makes me appreciate my darling wife more so. My wife is the best woman any man can have. I am really proud of her and love her very much. I hope we have a long and lasting life together on this earth. Furthermore, I hope our children outlive us. I love them all so dearly.
NAMC	22 Jan 1983	_____ and Bill Gordon were in plant today. We had a good discussion. The main theme I got out of the entire discussion is that I will have to spend 75 percent of my time selling. In a week, I will be going to the Los Angeles area to visit customers. As time goes on, I will be spending 50 percent of my time on the road.
NAMC	7 Feb 1983	I was surprised to come back to NAMC today to find out that _____, production manager, had laid off 32 people or 15 percent of our workforce. It seems that he is as impulsive as his father is. To take such an action without notifying me beforehand and making this decision in a matter of minutes just goes beyond me. He is running open loop! It's no wonder we now have fallen back into a bad morale problem…and after I started turning things around in my first two weeks on the scene, even. I leave for a week, and all Hades breaks loose. I just can't believe he did that.
NAMC	8 Feb 1983	It was a fairly calm day today. I forgot to mention that Randall Jones started working for me yesterday as Gyro Sales Manager. And today Jack McConnell started working as our QC Manager. I also hired Jack. Yesterday, I took Randall out to lunch; today I took Jack to lunch. It is really nice that _____ is in Europe on business. I can just imagine what it would be like if he were around here to get involved in running this operation. It would be difficult at best. The longer he stays away, the better things will be.

NAMC	21 Feb 1983	I had my first real confrontation with _____ today when I asked him if I could go ahead with establishing an engineering department at NAMC as he had suggested several weeks ago. Evidently, in the interim, he had changed his mind because his comment to me was that I would make this place go broke if I did set up an engineering group in plant. I mentioned to him that several of our customers and potential customers had expressed some concern that we didn't have on-site engineering support. That didn't phase _____ any, who then began to extol the virtues of the NEETA Corporation and how it serves the purpose well. The only problem is that I think the NEETA organization stinks, and that it doesn't give us the kind of support we need. And we have to pay $4,000 per week for that weak support. Well, the drama begins to unfold at _____ and the NAMC. I worked until 10:30 P.M. writing about a dozen letters for tomorrow. Oh, I might also mention that _____ probed me about hiring Randall Jones and the lack of his aerospace selling experience. He also questioned why I was focusing on selling in the Gyro line with Randall as opposed to concentrating in aerospace.
NAMC	23 Feb 1983	Well, today, _____ called me into his office to tell me that I should only be visiting prime contractors and not smaller companies. He also said that we should be going only for large assembly or system jobs and not piece-part, machined-to-print work. When I asked him his feelings about improving community relations with the Chamber of Commerce and Utah Valley Manufacturers' Council, he was negative at first. He was thinking that I would go out and solicit groups. However, when he found that they had come to us requesting a meeting in our plant and touring it, he changed his tune. That's how it went today. After all, he is the boss and owner of this company. Furthermore, I should remember that I have a lot more responsibility and authority now than I ever did have at HR Textron. Hence, I should be happy. That's what I will have to keep telling myself. I worked until 10:30 tonight. After I came home, I fixed myself some warmed-up canned chili and a tossed salad.

NAMC	24 Feb 1983	Today was a good day. _____ came in about noon, so I went to lunch with him. Then, in the later afternoon, Tom Summers came in for a visit. This is a fascinating person. He is 73 years old but doesn't look a day older than 60. He has over 60 U.S. patents to his credit. He's an absolute genius! After we chatted for over an hour, we went in to chat with _____ and _____. _____ hired Tom for $36K, plus he is paying him $9K for three months of work he has already done on a directional gyro and for his moving expenses back to California. _____, Bill Edwards, and I went to dinner at Big Boy's in Provo and had a nice discussion on the business. After that, I returned to the plant and worked until around 11:30 P.M.
NAMC	8 Mar 1983	Well, they say that it always comes to every top-level manager who works for _____. He waylaid into me this morning and told me that being on the road for only 50 percent of the time as I have been doing is unsatisfactory. He wants me to be on the road 100 percent of the time. Hence, I will only be a salesman with a big title. Tomorrow, I'll be flying to New York to visit Fairchild and Grumman. It was a miserable day for me today. _____ raised his voice at me and just nailed me to the wall. I really resent the way he did it. I am so mad that I am about to look for another job. Maybe I should go into business for myself. Time marches on.
NAMC	10 Mar 1983	I am still very upset at _____ and will try to get another job with either Martin Padway or Tavco. _____'s way of treating me has irked me to no end.
NAMC	13 Mar 1983	I typed up a letter to Martin Padway, president of Padway Aircraft Products Inc., to see if I can go to work for him.
NAMC	14 Mar 1983	I typed up a letter to W. Elwood Jae, president of Tavco, Inc., to be mailed to him either next Sunday or early Monday morning if Martin Padway doesn't respond by then to the letter I mailed him this morning. I am sick of the NAMC and want to get out ASAP.
NAMC	15 Mar 1983	Every day that goes by, I dislike more working for this wretched company. I hope Martin Padway offers me a position in his company. I'd like to jump ship next week if I can. I can't stand this company and some of the people anymore.

NAMC	27 Mar 1983	After church, we came home, ate lunch, and I read the *Los Angeles Times*. I typed out a couple of cover letters for job openings. I can hardly stand working for _____ anymore and can't wait to resign.
NAMC	29 Mar 1983	I worked at the _____ plant all day revising the _____Engineering Specifications (_ESs). I had my first bad hay fever attack today now that spring has sprung.
NAMC	30 Mar 1983	I worked on the _____ specs again all day at the Newbury Park plant. It was another headachy, stressful day for me. This has to come to an end soon.
NAMC	31 Mar 1983	I spent another painful day working on the _ESs. Fortunately, I completed them and dropped them off at the NEETA facility.
NAMC	3 Apr 1983	I am having another hay fever attack tonight. I took a 12-hour Contact pill, which usually makes me drowsy. I've completed 11 weeks with _____. I don't know how much longer this employment can and will last.
NAMC	19 Apr 1983	I really feel miserable about not being home so much and not being able to be more involved in Church. This job is so demanding on my time and energy that I get so exhausted after I get home that I don't feel like doing anything except lying around and resting. However, I have to say that this marketing and sales experience I am getting is very valuable. I am learning about many companies and government agencies, making a lot of contacts, and gaining confidence in my sales abilities. I wouldn't want to do this for more than a year though. The things that really depress me about this job are listed as follows: (1) _____ won't really let go, (2) _____ talks to me in a condescending manner, (3) _____ expects me to be on the road constantly, and (4) _____ has turned some of my decisions around (which says I really don't have total P&L responsibility).

NAMC	27 Apr 1983	It was another exhausting day at work. I find it quite difficult to motivate myself to work for this company because my heart isn't in it anymore. The proposal that I am working on for Hughes Helicopters is especially taxing on me. I had a splitting headache today. I guess it is all emotions. After coming home, I slept much of the evening between doing some reading. For dinner, I only had Campbell's vegetable soup. At noon today, I returned my phones to the phone company because they were costing me more than they were worth, mainly because I have been on the road so much selling for the company.
NAMC	15 May 1983	I got up around 6:25 A.M. to get ready to drive back to Utah. By the time I hit the road, it was almost 8:00 A.M. The drive took slightly over 12 hours to go 667 miles. I am exhausted. This is definitely not the kind of life I would want to lead indefinitely. I hope something comes up soon so that I can quit working for this lousy company.
NAMC	12 Jun 1983	_____, _____ VP and assistant to the chairman of the board, called me a couple of times tonight and ruined my evening with his boisterous talking and third degree questioning. I am really depressed to the point where I have been motivated to look for another job.
NAMC	15 Jun 1983	I'm getting sick of this job and _____ and _____. I'm ready to quit. I hope I get another job offer soon. Five months of this insane company is enough. I can't wait to turn in my resignation. This company is a real loser.
NAMC	6 Jul 1983	Dwight Haymond and I joined Rod Cockrell and Don and Karl Knapp at the Airporter Inn Restaurant, next to the Orange County Airport, for lunch. After that, I took Dwight back to NEETA. Then I went to _____ in Newbury Park for a 3:30 P.M. meeting with _____. He fired me today! I took it calmly as I was going to be gone sooner or later, one way or another. That is _____'s style. Nobody lasts long with _____. They either quit or are fired. I also have _____ to thank for bringing this about only after six months with the company. Anyway, I feel good to be out of this sorry organization. Now, the search begins for a new job. I will also be trying to get my business going quicker.

NAMC	10 Jul 1983	I prepared and mailed a letter to _____today proposing to offer my services to him as a manufacturer's rep for a retainer fee of $1,000 per month.
NAMC	18 Jul 1983	In the mail, I received a rejection from _____ of my proposal to do sales representing for him for a retainer fee of $1,000 per month.
NAMC	5 Aug 1983	_____ called me today to see if I was interested in the Administrative Engineer's position down at NEETA. Not wanting any opportunity to get by without my knowing all of the details, I acted as if I was interested. So, he called back later to see if I could be at the Newbury Park Plant in an hour to interview with Bernie Gira, the consultant that _____ knew for 40 years that he hired to straighten the mess out at _____. I told him I needed an hour-and-a-half. So, I took a shower, dressed, and drove over to Newbury Park. I arrived there about 10:00 A.M. This seems really strange that four weeks after _____ fires me, his boys are back talking about re-hiring me. I have to get an offer from them down in writing. This could be interesting and funny, when I turn them down. What a laugh. Bernie seemed interested in me after the interview. We'll see in a few days whether or not he will make me an offer. I think Norm had some guilty feelings about "stabbing me in the back" in getting me fired. I think this is why he recommended me for this position. What a laugh. This is one for Ripley's "Believe It or Not!"
NAMC	8 Jan 1984	Well, it's been six months to the day since I left NAMC. Today, I found out that _____ died on Thursday in a small airplane crash in Salt Lake City. I feel terrible about it because _____ and I worked closely together when I was up at the Spanish Fork plant. Now, _____ has to run it all by himself after _____ passes on. It's going to be a tough haul for him.
NAMC	11 Jan 1984	Karen and I attended _____'s funeral today at the Camarillo Stake Center. It was a beautiful service attended by hundreds of friends, relatives, and co-workers.

Promotion to General Manager	4 Sep 1980	This has been a monumental milestone day. Dave Stewart, my boss and vice president of the Controls Division, called me at home about 6:30 P.M. to inform me that he will be promoting me to general manager of the Air-Fuel-Firex Product Group at the APCO facility in Pacoima. My promotion will be effective on Monday, September 8, 1980. Needless to say, I am thrilled to death to have this opportunity to prove myself in this high-level management position.
SBA 8(a) Program	21 Jun 1984	I went to the L.A. SBA office for an 8:00 AM meeting on our 8(a) application. After that, I returned to my office and worked there for the remainder of the day.
Starting a Business	9 May 1983	We got our federal and state tax return today. The total came to $2,607.00. I will be putting $2,000 of it into a business account to start a company called Systems Technology Services Corporation. I went to the post office today to pick up an application form for renting a PO box. Tomorrow, Karen will order a business phone, open a bank account for the company, and call about getting a fictitious name published in *The Signal*. After I do all that, I will be able to get some letterhead and business cards. Then, I'll have to get a business tax and permit, and a federal employee ID number. I will also be incorporating soon.
Starting a Business	25 Aug 1983	It seems the farther ahead I get, the more behind I fall. I never can get through my "Things to Do Today" list. After I get some items completed, a bunch more are added. However, that's life in the starting up of a business. I am doing many things that a secretary would normally do as a matter of course.

Trial of Faith	2 Apr 1984	It seems like "when it rains, it pours." I am really going through my trail of faith at this time. We have had no income for almost nine months.
		I have been trying to get my new business going. My calling as first counselor in the bishopric has been keeping me hopping. And to add to it all, unexpected occurrences like the passing away of Bob Brockbank has been keeping me busy with arranging for the funeral services, etc.
		It's been just one thing after another, which has taken me away from my primary objective and priority, which is to provide a sufficient cash flow so that I can adequately provide for my family.
		With all of these trials, however, I know that the Lord will bless us and not let us go hungry. I know it with conviction that He will provide for us by allowing us to win a major contract soon. We are getting right out to the ragged edge, and I know He will not let us fall over the edge. But I do know that He will test us to the hilt so that we will become stronger from the experience. I know for sure that this experience has given us more understanding and compassion for those who make small incomes or who have gone unemployed for a long period of time. I have full faith and confidence that the Lord will see us through these trying times. I hope and pray it will be soon.

| Trial of Faith | 7 Apr 1984 | I am really beginning to feel the pressure now. It has been nine months since I lost my job with NAMC and started working full time in establishing and building my own company.
Our savings are depleted. Sears Machine Company stopped paying me the $250.00 per week as of last week. Our rent will be due in one more week, and we barely have enough to pay it. Then to top it all, we have gobs of bills that are due, but we have no money available to pay them. I can't count on anything coming from the Employment Development Department.
There are only two good notes that are coming up. We will be receiving about $2,900 tax return, which we should receive in a month. And, hopefully, I will have a consulting contract with GDC by May 1.
Other than that, I found out yesterday that we lost the NASA/MSFC contract on the "High Area Ratio Concept Investigation" study. And I had a really good feeling that we were going to win that one. I guess my senses are not really that good. I am really experiencing a trial of my faith.
I completed reading the book today on *Drawing on the Powers of Heaven* by Grant Von Harrison for the second time. It was a good book, which Bishop Thompson had recommended that I read.
Honestly, I really need the help of our Father in Heaven. I cannot go this road alone. It is all in His hands. I am trying to do everything I can to succeed at making AST go. I hope the Lord will bail us out soon. We are getting right down to our whit's end. Karen and I have fought like cats and dogs because of the stress and pressure under which we exist. If things don't work out soon, I may be forced to get a lower paying job somewhere just to get some money coming in. |
| Trial of Faith | 9 Apr 1984 | I'm beginning to feel the pressure more and more to get something going to get a sufficient cash flow. Something has got to break. I am praying so much that the Lord will help us out of this predicament. |

Trial of Faith	11 Apr 1984	I have been really sick today with both a headache and stomach pains. I don't know if my body wants to catch the flu or I am just having worrying problems because of our dire financial situation. I determined exactly what we owe and how badly we are in debt. It made me sick to find out that our credit cards show a debt of $7,270. And by next month, that will go up to $9000. Before we get sufficient cash flowing again, we will be over $10,000 in debt. This has been gnawing at me all day, which has contributed to my ill-feeling condition. By the end of this month, I have to pay out $2,157. But I only will have about $1,500 to cover it. So, I will have to cover it with the last credit card I have plus around $1,200 for fixing our car, which is still in the shop. After using up about $1,800 of the $2,000 limit, we are going to be in trouble until we receive our $2,900 tax return, which will barely cover us for May and June. If I don't get any of the money I am trying to get from unemployment insurance, we are going to be "up the creek" much more than we are right now. Something has to break for us. I have been sending out resumes this past week in hopes that I would receive a job offer to take off the pressure from us at this time. I also hope and pray that a GD-Convair contract comes to reality. The Lord is really trying my faith. I have got to persevere and prove that I have staying power. Satan will not overcome me. I know if I can hang in there, Heavenly Father will come to the rescue as long as I keep the faith, pray, and endure to the end and do all of the things I supposed to do.
Trial of Faith	14 Apr 1984	I received good news in the mail today, which I consider an answer to prayer. The Administrative Law Judge at the Van Nuys Office of Appeals made a decision in my favor and has now declared me eligible for unemployment insurance from August 28, 1983, onward. Now, it is a matter of how much the San Fernando Employment Development Department will give me since that time. This news really made my day.

| **Trial of Faith** | 16 Apr 1984 | I spent the day working in my office. Karen took my car back to the garage and found that I need a new radiator. That will be another $200 of expenses. Murphy's Law is really working on us. Everything is going wrong.

One good note, however. Don Knapp called me this morning and said that he will be investing $12,000 in the company. That will save us for another six months. We should get this business going in the next three months.

We received our first order (about $45) for J&S Chemical Corporation products today. It is small, but it is a start. |

Trial of **Faith**	21 Apr 1984	The Lord is beginning to answer our prayers and to help us. Karen sold three dolls this past week and made $60. She received a raise from $3.35 per hour to $3.75 per hour at Howard & Phil's. I received the RFQ (request for quotation) from GDC (General Dynamics-Convair) today to prepare a System Engineering Management Plan on the Small ICBM Weapon System Program. It will be a three-month job, which I will be bidding about $20,000 for it. The deadline for my quote is this coming Tuesday. I also received in the mail today an appointment for Wednesday at 2:30 P.M. with the Employment Development Department. I think we will be receiving some money from them for my unemployment insurance, which they stopped giving me last August 28th. I hope we can justify receiving about a couple of thousand dollars. Don Knapp sent me our signed agreement for him to invest $12,000 in the company by buying 120,000 shares of AST stock. He will also become AST Corporate Vice President and will start working full time for the company on April 30. He will be in charge of the Manufacturers' Rep side of the business. The $12,000 check should be arriving here this next week. We received a small order this week from Megadiamond Industries, Inc. for some rust remover chemical. It's a small start but could grow in the future. I mailed off the preliminary proposal to the AFOSR (Air Force Office of Scientific Research) today. It's good to have another one under our belt. Our $2,900 tax return should be coming soon. When we get that, we will be in good shape for a couple of months. This has been a tough 9½ months since I was fired from NAMC. But I have full faith and confidence we are going to make it. I know the Lord will not let us down. Karen went to work today and sold over $1,000 worth of goods. The whole store only sold a little over $1,500. Thus, the two other guys in the store sold only $500 worth of goods between them. I think Karen is an outstanding salesperson.

Trial of Faith	25 Apr 1984	I did a few things in the office before going to the Employment Development Department in San Fernando to go over my expense lists. We will be receiving a check either this Friday or next Monday for back benefits since August 28, 1983. I hope we get at least a couple of thousands of bucks. We need it badly.
Trial of Faith	26 Apr 1984	I sent the GDC quotation on the "Preparation of a System Engineering Management Plan (SEMP) for the Small ICBM Weapon System" by Express Mail this morning. I quoted $19,750.50 for 3½ months of work and a 225-page document. We'll be in good shape after we win this subcontract. Don Knapp gave me a check for $12,000.00 today to purchase 120,000 shares of AST common stock at $.10 per share. Don saved the company from going under. I am thankful to Heavenly Father for making Don feel all of that confidence in AST and me. These are great days for us, even though we have been struggling financially over the past 9½ months. It has taught us a lot of things. I'm really thankful to our Heavenly Father for helping us in our time of great need.
Trial of Faith	2 May 1984	Good news today! We received in the mail from the Employment Development Department 21 checks totaling $1,649 for back payments of unemployment insurance since August 28, 1983. This windfall was heaven sent, as we didn't have any money, our bank accounts were overdrawn, and our credit cards are over the limit. This was a very good day in the life of the Uda family.
Trial of Faith	3 May 1984	This morning Karen, Heather, and I drove around the area to look for office space to lease. I am going to lease a facility this month for AST. Today, I received a $3,500.00 line-of-credit from the Chase Manhattan Bank on their Chase Advantage Credit Program. I have a book of personalized checks that we can write checks for any purchases of $100 or more.
Trial of Faith	5 May 1984	I received another sole source RFQ from GDC today in the mail. They specifically want me to provide system engineering and analysis services on risk assessment for the Hard Mobile Launcher (HML) program. Things are really looking up for AST and us. I have only to thank Heavenly Father for blessing us.

Trial of Faith	21 May 1984	I hope something breaks for me this week. This can't go on like this much longer. Something good and positive has got to happen.
Trial of Faith	22 May 1984	According to a call from the GDC buyer, we should be receiving the contract by the end of the week.
Trial of Faith	24 May 1984	Today, we received a $353.00 check for our tax refund from Utah. Now, if we will receive our refund from the federal IRS, we will be in good shape for a couple of months.
Trial of Faith	1 Jun 1984	I talked to the GDC buyer this afternoon. She said that she would be sending me the P.O. today. She gave me the P.O. number. So, it looks like we will be receiving a contract either tomorrow or Monday.
Trial of Faith	4 Jun 1984	I worked in my office all day. The P.O. from GDC did not come in the mail today. Bad news! Our federal income tax return has not arrived yet also. We have just got to get it this week or we will be in deep yogurt.
Trial of Faith	7 Jun 1984	I went for an interview at Northrop Electronics this morning. The guy who interviewed me, Joe Coulter, liked me so much that he said that they will be making me an offer. After I got home, a Federal Express package was waiting for me. It was the purchase order from GD-Convair for a three-month contract to prepare a SEMP (systems engineering management plan) on the Small ICBM Program. I think AST is finally on its way to become a viable business. In the evening from 7:30–9:00 PM, I held a PPI with Sis. Jeannie Groff, our ward activities chairman. After that, I spent the rest of the evening working in my office.
Trial of Faith	8 Jun 1984	I worked in the office all day today. In the afternoon, Karen and I went again to look at office spaces in the Hillside Professional Center. Karen went to work at Howard & Phil's for the last time today. The boys and I left for the Father and Son Overnighter at Carpinteria Beach. We also took Jay and Christian Barney and Joey Groff along with us. Apricot dumped in my office some time during the night. Boy was I mad at her.
Trial of Faith	10 Jun 1984	Well, it has been 11 months since I departed from NAMC. I start receiving a salary starting tomorrow from AST. I will be receiving $20.00/hour.

Trial of Faith	14 Jun 1984	I received a copy of a letter in the mail from Lockheed-California Company informing Tavco that they were going to buy a couple of Freon Pressurization systems and a couple of pressure vessels. That will be about a $50K contract of which we will receive a 5 percent commission. Things are really looking up for us. I thank Heavenly Father for answering our prayers.
Unemployment	11 Jul 1983	In the early afternoon, I went to the Unemployment Office in San Fernando to pick up the forms to fill out to get unemployment insurance. It was a strange feeling in there. I felt the same way in July-August 1974, when I resigned my commission in the USAF and was without work for about a month-and-a-half. I will have to go back to the Unemployment Office tomorrow at 2:00 P.M. for a group orientation. This was my first full day of unemployment. I am pursuing two options. First, I am sending out resumes to get another job. Secondly, I am trying to get my business going. If I can get five companies to give me $1,000 retainers per month, I will be able to get the Sales Representation Division of my company (Systems Technology Services) going full force. Then, I won't have to get a full-time job working for somebody. I can work for myself, which is what I ultimately want to do anyway.
Unemployment	12 Jul 1983	This afternoon at 2:00 P.M., I went down to the Unemployment Office again to fill out the bunch of bureaucratic forms to apply for unemployment insurance. They herded us through like cattle. It is really demeaning and insults one's intelligence to have to go through this embarrassing ritual to get a measly $166.00 per week of unemployment insurance.
Unemployment	3 Oct 1983	Then, at 3:05 P.M., I left for the unemployment office in San Fernando for an interview there. They are giving me hassles about my itemized business expenses. I think they are going to try to shut off my unemployment insurance, which they have not paid in over three weeks. That bureaucratic organization is a waste of taxpayers' money. They are manned by nothing but incompetents. I already went through this hassle once before with another examiner. Now, because they changed the examiner, I have to start all over again with this really sad person. The hassle almost doesn't seem worth trying to justify getting the $166.00 per week. I'll have to call them again tomorrow to get their verdict on this case.

Unemploy-ment	4 Oct 1983	I received a call this morning from a Mrs. Johns of the San Fernando Employment Development Department, who said that my unemployment insurance benefits would cease as of week ending 9/3/83 and indefinitely thereafter. I was so upset about this unilateral decision on her part that I spent the entire afternoon drafting and typing up an appeal letter to the director of that office. I hope he will have enough sense to apply the "spirit" as well as the "letter" of the law.
Unemploy-ment	8 Oct 1983	I got a letter in the mail that stated that I was ineligible for any more unemployment insurance, because I supposedly was not actively seeking full-time employment. I wrote a two-page letter with about 45 pages of attachments justifying my position in an attempt to appeal the decision. I think I have them with all the facts to back my position up.
Unemploy-ment	21 Oct 1983	I have a good feeling that my appeal for my canceled unemployment insurance over the past couple of months will be approved. That will be a big help. It may pay another month's worth of rent.
Unemploy-ment	22 Nov 1983	I worked in my office all day today. However, between 9:45 A.M. and 12:45 P.M., I went to the Employment Development Department in San Fernando to attend my appeal hearing on being reinstated to receive unemployment insurance. I was sick with the way it went in that hearing. It is now up to Heavenly Father to soften the heart of Judge Stopol to get her to give us a break and provide us with some funds to live on beyond January 1, 1984. I hope and pray we get something or I am going to shut down STS and go out and really get a job working for someone.
Unemploy-ment	8 Dec 1983	When I came home, I was depressed to find the result of my appeal hearing with the Administrative Law Judge was negative. I guess I am going to have to appeal it one more time.
Unemploy-ment	13 Dec 1983	This evening, I started drafting my letter of appeal on my unemployment insurance stoppage decision. This has been a real hassle to me. I hope we can get a favorable ruling this time. They say, the third time is a charm. I hope so anyway.
Unemploy-ment	14 Dec 1983	After that, I returned home for some lunch and to assemble my appeal report to the Van Nuys Appeals Board. Then, I went to the post office followed by driving to Van Nuys to deliver the appeal report.

Unemploy- **ment**	10 Jan 1984	Brother and Sister Gratrix came over this evening and brought me a couple of quarts of Perrier water. It's an expensive drink (carbonated water), which I had stated in my testimony on Sunday that I couldn't afford to drink anymore. I got a good laugh over their bringing me those two bottles.
Unemploy- **ment**	28 Mar 1984	I am really beginning to feel the financial squeeze. Our bills are stacking up, and I am finally beginning to have a hard time making ends meet. This week is the last time we will be receiving $250 from the Sears Machine Company. That is really going to hurt us next month. I hope and pray the Lord will bless us by making the Employment Development Department people give us some back payments on our unemployment insurance. We need that money badly. In the next couple of days, we will receive from our tax consultant our tax return papers to sign. It will probably be May 1st before we receive our tax return check. We are going to need that money badly at that time. Something has to break for us. I am waiting on the verdict from NASA/MSFC on the proposal we sent them and also the consulting work with GDC in San Diego. If one of those things happens by next week, we will be in good shape. Something has to happen soon. This is the most I've struggled in my entire life. I guess the Lord is putting us through the "refiner's fire." This is a real humbling experience. I really don't know how much longer this will go on. It's really teaching me many good lessons. I've started reading *Faith Precedes the Miracle* by Spencer W. Kimball and *Drawing on the Powers of Heaven* by Grant Von Harrison. Bishop Thompson (during my temple recommend renewal interview last night) recommended that I read the latter book. He also recommended that I read *Lectures on Faith*, which I will try to get soon.
Vacation/ **Holidays**	6 Jul 1979	This vacation/holiday period is sure going by quickly. I only have two more days out of a total of nine before I have to return to work. It never seems long enough.
Vacation/ **Holidays**	8 Jul 1979	My nine-day vacation from work has come to an end. Tomorrow morning, I will be going to work at CTS (Capistrano Test Site). These vacations (holidays) never seem to be long enough. I really need about a month's rest from work to really recuperate.

| Vacation/ Holidays | 4 Jan 1981 | I'm glad my 12-day vacation is over. Now, I can go back to work and recuperate. |

12

Educational Things

*A*nother huge part of my life has been my educational pursuits. I strongly believe that education and training are lifelong endeavors. Learning new things should never stop. I have two bachelors and two master's degrees. Throughout my life, I have always wanted to earn a doctorate degree. I still may do it starting next year. As in reading and writing, I find great solace in studying and learning.

Books	3 Jun 1979	Brother Emerson Snider gave me another box of old books he didn't want any more. I value almost all books and will gladly take them off people's hands to stock my bookshelves. I am an avid reader and love all kinds of books.
Executive Program at UCLA	8 Jul 1981	Today, we received a letter from Industrial Relations, which said that they would nominate me to attend the Executive Program at UCLA starting in January 1982. It is a two semester "gentlemen's course," which will cover a whole year. Thus, if I am selected to attend it, I will complete my University of Redlands MAM (Master of Arts in Management) program in December and start on the UCLA program in January. Now I am going to have to complete my thesis by the end of January 1982.

Executive Program at UCLA	7 Feb 1982	I left at 11:30 A.M. for Avila Beach to attend the UCLA Executive Program in-residence retreat being held at the San Luis Bay Inn in Avila Beach. I will be here until Wednesday afternoon (2/10/82). I arrived at the hotel at about 2:55 P.M. The program started at 3:00 P.M. We met in session until 6:30 P.M. After that, I checked into my room and called Karen to see how things were going back at home. Between 7:00–7:30 P.M., there was a cocktail party. At 7:30 P.M., we all went to dinner in the hotel's dining room. I got back to my room at about 9:00 P.M. and read the *Los Angeles Times*. Jay Barney (of our ward) is up here too but as one of the instructors of the UCLA Business School.
Executive Program at UCLA	8 Feb 1982	I got up this morning at 6:30 and went to breakfast at 7:30. The session started at 8:30. Jay Barney taught the afternoon session and did pretty well. We ended at 4:00 P.M. I rested in bed and watched TV from 4:00 to 6:00 P.M. Then I called the family and found that all was well at home. We had another no-host cocktail party from 6:00–6:30. At 6:30, we went to dinner. I went back to my room at about 8:15 P.M. and read the paper, watched TV, and read some material.
Executive Program at UCLA	9 Feb 1982	We had a full day with Dr. Tony Raia on group dynamics and organizational design. For dinner, we had a barbecue chicken dinner. This has been an enjoyable retreat. Tomorrow we will meet for the morning with Jay Barney to do a case study. Then at noon, we will leave for home.
Executive Program at UCLA	10 Feb 1982	We met in the morning with Jay Barney to cover conflict resolution and to do the case study on Diversified Industries. The live-in retreat ended at 12:00 noon. I left the hotel for Pacoima at 12:45 P.M. It rained for most of the way. I arrived at the plant at 4:10 P.M. and worked until about 6:30 P.M. I got home at about 7:00 P.M.
Executive Program at UCLA	11 Feb 1982	At 2:45 P.M., I left for UCLA to attend my first class on campus on the Executive Program to which HRT is sending me. It cost the company $4,200 to send me to school there for a year.
Executive Program at UCLA	11 Nov 1982	I attended my UCLA class from 4:00–9:00 P.M. and heard a lecture from Dr. Bill Ouchi, author of *Theory Z*. It was an extremely stimulating and interesting lecture. Bill Ouchi is an extremely intelligent and learned man.

Executive Program at UCLA	9 Dec 1982	It was an average day at work. At 3:10 P.M., I left for my UCLA class. It was our last formal classroom session. It was a good course, but I'm glad it's over. Next week Wednesday, I'll be attending the UCLA Forecast, and our Graduation Dinner/ Dance will be next Friday evening.
Executive Program at UCLA	17 Dec 1982	It was an average day at work. Willadean Bryant, my secretary, took a vacation day off. Unfortunately, at about 9:30 this morning, she slipped on some ice on her driveway and badly broke her ankle. She ended up in Henry Mayo Hospital. For lunch, we went to a restaurant to celebrate Blaise Revay and Ardis Martin's birthdays. Blaises' wife, Mary, also came to the luncheon party.
		After work, I stopped off at Weinerschnitzel to buy dinner for the kids. I also stopped at Alpha Beta to buy some flowers and a get-well card for Willadean. Then, I got home, took a bath, and dressed to go to the UCLA Executive Program Class 57 Graduation Dinner/Dance. Before heading for LA, Karen and I stopped at Henry Mayo Hospital to visit Willadean. Her husband, Bill, was there with her.
		We then went to the graduation and got there as they started eating dinner. It was an enjoyable event. I received a large certificate, which was decoupage on a wooden plaque. Karen wasn't feeling well, so we left about 10:15 P.M. for home. We arrived home at about 11:00 P.M. Becky Moody baby-sat the kids for us while we were away.
Night School	30 May 1979	I attended my Microeconomics class tonight and got an 80% on the weekly quiz. It appears to me that if I am going to get an A in the course, I am going to have to get a 100 on the final exam. It's going to be tough, but I'm going to *give it that old college try*. We only have two more weeks in this semester. Thank goodness. It really has been a long semester.
		I'll be glad to start on the quarter system at CSUDH (California State University at Dominguez Hills). A quarter is only 12 weeks long, whereas, a semester is 16 weeks long. I usually start to "burn out" around the 12-week point. So, 12-week quarters are just fine to me.
Peter Drucker	12 Dec 1980	Today, I attended an all-day seminar at the Ambassador Hotel in Los Angeles, where I listened to Dr. Peter Drucker. It was a very interesting and inspiring lecture.

Peter Principle	11 Nov 1980	After work today, I attended the Management Club meeting at the Odyssey Restaurant. After the delicious roast beef dinner, we listened to an entertaining speech by Dr. Lawrence Peter, the originator of the Peter Principle. It was an excellent speech.
Pre-school	4 Aug 1981	Karen taught her first pre-school class this morning in her new job (part time) with the Parks and Recreation Department with the City. Karen makes $5.50 per hour in her job as pre-school teacher.
Reading	3 Feb 1979	I spend most of the day reading. I have such a great thirst for knowledge that I find myself reading about a half dozen books simultaneously. I try to read the scriptures daily.
Reading	8 Feb 1979	I did more reading tonight. I have about a half dozen books going simultaneously. Reading is one of my favorite pastimes. I have a great desire to read as much as I can on Church history and on Gospel doctrine. I want to be more knowledgeable about the Church. I'm sort of making up for lost time, as I goofed off during my youth and never really had a good knowledge of the scriptures and about Mormonism in general. My knowledge of the Gospel is expanding and progressing by leaps and bounds daily. I hope that some day I will get to the point where I will be comfortable in answering any gospel question that anyone asks me. As it is right now, I feel rather ignorant. I read the scriptures religiously almost daily. It is my personal goal to also write in my journal on a daily basis. I think it is important for my posterity to know about the life of Robert Takeo Uda.
School Planning Board Meeting	11 Sep 1984	Karen went to a school planning board meeting this evening. She was one of a few people in the community appointed to that committee by the school district superintendent.
Seminar	28 Jun 1984	I attended the "Risk Management" seminar all day today at the Sheraton-Newport in Irvine.
Seminar	29 Jun 1984	I drove to Orange County to attend the second and final day of the "Risk Management" Seminar. It was an excellent seminar. Now, I am an expert. I'll now be able to do risk assessment and analysis on the HML program when I get my second subcontract from GDC.

Sex Education	26 Jun 1982	I had a personal priesthood interview (PPI) with Atom to discuss sex, the reproductive process, and masturbation. Karen has been after me for months to talk to Atom about these matters because he is rapidly approaching puberty and his teen years. If we do not teach children these things at home, they will surely learn them from their friends, which may not be very accurate and within the context of the Gospel. Atom understood fully what I talked about on how babies come about and when sex should be engaged in.
Study Technique Using Tapes	13 Feb 1979	I tape record the lectures in my Microeconomics class and listen to the recording over and over going to and coming from work. It works fine. You are "brainwashed" with the tape. It helped me "ace" Business Law last semester.
Study Technique Using Tapes	19 Feb 1979	I spent the rest of the evening writing notes from my tape recording of last week's Microeconomics class lecture. I usually listen to these tapes while driving to and from work. It works pretty well. I am "brainwashed" into remembering what was said in the lectures. The batteries do get expensive though, as I have to purchase a new set of four batteries at least once every two weeks.
Teaching	8 Aug 1983	Karen went in for her interview for Pre-School Teacher (3-year olds) for Leona Cox School in Canyon Country and was selected over two other candidates. She will be making about $50 a week for eight hours a week of paid time, which includes preparation and traveling time. That's not bad! I am really proud of her.
Textron Executive Development Program	18 Mar 1981	I failed to mention yesterday that Sam Garcia, HRT president, called me and said that he was nominating me to attend the Textron Executive Management Seminar in July. It will be held at the corporate headquarters in Providence, Rhode Island, and will be taught by the faculty of Harvard Business School.
Textron Executive Development Program	10 Jul 1981	Tomorrow, I will leave for a two-week trip to Rhode Island. I will be attending the Textron Executive Development Program at Bryant College in Smithfield, Rhode Island.

Textron Executive Development Program	11 Jul 1981	Karen and the kids drove me to the Los Angeles International Airport for my United Airlines flight #90, which departed at 12:45 P.M. I arrived at Logan Airport in Boston, Massachusetts, at 9:00 P.M. Actually, this is only 6:00 P.M. California time. I am spending the night at the Logan Airport Hilton Hotel. Tomorrow, I will be catching a chartered bus from the American Airlines terminal at 2:30 P.M., which departs for Bryant College in Smithfield, Rhode Island. We should arrive at the college at about 4:30 P.M.
Textron Executive Development Program	12 Jul 1981	Since I went to bed at 3:30 this morning, I slept in till 10:30 A.M. I got seven hours of sleep. After that, I took a shower and got ready to check out, which I did at 12:00 noon. Then I had clam chowder and milk for lunch in the Hilton Coffee Shop. I then waited in the lobby for about two hours before catching the Hilton shuttle bus to the American Airlines terminal. The chartered bus to Bryant College was waiting for us there. At 3:00 P.M., we headed out for Bryant College, arriving there after 4:00 P.M. Then we checked into our assigned rooms, which were in townhouses on campus. At 5:00 P.M., we went for a brief orientation session. Then we had dinner till about 7:30 P.M. After that, we went back to our rooms to spend the rest of the evening reading and preparing for our case study group discussions starting tomorrow.
Textron Executive Development Program	13 Jul 1981	I went to bed at 2:30 this morning (studying till then). I got up at 6:30 A.M. to take a shower and get ready for breakfast at 7:15 A.M. Our sessions started at 8:15 A.M. I was so tired from only four hours of sleep that I dozed off a couple of times during the day. After our session ended at 3:30 P.M., I came back to the room and slept for two hours before going to dinner at 6:30 P.M. After dinner, I came back to the room at about 7:40 P.M. and started studying for the rest of the evening.

Textron Executive Development Program	14 Jul 1981	I went to bed at 1:30 this morning and rose at 7:00 A.M. We went through the same schedule today as we did yesterday. After our sessions ended at 3:30 P.M., we had a group photo taken. Then I came back to the room to do some reading, and I also took a 1–1/2-hour nap. After dinner, I spent the rest of the evening studying my case studies for tomorrow. This is a really grueling seminar, but I am really learning a lot. This is only the third day, and it already feels like I've already been here a week. One beneficial thing I am experiencing is the interchange of discussion among all of the different managers from the various Textron divisions who are attending this seminar. It gives one a better perspective on how others think and how different divisions do things.
Textron Executive Development Program	15 Jul 1981	It was a usual day today with the exception of having four Textron executives here with us for lunch. This going to school is really exhausting work. It reminds me of my two years at AFIT on my MS in Astronautics program. The professors who are teaching us here are really top notch. It's no wonder Harvard graduates are, on the whole, better than the average business school graduates from average universities. The recent instructors I have had at Golden West College, Cal State University at Dominguez Hills and Northridge, and University of Redlands are no comparison to the instructors I am experiencing in this Textron Executive Development Program.
Textron Executive Development Program	16 Jul 1981	It was a typical day today–just the same old grueling pace. I can hardly keep up with the volume of reading material, much less write out the answers to the cases. But I am learning a lot, though.
Textron Executive Development Program	17 Jul 1981	It was a usual day today–hectic. I get up at 7:00 A.M., take a shower, get dressed, go to breakfast, attend classes, take a 20-minute morning break, go back to classes, go to lunch, have an hour study break after lunch, go back to classes, get out at 3:30 P.M. Then I go back to the townhouse room I am staying in and study till 6:30 P.M. Then I go to dinner and then back to doing homework from 7:30 P.M. to the wee hours of the morning. I have gone to bed every morning anywhere between 1:00 A.M. and 3:30 A.M. The next morning starts the whole routine all over again. There's not much excitement, but I am learning a lot.

Textron Executive Development Program	18 Jul 1981	We had the usual day today. At 2:15 P.M., we climbed into a chartered bus and headed for Newport, Rhode Island. We picked up a tour guide there who gave us a tour through the old historical area, viewing some of the homes of the very rich who owned them. We also had a guided tour through the Breakers, the home of Cornelius Vanderbilt. After that, we had a fantastic seafood dinner at the Clark's Cook House Restaurant. I had escargot, spinach salad, and lobster for my meal. We got back to the townhouses at about 11:30 P.M. After that, I did some studying for a couple of hours. It was a great day. The evening was a nice break from the grueling past week. After tomorrow's day off, we will be ready for the next grueling week of case studies. I made a call to Karen earlier in the day. Everything appears to be going okay back home.
Textron Executive Development Program	19 Jul 1981	I slept for 9–1/2 hours last night. That's about twice the average hours of sleep I have had each night for the past week. After I got up, I took a shower, got dressed, and then did my laundry. I studied a bit in the afternoon until the start of our cookout at 4:00 P.M. We had steaks and barbecue chicken cooked on an outdoor grill. After dinner, I studied for the rest of the evening.
Textron Executive Development Program	20 Jul 1981	This was a typical day today with the exception that we had a corporate attorney from Textron headquarters talk to us about anti-trust laws. We also had a meeting this afternoon on our mock labor-management negotiations we will be having tomorrow. I am on the labor union team going against the management team. I received my laundry and dry cleaning back today, but I think I am short one dress shirt.
Textron Executive Development Program	21 Jul 1981	Bob Straetz, chairman and CEO of Textron, Inc., had lunch with us today. We also were visited by Group Vice Presidents Frank E. Grzelecki and George H. Hartmann. Furthermore, this afternoon, we held our union-management negotiations. I am sorry to say that on both of our cases, we came out at a stalemate and had to go to arbitration.

Textron Executive Development Program	22 Jul 1981	It was a normal day today. The New England Patriots rookies are on campus this week in their tryouts. The veterans will be coming in this Friday. After dinner, I spent the entire evening reading my case studies for tomorrow. Even though it's great to be here, I am beginning to get anxious to return home—just two more days!
Textron Executive Development Program	23 Jul 1981	Well, these two weeks of the Textron Executive Development Program are finally winding down to an end. Tomorrow morning will be the last of our case studies. It has really been a grueling two weeks, yet it has been enjoyable. I will always remember these two weeks with 31 other Textron division managers from throughout the United States and England (we had one guy from England). At dinner today, we were presented with a group photograph of all 32 of us plus a nice big Harvard University beer mug. It will be a nice memorabilia. This evening, I did the last of my laundry. This will be the first time that I will have returned from a trip without dirty clothes for Karen to wash. Tomorrow, at about 3:00 P.M., the bus will take us to Boston airport. I will be staying the night again at the Logan-Hilton Hotel and will fly home on Saturday morning.
Textron Executive Development Program	25 Jul 1981	This was our final day of the Textron EDP. At lunch, we heard a speech from Bill Ledbetter, vice president of administration and planning. We left for the airport at 2:45 P.M. I am spending the night at the Hilton Hotel next to the Logan Airport in Boston. Tomorrow, I will be catching the 9:30 A.M. United flight #91 for LAX. Karen and the kids will be picking me up at about 1:00 P.M.
Textron Executive Development Program	26 Jul 1981	I arrived at LAX at about 12:30 P.M. today. Karen and the kids picked me up at about 1:00 P.M.... It's really great to be home. I brought Karen and the three kids some gifts. Most of it was a lot of junk stuff I had picked up at the hotel and at Bryant College.
TMSA Conference	13 Aug 1984	I got up at 5:00 AM (having had only 4 hours and 20 minutes of sleep) to attend the Technical Marketing Society of America (TMSA) Conference on Army Marketing Opportunities at the Amfac Hotel in Los Angeles. Steele Oman had gotten me into the conference free, which would have otherwise cost me $475.00.

13

Life Experiences

O ur life has been full of trials and tribulations. I am convinced that these trials and tribulations have been for our good. They have strengthened us. They have helped us to be more understanding and tolerant of things. We have learned how to deal with challenges and either resolve them or endure them. We have been immeasurably blessed. Life has been tough, but it has been worth it. Actually, life is great!

Abortion	3 Nov 1983	Atom received a letter of response from Senator Alan Cranston today regarding Atom's concern about legislation on abortion. Senator Cranston, the fink, is for abortion. To bad. And he wants to run for President of the United States. Fat chance for him to win.
Airport Visit	27 Dec 1982	The boys took their baths around noon to get ready for our going to LAX to meet Lowell and Joan there on a 2–1/2-hour layover. We left for LAX around 2:40 P.M. and got there around 3:45 P.M. Their plane was supposed to have come in at 4:00 P.M., but by the time they finally walked into the Western terminal, it was about 4:15. We also met Joan's cousin, Dean, and his wife (Bonnie) and child (Amy) there, who came from Whittier to see them. We all ate dinner at the airport cafeteria and spent a good two hours chatting and visiting with them. They had a 6:30 flight back to Helena, Montana. Lowell brought some *laulau* and poi from my parents' in Hawaii. After coming home, I prepared the poi, cooked the *laulau*, and had some. It was soooo delicious. It had been over a dozen years since I last had some good Hawaiian *laulau*.
Assassination	6 Oct 1981	In Egypt today, someone assassinated Egypt's president, Anwar Sadat.

Auto Accident	16 Mar 1979	The clutch on our orange Honda Coupe finally gave out today at the Pennys Shopping Center about two miles from home. Hence, after the lecture I had attended at Orange Coast College, we went out about 10:00 P.M. to haul the car home. I was rather leery about going to pick up the car because it was dark and also raining. However, since Karen insisted, we went. Unfortunately, as we were towing the car home, a young 18-year-old boy ran right into the rear of the orange car. I was pulling with the gray Honda Civic, and Karen was steering the orange Honda. The crash completely smashed in the back end of the orange car. After the police came and recorded all the information on the accident, we towed the battered and destroyed orange Honda home.
		None of us were hurt except Karen, who had a bruised knee. The boys were with me in the gray Honda and were okay. We are all thankful to our Heavenly Father for watching over us and keeping the accident from being worse than it really was. We were glad that the boy who hit Karen was unhurt. His front end was smashed in a little, but it wasn't as badly damaged as our orange Honda.
Auto Accident	17 Mar 1979	Karen went to the doctor to get a checkup to see if there was any serious injury from last night's traffic accident. The doctor said that there was no injury to the baby. But she did bandage up Karen's knee, which was paining her pretty badly. She is limping around. The doctor also said that her body was stressed like someone who had done very hard labor.
		Other than that, she is to be on the watch for any vaginal bleeding, nausea, and other symptoms of possible internal injury or injury to the baby. I really feel that the Lord is watching over us to keep us safe because we have much yet to do in this earth life.
Auto Repair	26 Jun 1984	I took my car into the garage today to get the air conditioner and brakes fixed. It cost me $130 for the job. I wonder what's going to break down next.
Auto Repair	30 Jun 1984	We took my car back into the garage again today because the air conditioner stopped operating again and the radiator or hose was leaking.
Auto Repair	5 Nov 1984	I took my car in for a tune up, which cost me about $82 for labor and material.

Auto Repair	9 Nov 1984	I worked in my office all day. My car transmission had to be fixed today, which cost me $460. I think I have fixed everything on the car this year, which has totaled about $2,500. We had a rebuilt engine put in, new radiator, brakes, muffler and exhaust pipes, tires, battery, shocks, lights, and I don't know what else.
CIF Champs	7 Dec 1984	Atom went to the Canyon High Playoff Game at the College of the Canyons (COC). Canyon High won the California Interscholastic Federation (CIF) football championship 33 to 6!
Craig Mc-Creary Visit	9 Sep 1984	I ran around all day today getting things ready for the start of seminary. Craig McCreary dropped by for a couple of hours before going back East. I was so busy preparing the seminary enrollment statistics and rosters that I hardly could spend any time with him. Fortunately, Karen was able to spend some time with him and feed him some brunch. They dropped by the office for about 20 minutes before he headed off for LAX.
Darcy Dick	15 Nov 1980	Darcy Dick has decided to go home in January after the next school-break. She says that she misses her mother. Though I will not force her to change her decision, I feel she is making a grave mistake because she hasn't really made the internal changes necessary for her to have the internal conviction to keep from returning to previous behavior. However, she has to make her own decisions and learn that running away from reality isn't always the best thing to do. I hope my feelings are wrong because I want the best for Darcy. She has a lot of potential for good if she can maintain the right kind of friends and exist in an environment that would be conducive to healthy spiritual and emotional development. She needs to develop a more positive self-image in an atmosphere that is non-threatening and low stress along with proper discipline and concern. I hope she returns to a changed previous environment. Only then will she be able to refrain from falling back into a previously unhappy behavior. But, life must go on. I just hope that all the people involved will make the necessary changes to make things better.
Darcy Dick	29 Jan 1981	Karen held a party for Darcy with some of her girl friends. Darcy will be flying home tomorrow night.

Darcy Dick	30 Jan 1981	After coming home, I took the family to the Sizzlers Restaurant for dinner. Then we took Darcy to the Los Angeles International Airport for her Eastern Airlines flight to Atlanta, Georgia, and then on another flight to Cleveland, Ohio. She should be home about 8:30 A.M. tomorrow. It has been quite an experience having Darcy live with us for four months and ten days. We sure learned a lot from this experience. I hope Darcy learned something. The next six months will tell whether or not she learned anything from staying with us for that time period. I hope she will have the strength to overcome her weaknesses and Satan's temptations. She has lots of potential, if she can only get the proper help, assistance, guidance, and support from her parents.
Dog Bite	9 Nov 1979	Karen tells me that the collie down the street bit Atom on the heel on his way to school while riding his bike. The collie just had puppies, so she must not be feeling too well. It was the same dog that I hit with the car earlier this year. Since Atom had his shoes on, his heel was only slightly nicked. Karen tells me that the owner came over to apologize and said that his dog had all of the required shots. Atom came home bawling. Karen spent some time treating the slight wound and sent him off to school. He was a little late for school because of this minor altercation.
Dog Runs Into Car, Not Vice Versa	17 Jun 1979	Karen had forgotten to bring the music sheets she needed for a song practice after Sunday school, so I went back home to get them. Earlier, on the way to Sunday school, a dog down the street ran into our car. The dog's eye, nose, and mouth were bleeding. The owner took it to the veterinarian and left it overnight for X-rays and observation. I think the dog will be okay. Karen was very upset about it. That is why I had to drive home for the music sheets.
Eclipse of the Moon	5 Jul 1982	There was an eclipse of the moon tonight around 11:38 P.M.
Election Day	4 Nov 1980	Today was election day. I voted for Ronald Reagan for president, who won. Now, things will start getting better again. Poor President Jimmy Carter was not meant to win a second term. He just was not an effective president.

Election Day	5 Nov 1984	Tomorrow is election day. President Ronald Reagan is going to wipe out Walter Mondale–that is my prediction. Karen and I are Republicans. I just cannot see how anybody can be a Democrat. They are so tax happy, socialistic, and welfare happy. As do the Republicans, they just do not really believe in the free enterprise system, a strong national defense, and personal independence. When President Jimmy Carter was in office, everything went to pot. Since President Reagan has been in there, things have really improved. I'm for giving him another four more years.
Election Day	6 Nov 1984	I voted for President Reagan this morning. At this time of the evening, President Reagan has won by a landslide. Poor Fritz Mondale and Geraldine Ferraro, they were smeared to the wall. I just couldn't see how anyone could vote for them anyway. Well, the people spoke. It's four more years for the Reagan-Bush team. Thank goodness.
Extortion	11 May 1983	After I came home tonight, I found that, this past week, Atom was being blackmailed for his milk money by a punk in his school. That punk threatened to beat Atom up if he didn't pay him money every day. Boy, was I mad. I told Atom to beat that kid up even if he would have to take a beating himself. I couldn't believe Atom would allow himself to be intimidated to that extent where he would be afraid of that bully. In a free country, you can't let punks like that get away with threatening you. If you let a kid like that get away with it, what will he do when he becomes an adult! He'll become an extortionist. Anyway, I hope Atom will stand up to him tomorrow and fight for his rights. This is not a communist country. Good people cannot and should not tolerate bad people doing these kinds of things.

Good Deed	14 Oct 1979	We got up this morning about 7:30 and got ready for Stake Conference. Karen fixed us some bacon and eggs, toast and margarine, and orange juice for breakfast. We left the house about 9:25 for the new Huntington Beach Stake Center. Conference lasted from 10:00 A.M. to about 12:10 P.M.

By the time we got to the Stake Center, the parking lot was already full, so we had to park on the street about a block away. When we were seated, we were about $^3/_4$'s of the way back in the cultural hall. Bishop H. Burke Peterson (1st counselor in the presiding bishopric) presided at the conference. It was a very enjoyable general session.

After we came home, Karen fixed us a roast beef lunch, which included potatoes, peas, biscuits, sliced tomatoes, and milk. Since Karen wasn't feeling well and Marc and Heather had to be put down for their naps, they stayed home while Stan Moon (who was visiting us while out here in California on business), Atom, and I returned to the Stake Center for a 2:00 P.M. building dedicatory session.

By the time we got there, the parking lot was again full, so we parked in the same location we did for the morning conference session. However, while we were crossing the intersection, a young lady with two children in a VW van had car trouble in the intersection.

We tried pushing them to get the van started, but it wouldn't start. Evidently, she had flooded the engine while trying to restart it. I saw her pumping the accelerator while trying to restart the van. I'm pretty sure it was flooded.

Stan brought his rented car up to the van, which we had pushed to the side of the road. Fortunately, the lady had some jumper cables, and we were able to jumper the battery to get the van restarted. They went merrily on their way.

We were about five minutes late for the dedication because of our good deed. However, it felt good to have helped someone else even if it caused us to be late for the church meeting. I think the Lord will forgive us for being late in this situation. The meeting lasted until about 3:20 P.M.

After we got home, Karen had fixed us some dessert, which consisted of chocolate syrup and whipped cream on some pound cake that she had baked. It was so delicious, I had to have two servings. Brother Moon left for San Diego at about 4:00 P.M.

Group Dat-ing	23 Feb 1979	We had Shantal Hiatt baby-sit for us again. Shantal is in the process of trying to save up about $30.00 for a big "Sadie Hawkins Girl-Ask-Boy Dance" that will take place at her high school on March 9. She had asked a boy from another ward who is out of high school. There is a 4–1/2-year difference between them, and she is quite excited about the forthcoming event. I get a feeling that Shantal really likes this fellow a lot. Therefore, I have been trying to set up many occasions where we would need her to baby-sit for us. She already has about $10 saved up and needs about $20 more. I'd like to do everything I can to help her earn the $30 she needs. The money is for admission, snacks, and a big dinner they will be going to at a restaurant with the rest of the Mormon girls and their chosen dates from our ward. *I think that's a great idea for all of them to be together in one big shindig like that as opposed to going only as couples.*
Holiday Bowl Game	21 Dec 1984	After I came home to a fried potatoes and sloppy Joe dinner, Atom and I watched the BYU-Michigan Holiday Bowl game on TV. It was an exciting seesaw game, which ended at 24 to 17 in favor of BYU. I am thrilled to see BYU as, in most likelihood, the Number One Team in the nation. They are the only unde-feated major college football team in the nation this year. This great publicity is going to be great for the Church and gospel.

Jury Duty	9 Oct 1979	At 9:00 this morning, I went to the Orange County Courthouse for jury duty. I sat around for most of the day waiting to be called. During that time, I did a lot of reading in my Marketing Systems and Human Resources Management textbooks. Finally, at around 2:00 P.M., our panel was called to report to Superior Court #32 on the ninth floor of the courthouse. The rest of the afternoon, until 4:40 P.M., was spent in trying to select the members of the jury. The defense and prosecuting attorneys did not finish their selection when the court was recessed at 4:40 P.M., so we will have to report back tomorrow to complete the jury selection. I have yet to have my name pulled out of the file box. So, I have been diligently waiting to be called on in the spectator seats. The young man that is on trial is charged with three counts of burglary, one count of robbery, and one count of aggravated assault with a deadly weapon (a pipe). It looks like this will be another long trial as the prosecutor has about 24 witnesses to call to the stand. After sitting through a couple of jury selections, I now know why court cases take so long to dispose and why the court is so backlogged on their caseloads. The attorneys and judge ask so many stupid questions, which waste a lot of time. Some of the questions they ask make them look like clowns. Several times, we broke down laughing at them, not at any funny joke or something like that, but because of their blunders and stupid comments and questions. It almost makes a mockery of the justice system.
Jury Duty	10 Oct 1979	I went to the Orange County Courthouse at 9:00 this morning. The attorneys completed selecting the jury, and I was selected as an alternate juror! So, I was able to stay for the rest of the day for the trial. The prosecutor brought in 6 of the 24 witnesses for the people to testify. Since the judge has other duties on tomorrow and Friday, the next time he will reconvene the trial will be on Monday next week. The trial seems like it will be a long one, which should last through two weekends. It has been a very interesting and educational experience thus far. We adjourned for the day at 4:30 P.M.

Jury Duty and Earth-quake	15 Oct 1979	I got up this morning at about 8:00 since I didn't have to report for jury duty until 10:00 A.M. Since one of the key witnesses was late, it was not until about 11:00 A.M. before we got started. Fortunately, I have been able to get a lot of reading done on my courses during all the breaks and waiting times during the days I am on jury duty. We completed seven more witnesses today and even repeated a couple previously done for additional testimony.
		An exciting thing happened today while the court was in session. There was a large earthquake at about 4:16–4:18 P.M., which really shook the building. We were on the ninth floor of the Orange County Courthouse. The building swayed six inches to each side. Many of the women in the court were scared to death.
		The radio reports gave differing information. The strength of the quake was given as 6.4, 6.5 to 6.7, and 8.0 on three different radio reports. The radio also reported that there were a series of seven quakes. The epicenter of the quake was determined to be about 14 miles east of Calexico in the Imperial Valley.
		Radio reports stated that there was one death and 76 injured in the El Centro and Calexico area. Many buildings caved in. The radio said that that was the worst quake they have had in that area since 1940. Karen said that she didn't feel it at all in the Westminster area.
Lesson Learned	5 Dec 1984	I got back to the office at 8:45 PM and continued working. Then, at around 10:00 PM, Karen called me to get me to pick up Atom and Eric Foyt at the high school. They had just returned from the basketball game that they won. However, Atom and Eric didn't get to play.
		They did a foolish thing in that they started walking to Eric's house because he was cold. So, I missed them and went home. Then, Karen went out to look for them and found them at Eric's home. Needless to say, Eric's mom and Karen chewed out both Eric and Atom when she got there. I hope they learned a lesson to stay put when they call someone to pick them up.
		After that fiasco, I went back to my office to finish up what I was doing on the SEMP. By the time I got home, it was 11:40 PM. I can't believe I have to get up at 4:00 AM to drive to GDC–San Diego.

Near Acci-dent	21 Oct 1979	When Karen and the kids came back for sacrament meeting at 1:00 P.M., Heather was in a bad mood because, on the way to the chapel, Karen almost ran into a stupid kid who was riding a bicycle, without looking, right into the path of our car. Karen jammed on the brakes, which then caused Heather to fly out of her seat and onto the front floor of the car. Evidently, she hit her head on the dashboard because she had a slight scratch and bruise on the side of her forehead. Karen said that Heather started crying hysterically. Karen really yelled at the nine-year old kid, "reading him the riot act." The kid's father was nearby, and he also started yelling and chewing out his son. The poor kid will probably never forget this incident.
Oil Crisis	13 Apr 1979	The oil crunch is on us again. Many gasoline stations are closing early. The radio announcer said that 70 percent of gas stations would close on Sundays. That's good anyway. That will get more gas station owners and workers keeping the Sabbath day holy. Regular gasoline now ranges from about 76.9 cents per gallon to 83.9 cents per gallon. Ethyl and non-leaded gas are in the 80 cents range up to 90 cents per gallon. I don't see inflation stopping there. It'll probably be over a dollar a gallon before long.
Oil Crisis	7 May 1979	I attended my Statistics class at GWC (Golden West College). My instructor, Mr. Gene Cotton, was in an accident before coming to class. Evidently, he was driving his motor bike through a service station and was hit by a car driver who thought it was someone who was trying to cut in line. Since the gasoline crisis is upon us again, it brings out the worst in people. It seems as though there have been many people trying to cut in on the long lines of waiting drivers at gas stations. And when they do, the other drivers would run into them, fight them, etc. It's really unbelievable what people will do without gasoline. Imagine what people would do if there was a shortage of food for over a year. People without their year's supply of food would really be in a fix then. Anyway, my instructor was banged up to the extent that he was limping with pain. So, we had a short class session. After a half-hour, he let us go.

Oil Crisis	21 Nov 1979	Governor Jerry Brown has put us back on the odd-even gas-rationing plan again because of the cutoff of oil from Iran. Since today was an odd-numbered day and my Honda Civic has an even-numbered license plate, I was not entitled to fill my gas tank. However, I didn't have enough gas to make it home from work. The first gas station I went to wouldn't allow me to get any gas. Fortunately, the next station I went to didn't pay any attention to the license tag numbers, so I was able to fill my tank and make it home okay.
Lazy	1 Sep 1979	I spent the entire day today preparing the Mutual newsletter, a special meeting (for tomorrow) notice and agenda, and stuff for the Youth Leadership Training Seminar. Interspersed throughout the day, I went to get some Xeroxing done, played with the two boys, watched TV, took care (baby-sat) of Heather, and bathed Puffy. I really did not get much done today mainly because I was lazy.
Palmdale Land	3 Jan 1981	We drove out to Palmdale today to look at our 4–1/2 acres. It was still there. We stopped at a real estate office to find out the going rate of land out there and found that our land could be sold for anywhere between $25K–$40K per acre. If the Palmdale International Airport goes in there, the land value should skyrocket by at least double.
Parents' Marital Problems	10 Sep 1979	Karen has been really upset these past few days because her parents are having marital problems. Things look pretty bad for them as of this date.
Parents' Marital Problems	11 Sep 1979	Karen's brother, Rick Rowland, called tonight and talked to her for over an hour about the problem their parents are having.
Parents' Marital Problems	13 Sep 1979	Karen's mom and dad are separating for a while so her mom can think through the problems they are currently facing.
Parents' Marital Problems	20 Sep 1979	Karen went to the doctor this morning to check out her hives. Apparently, Karen has been breaking out and really itching because of a nervous condition probably brought about because of the situation with her parents.

Parents' Marital Problems	28 Sep 1979	Karen went to the doctor today because of pains she has been having in her stomach. The preliminary diagnosis shows she may be in the beginning stages of a stomach ulcer. Evidently, the stress and strain she has been experiencing over the past couple of months (particularly with the marital problems her parents have been having) has been really getting to her. At any rate, she has to take Mylanta and get herself on a bland diet. I know all about this because I also have had ulcers.
Parents' Marital Problems	8 Oct 1979	Karen told me that she called her mom to encourage her to come out and stay with us for a couple of weeks so we can help her work out her marital problems. But she declined saying that she had to work things out for herself.
Parents' Marital Problems	3 Jul 1980	Karen's dad's and mom's divorce was finalized today.
Passing of Bob Brock-bank	1 Apr 1984	At about 11:00 P.M., the Brockbanks neighbor called and said that something had happened to Bob Brockbank, and that the paramedics were there. I got dressed quickly and went up there to their home. Bob had a severe heart attack and expired. The paramedics took him to Henry Mayo Hospital were he was pronounced dead. I drove Bonnie Brockbank down to the Emergency Room at Henry Mayo Hospital. The attending physician broke the official news to us there. Sister Brockbank really was in bad shape at that time, though she carried herself well. Bishop Thompson and Brother and Sister Houck were at the hospital with us. After the bad news, I took Sister Brockbank back home. Karen and Sister Linda Bradford came over to stay with Bonnie until her relatives arrived. We also had some help (well-needed help) from their good neighbor friends from across the street. By the time I came home, it was 1:00 A.M. in the morning. I hope to stay up for the remainder of the night catching up on some backlogged work. This has been quite an eventful day for us.

Passing of Bob Brockbank	2 Apr 1984	I spent much of the day today making phone calls in behalf of getting arrangements made to release Bob Brockbank's body to the coroner. I also got a funeral home to do the work of conducting the necessary things for the funeral services, etc. At 1:00 P.M., I took Bonnie Brockbank and Paul Penrod (a brother-in-law) to the Hilburn's Funeral Chapel in Newhall to give them the necessary information and sign the papers to get the ball rolling on the preparation of the remains. That took an hour at the funeral home. Then we went back to the Brockbanks' home and drew up a preliminary program for the funeral services. After that, I came home and started making phone calls to get the necessary commitments.
Passing of Bob Brockbank	3 Apr 1984	I worked in my office for a while before having dinner. Karen made a delicious rice casserole for the Brockbanks and us. After dinner, Karen and I went for our temple recommend renewal interviews with President Shaw.
Passing of Bob Brockbank	4 Apr 1984	In the evening from 5:00–8:00 P.M., I attended Bob Brockbank's viewing at the Hilburn's Funeral Chapel in Newhall. I touched Bob Brockbank's hand, which was hard and cold. That was the first time I had ever touched a dead person's body.
Passing of Bob Brockbank	5 Apr 1984	At 10:30 A.M., I met with all of the others who participated in Bob Brockbank's funeral service in a prayer meeting in the bishop's office. Bishop Thompson officiated. After that, we had a brief prayer meeting in the Relief Society Room. Because the flag was late, we started about 11:10 A.M. with the funeral service. The flag was brought in and draped over the casket after the special piano number. I spoke in the services along with John Houck, Jim Baynes, and Bishop Bill Thompson. The services lasted about 35 minutes. It went really well. We all will miss Brother Bob Brockbank. He was a good man. Our condolences go out to Sister Yvonne "Bonnie" Brockbank. Bob's body will be flown to Orem, Utah, where it will be laid to rest. Sister Brockbank and the others in her family will be driving up to Utah today and tomorrow.

Passing of Bob Brock-bank	22 Jun 1984	In the evening, Karen and I visited Sis. Yvonne Brockbank was having a difficult time because she found that she may not be the beneficiary of her husband's life insurance. It seemed that he had changed it to his niece many years ago and never did change it back to Yvonne. She was really upset about that.
Passing of Jim Sorbo	12 Sep 1984	After I got home around 7:30 PM, I took a shower. At 8:00 PM, Karen and I left for a funeral hall in Northridge to view the body of Jim Sorbo who had passed away on Sunday. Jim was a good friend of mine who worked for me as a program manager when I was general manager of APCO in Pacoima. After the viewing, we went to his and Helen's (Jim's wife) daughter's home for some light refreshments before going home. Helen Sorbo (the widow) was very pleased that we came. We had gone to dinner with Jim and Helen and customers a couple of times when I was working for HR Textron. Jim was a great guy whom I liked very much. We will miss him, but he had a good 67 (almost 68) years of life on this earth.
Poetry	14 Feb 1979	I wrote three poems today. They were on "Success," "Positive Attitude," and "Faith." I hope to publish a book on poetry one of these fine days.
Pumpkin Pie	23 Nov 1983	Chris Moody brought over a pumpkin pie that she had baked. I had a piece of it, and, oh, how delicious it was. She can make me pumpkin pie anytime.
Record Keeping	24 Feb 1979	I spent the entire afternoon going through my files and organizing all of my correspondence (both those we have written and those we have received from others). I am going to bind all of my correspondence together by years (chronologically) so that it will provide a history of what we wrote about since 1974. It really is a gargantuan task getting all of my paperwork in order.
Ronald Reagan Inaugu-rated	20 Jan 1981	Today has been a significant day in history. Ronald Reagan was inaugurated as the 40th President of the United States. The 52 hostages were flown out of Iran to freedom. President Jimmy Carter returned to his peanut farm in Plains, Georgia. Now we can start our Country back to economic normalcy. In this day, we are suffering from run-away inflation, high unemployment, business recession, high crime rate, high interest rates, high taxes, high cost of living, poor national defense posture, and on and on. We have only one way to go, and that's up.

Ronald Reagan Shot	30 Mar 1981	President Ronald Reagan was shot in the left chest by an attempted assassin. Press Secretary Jim Brady was shot in the forehead. The gunman also shot a Washington, D.C., police officer and secret service agent. Fortunately, President Reagan will live. The attempted assassin was a 22-to-25-year-old man from Colorado. We had a short (one-hour) class session this evening because our instructor, Gary Strickley, had to attend an important meeting. So, I got home at about 7:15 and watched the news about the shooting of the President till about 9:00 P.M.
Ronald Reagan Shot	31 Mar 1981	It was a usual day at work today. President Reagan is okay and will recuperate well.
Space Shuttle	12 Apr 1981	I got up at 3:30 A.M. to watch the first Space Shuttle launch from Kennedy Space Center, Florida, at 4:00 A.M. PST. I watched the TV till about 4:30 A.M. before falling back to sleep.
Space Shuttle	11 Nov 1981	Tomorrow morning at 7:00 PST, the second Space Shuttle will be launched from Kennedy Space Center, Florida. I plan to watch it on TV.
Space Shuttle	12 Nov 1981	The second Space Shuttle was successfully launched at about 7:10 A.M. today. It was beautiful.
Space Shuttle	14 Nov 1981	The Space Shuttle Orbiter landed safely at Edwards Air Force Base this afternoon.
Space Shuttle	22 Mar 1982	The third launch of the Space Shuttle was successful today.
Space Shuttle	5 Sep 1983	Today was Labor Day holiday. I saw the Space Shuttle land at Edwards AFB on TV about 12:30 A.M. last night. It was a perfect nighttime landing. Atom and the Nichols drove out to Edwards AFB last night to watch it land, but they couldn't get on base nor see the Shuttle in the dark. So, they drove back to their home and watched the landing on TV too! Atom stayed there for the night.

Speeding Ticket	7 Nov 1983	I got up at 5:10 A.M. to get ready to leave for Sierra Vista, Arizona. I left the house at 6:15 A.M. and drove for 11.5 hours before arriving there. I had to stop twice to sleep for a while. Just outside of Blythe, I received a ticket from the California Highway Patrol for speeding. The officer said I was going approximately 70 mph. This is the second ticket I have received since my speedometer broke. It has gotten expensive not fixing it. And this ticket came at a most inopportune time–when we don't have the extra money to spend on such a thing as a speeding ticket. Needless to say, I was very careful the rest of the way to Sierra Vista.
Tax Returns	11 Apr 1979	I received a call tonight from our tax consultant, Brother Belliston, who said that we will be getting back from the federal income tax of about $2750 and about $450 from the state income tax. That doesn't seem to be too shabby.
Tax Return	20 Mar 1982	We received our completed tax forms today from our tax consultant (Alan Rosenberg). We will be receiving a total of over $4,800 back from the federal and state tax refund.
Tax Return	14 Jul 1984	We received our tax return today of $2,772.00. We received $65.00 extra because they had kept our return for so long. They had it for 3–1/2 months. Initially, they said that we had a problem. But, I guess, after they had investigated it, they couldn't find anything wrong. So, they paid us interest.
Temperature	29 Aug 1984	It was another miserably hot day again today. I hope this summer ends soon. It has really been a long, hot summer. Thank goodness for my air-conditioned office and car. If it weren't for that, I would be miserable all the time. Karen runs the house air conditioner, but she only sets the thermostat at 80 degrees. So, it is still hot in this house. Over the last four months our electric bill went from around $20 to $40 to $112 to $144 this last month. The increase has been mainly the use of the air conditioner, yet I haven't noticed the coolness it should cause. I hope the bill starts going down after this month. It is absolutely ridiculous to pay that much more for electricity just to get the house cooled down to 80 degrees. I keep my office thermostat set at 70 degrees, which is just nice.

| Volcano Eruption | 7 Aug 1980 | At about 4:28 P.M., Mt. St. Helens erupted again. We were able to see the smoke rising up into the sky. To think, we flew almost directly over the crater at about 17,000 feet in the morning on our way to Seattle. I mentioned to the people around me that it would be exciting if the volcano erupted while we were flying over it. Then, in the afternoon, it blows. |

14

Marriage and Family Relations

Our marriage and family relations have been full of activity and challenges. I am sure of one thing. I am happy that I married the beautiful woman that I did. After all, I chased her and chased her and chased her until she finally caught me. If it weren't for Karen's strong testimony in the gospel, I probably wouldn't be as strong in the church as I am today. Our kids have turned out to be wonderful adults. They are now great parents to their children. We are very blessed.

Apples of My Eye	23 Sep 1982	Karen went to Marc's student conference with Mrs. Primus, his teacher. Marc seems to be doing really well in school. He is considered as one of the top four students in his class by Mrs. Primus. I am really proud of all three of our children. They are the *apples of my eye*.
Apricot, the Dog	23 Oct 1982	We put a down payment on an apricot poodle today. We will pick it up next Saturday. It will cost us $200.00.
Apricot, the Dog	26 Oct 1982	Karen found out today that we could bring home our new poodle on Thursday.
Apricot, the Dog	28 Oct 1982	Karen picked up our new poodle today, which Heather named Apricot.

Apricot, the Dog	24 Dec 1982	Apricot gave me a panic today while Karen was out shopping. When I stepped out of the front door to check the mailbox, she darted outside without my even knowing it. I looked all over the house for her until I finally believed Heather saying that she saw Apricot run out of the house. I already went outside twice before looking for her and didn't see her anywhere. That's why I doubted Heather. But after finally realizing that she wasn't in the house, I looked way down the street and saw a kid chasing Apricot. So, I went down there and caught her and brought her home. I was more afraid of the wrath of Karen than the thought that Apricot was gone.
Apricot, the Dog	11 Mar 1984	Apricot was really happy to see us. However, she had a whole clump of doodoo stuck to her hind end, which Atom and Marc had to clean up. Needless to say, they did not enjoy the task. To get her really clean, they finally had to give her a bath. It was quite an ordeal for both the boys and the dog. So, by the time they finally had their baths and got to bed, it was after 10:30 P.M.
Atom	12 Jul 1979	We went to Atom's soccer game. Today, Atom's team, the Blue Bombers, beat the yellow-shirt team 3 to 1. Atom was so proud. I think Atom is gaining a lot of confidence. He is running more and trying to kick the ball more often. He is beginning to really like soccer.
Atom	4 Aug 1979	This morning, we attended Atom's soccer game. His team tied the other team 1 to 1. Atom is improving well in his playing. He kicked the ball well several times. The assistant coach even mentioned that Atom was improving well, and that he is a good listener and follows instruction well.
Atom	11 Aug 1979	This morning, I got up about 8:00 o'clock, watered the garden, had breakfast, and took a shower. Then, we went to Atom's soccer game, which they won (beating the gold team) by a score of 4 to 3. Atom's team, the Blue Bombers, ended up in second place in league play. Atom had the best coach and assistant coach. He was really fortunate to have started his first season in soccer with such good coaches. After the game, the entire team went over to one of the team member's homes (the Wittakers) for lunch and a swim party.

Atom	16 Feb 1981	Atom's soccer coach, Bill Becker, brought over Atom's certificate, patch, and a plaque, which he received for "Best Sportsmanship." It was voted upon by all of his teammates. Of all awards to win, I think that is the most meaningful one because it shows how much his fellow teammates liked and respected him. I am very proud of Atom for being such a good sportsman and in winning this award. I hope this motivates him to continue being the good kid that he is.
Atom	3 May 1983	Atom is so good now that he takes care of cleaning up the kitchen after dinner.
Atom	31 Jul 1983	While driving home from Church today, Atom asked me, "How do we live?" I said, "What do you mean?" He said, "Well, we don't have any money coming in (because of my unemployment)." I expressed to him that we have several thousands of dollars saved up. So, I stressed the importance to him of saving for a rainy day. I also told him that we have a year's worth of food storage in the garage, and that I am receiving $166 per week of unemployment insurance from the State of California. My new business will also be receiving $250 per week from the manufacturer's rep contract I got with Tavco, Inc. So, it was a good teaching moment. I told Atom it was important for him to take odd jobs such as cleaning yards whenever he could and to save his earnings instead of spending it foolishly. He should save for his mission, his college education, and for rainy days such as what we are now experiencing. It is really neat to see the concern that Atom has about my present unemployment. He is really cute being concerned as he is about the possible lack of food to eat in the future. He doesn't have to worry, though. The Lord will provide.

Atom	22 Aug 1983	A cute thing happened tonight. Atom went to my wallet to get the $2.00 he earned washing my car. He noticed that I had only a $10.00 bill and a $5.00 bill in it. He got quite worried about my running out of money. I noticed his concern about something, so I had a personal priesthood interview (PPI) with him and asked him if he had any problems or was worried about anything. This is when his feelings were revealed to me of his concern about my running out of money. So, we had about a half-hour chat, where I alleviated his fears about us running out of money and starving. I told him, we had about $6,000 in the bank. Also, we had about $30,000 of equity in this house. Then, there is the quarter share of land we own in Palmdale, which is worth about $25,000 to us. Also, we have cash value in our life insurance policies. Furthermore, we have a year's supply of food in our garage. Then, if worse comes to worse, there is the bishop's storehouse, where we can get food. I told him I could also go out and get any old job. I also told him that the Lord will provide a way as long as we obey his commandments. I told him that is why we have paid tithing, budget assessments, welfare, fast offerings, etc. all these years. Also, that is why we worked on church farms and canneries all these years. All the work we put in is insurance for us in times of need. So, I told him that there is nothing to worry about and that the Lord and I have everything under control. We must think positive, pray, and work hard to make this new business I started a success. So, now, Atom has a different appreciation about going to work on the pear farm this Saturday morning. He is now gung ho; whereas, before, he was reluctant to go. I told him that Heavenly Father will be pleased with us working on the farm and will bless us for it. I think the main thing Atom was worried about was whether or not our money will last through his birthday on November 9th. I think he was concerned about whether or not he was going to get anything for his birthday.

Atom is really cute. He is so aware of what's going on. Marc and Heather haven't a clue that I am unemployed and not receiving an income. But Atom, on the other hand, is really concerned about us running out of money and, consequently, food.

I told him that he could help us out by digging up the back yard to put in a garden. He could also help us turn off all lights when not in use to save on electricity. In addition, if he would wash my car, we could keep the money in the family instead of my giving it to the car wash people if I took it to the car wash. Then, also, we should eat all of our food and not waste any.

All of these little things help us conserve money, which would allow us to survive longer if we really were forced to. So, he finally went to bed feeling secure and assured that there is nothing to worry about if we trust in the Lord. I was really verbose tonight!

Atom	21 Oct 1983	Atom took it upon himself to mow the front lawn this evening. I was pleasantly surprised that he did that without any prompting from us. He also heated up and served the dinner that Karen had prepared for us before she left for work.
Atom	19 Jan 1984	Atom was really cute tonight when he counseled me not to get mad at mommy so that we won't get into any arguments. He's such a good kid to keep his old man straight. I hope he remembers these things and treats his wife as good as he thinks he will. I really think Atom is a very sensitive boy, a peacemaker. He should make a good bishop and stake president one of these years. He's a really good boy.
Atom	28 Jan 1984	In the afternoon, I played basketball with Atom for about 15 minutes. Atom washed my car and gave Apricot a bath today, which made me really happy because both car and dog were really dirty.

Atom	5 Jun 1984	After I got home, I fed the kids and then went to pick up Atom from his baseball game, which his team won. They are now in first place. Then, I took Atom to the Mutual Combined Activity, which was a swim party at Monte and Kathy McKeon's home in Sand Canyon. After we came home, the kids had their baths. Karen came home from work, and she, Apricot, and I took a walk up and down our street.
Atom	14 Jun 1984	We went to Atom's junior high school graduation. Karen bought him a suit today. He really looked sharp all decked out in his new two-tone blue suit. After the graduation, Atom went to a party with his friends. Karen took Marc and Heather to buy dinner at Kentucky Fried Chicken, and I went to a Stake Presidency–Bishoprics Meeting.
Atom	17 Jun 1984	Atom was really proud wearing his new suit to church today. He really looks sharp in it.
Atom	19 Jun 1984	Atom started playing on the Freshman basketball team at Canyon High School. He has his first game tomorrow.
Atom	20 Jun 1984	In the evening, I took Atom and Eric Foyt to their Freshman basketball game at Hart High School in Newhall. They lost.
Atom	3 Sep 1984	I forgot to mention that, last night, Bishop Dale Sutherland called Atom to serve as president of the deacons quorum. I'm really proud of Atom and hope that he will take this calling seriously since he has only two months to serve in this calling before he becomes a Teacher.
Atom	11 Sep 1984	Atom is all fired up to get straight A's this year in school. He has started reading the New Testament for seminary. I hope he maintains that enthusiasm throughout his high school years.
Atom	16 Sep 1984	Atom was set apart today by Bishop Dale Sutherland as deacons quorum president.
Atom	4 Oct 1984	This evening, Atom babysat for the Williamses. He is also selling tickets for the Booster Club and is up to 80 sold tickets. He has sold the most of all the kids on his basketball team. He will be shooting for 100.

Atom	11 Nov 1984	After sacrament meeting, I ordained Atom a teacher in the Aaronic Priesthood. Then, I attended the Stake General Priesthood meeting, which was attended by over 400 brethren. After that, I attended the Stake Library meeting. It was a full day for me. We had a belated birthday cake for Atom today for lunch. I am happy for the opportunity to ordain Atom a teacher today. Those that assisted me in ordaining Atom included Bishop Dale Sutherland, Brother Dave Orme, Brother Rich Nichols, Brother Roland LaBass, Brother Ollie Myrvang, and Brother Rob Klein.
Atom	23 Nov 1984	Atom played in his first basketball scrimmage game today, but they lost. He is on the Canyon High School "Cowboys" freshman team. He said he got to play for about 10 minutes. Their opponents smeared them something like 47 to 31.
Atom	28 Nov 1984	Atom had basketball practice this afternoon. He said that he got an 85 percent on his "Introduction to Physical Science (IPS)" class test yesterday. He said next quarter he will receive four A's and one B. If he gets on the honor roll, Karen said that we would give him $50.00. I do believe he will be going after it.
Atom	1 Dec 1984	Atom played for about 10 minutes in his basketball game today. He even made a basket (two points)!
Atom	9 Dec 1984	I went back to the chapel to assist in setting Atom apart as Teachers Quorum secretary. After that, we came home for dinner. Then, Karen and I went to a missionary farewell open house for Elder George Sagen at Bishop Thompson's home.
Baby Sitter	23 Jan 1982	After we got home, our baby sitter was sleeping so soundly that Karen broke into the front door after 10 minutes of knocking and calling for her. I guess Karen panicked and put her shoulder to the door while assisted by a lot of adrenalin.
Baby Sitting	24 Feb 1979	I baby-sat the boys all afternoon. It's quite a job to take care of a couple of young 'uns all day. They get into their little hassles and ask me questions all the time.

Baby Sitting	20 Oct 1979	I baby-sat the kids during the entire time Karen was away. Fortunately, Heather slept for most of the day. Atom was really helpful. He fed Heather twice, wound up her music carousel about a dozen times, and washed a dirty diaper for me in the toilet. I don't know what I would do without Atom. He really is a great help to me. He's such a good boy.
Baby Sitting	5 Aug 1980	The Ward Primary Board held a year-end party at our home tonight. I baby-sat the three kids in our bedroom. I took a snooze and did some reading. The boys played with their Legos. Heather was in everything as usual. Karen brought in food from time to time, which we devoured with little difficulty.
Baseball	3 Apr 1981	Atom got ready for his baseball game. At 3:45 P.M., we were off to his game. Eric Illera (our next-door neighbor's boy) accompanied us. Atom's team, the Angels, slaughtered their opponent 12 to 4. Atom scored once and brought a man in.
Baseball	7 Apr 1981	I picked Atom up after work from his baseball game. His team stomped their opponents something like 17 to 2.
Baseball	15 Apr 1981	After work, I picked Atom up from his baseball game. His team, the Angels, won again, 7 to 0. They are presently in first place in their league.
Baseball	9 May 1981	Atom won his baseball game again today 12 to 10. His team is the number one team in the league.
Baseball	12 May 1981	After I got home, I changed and went with Marc to Atom's baseball game. Atom's team won again (ho-hum) 16 to 5.
Baseball	13 Jun 1981	At 1:00 P.M., we went to see Atom's team, the Angels, win another baseball game. This time the score was 17 to 5…another route.
Baseball	25 Jun 1981	After work today, I went to the Hart Park to see Atom's ball game. Karen was there and left for class after I was there for about 15 minutes. Atom's team beat their opponent 16 to 1.
Baseball	26 Jul 1981	When I left for Rhode Island two Saturdays ago, Atom received two trophies for his baseball participation. He got a smaller trophy for being a member of the team and a large trophy (about 18 inches tall) for being a member of the championship team (the Angels).

Baseball	26 Mar 1983	We all attended Atom and Marc's baseball season opening ceremonies at 8:00 A.M.... At 1:45 P.M., we went to see Atom's first ball game. Atom's team (Giants) beat the other team 16 to 5. Atom hit a triple, so Atom got $3.00 from me.
Baseball	4 Jun 1983	I took the boys at 7:30 A.M. to their baseball games. Karen stayed home with Heather, who was still sick. Atom's game started at 8:00 A.M. They won 25 to 0. Atom made a nice catch on a pop up and also tagged a runner out at second. Marc's game started at 9:30 A.M. His team beat their opponent 24 to 19. Marc's team, the Astros, won every game except one thus far. Marc hit a couple of singles.
Baseball	11 Jun 1983	After the recital, we went to see the ending of Atom's baseball game, which they lost 10 to 3. Atom batted 2 for 3. He had two singles, drove in a run, and made a neat play at second base getting a runner out there.
Baseball	25 Jun 1983	I almost forgot to mention it that Marc's team, the Astros, came in second place in the league. The Dodgers won all of their games and came in first. The Astros lost only one game, and that was to the Dodgers.
Baseball	26 Jun 1984	Atom's team won their playoff game today and thereby became the champions. This is the second championship baseball team on which Atom has served.
Birthday, Atom	9 Nov 1980	Today was Atom's 10th birthday. I got him a digital watch, which he was thrilled to receive. In the evening, we had pound cake covered with chocolate icing. Karen baked the cake. It was really delicious. We all gave Atom 10 spanks, plus 1, plus "a pinch to grow an inch." Brother and Sister Roland LaBass came over to give Atom a birthday card with a dollar in it. It was really sweet of them to do that.
Birthday, Atom	7 Nov 1982	In the afternoon, I took Atom over to the chapel for an interview with the bishop. Atom will be 12 years old on Tuesday and will be conferred the Aaronic priesthood and ordained a deacon next Sunday.

Birthday, Atom	9 Nov 1982	Today was Atom's birthday. He is 12 years old. Our kids are really growing up. Next thing you know, he'll be in high school, then in college, then on a mission, then marriage in the temple, and then kids. For his birthday, we got Atom a genuine leather football, a couple of shirts, etc.
Birthday, Heather	12 Aug 1983	Karen held Heather's fourth birthday party today from 2:30 to 3:30 P.M. She was assisted by Marie and Kathy Illera, who helped decorate the house and serve the cake, ice cream, and green river punch. Heather had about 20 guests at the party, and she received a good bunch of presents. Actually, Heather's birthday is tomorrow.
Birthday, Karen	2 Dec 1983	At around 7:15 P.M., I took the three kids shopping at K-Mart for Karen's 32nd birthday tomorrow. The three kids got their mom a couple of necklaces. I got a birthday card and baked a cake.
Birthday, Karen	3 Dec 1983	Today was Karen's birthday. She is 32 years old. She has received tons of cards and gifts from many of the sisters in the ward. Karen is so good to many of them that they reciprocate abundantly on her birthday. She really does well with many of the sisters.
Birthday, Karen	30 Nov 1984	Karen and Chris Moody went to the movies tonight. Chris was taking Karen out to celebrate her 33rd birthday, which is coming up next Monday. Karen sure is getting old. We married on June 8, 1968.
Birthday, Marc	3 Jun 1976	A significant event occurred in our lives today. Marc Edward Uda, 7 pounds 10 ounces, was born at 4:16 P.M. on June 3, 1976. I took Karen to Jess Parish Hospital at 6:00 A.M., where she began receiving shots to induce labor as she was already 17 days overdue. It was quite a tiresome wait for me and, I'm sure, painful for Karen. I spent most of the day either reading or dozing off. The baby and Karen are doing fine. Atom was happy to have a younger brother.

Birthday, Marc	2 Jun 1979	At about 12:30 P.M., the whole family left for Knott's Berry Farm to celebrate Marc's birthday, which is really tomorrow (3 June). We took the kids through a small jungle park. Then we went on a choo-choo train ride, then on a steamboat ride, and finally on a merry-go-round ride. Along the way, we purchased some corn to feed the ducks and chickens. We had some fun feeding a hen and her litter of chicks. Atom petted a couple of the chicks. I picked one up and let Marc pet it. It was a neat experience for the boys. After that, we went to Farrell's Ice Cream Parlor, where we bought a late lunch and topped it off with ice cream dishes for dessert. Marc had a free chocolate sundae because of his birthday. Everyone there sang "Happy Birthday" to him. We got home about 4:30 P.M.
Marc	11 Sep 1984	Marc will be seeking the office of Athletic Director at Cedar-creek School. He only needs three more signatures for his application petition to run for that office.
Birthday, Marc	3 Jun 1983	Karen was holding Marc's birthday party at the house. We had about a dozen screaming little boys here celebrating with Marc. He got a load of presents.
Busy Little Beaver	13 Oct 1979	While we were gone to Atom's soccer game, Karen bathed Puffy and Heather, cleaned the kitchen, did two loads of laundry, cleaned the bathrooms, fed Heather, and set her hair. She said that she was a busy little beaver while we were gone.
Broke-chanics	20 Jan 1984	The kids and I installed the new garbage disposal unit that Karen had bought this morning. It took us over two hours in the early evening to do the job, but we finally got it in and without any leaks! That is quite an accomplishment for a bunch of broke-chanics. Marc sure loves to work with his hands and to tear mechanical things apart. I'm really glad he likes to do that. He'll be a lot more useful than I am when he gets married and raises a bunch of kids.
Carnations	18 Nov 1982	It was a normal day at work. I attended my UCLA class from 4:00–9:00 P.M. It rained while we walked from our classroom building to the parking lot. As the distance was about a third of a mile, we got pretty wet during the walk. On my way home, I stopped at Alpha Beta to buy Karen a bunch of carnations.

Changing Times	2 Jan 1981	In the afternoon, I took Darcy and her two friends (Julie and Kelly) with me to the post office, then to fill my Honda with gas, then to the department store to buy some envelopes, and finally to the car wash to vacuum the rugs in the Honda. At Newberry's, the girls bought a fistful of candy each and gorged themselves on candy. Times seem to have really changed since I was a teenager. The girls now days seem to be boy crazy. They just yell and wave at anything that wears pants. It seemed as though every boy they passed was cute.
Chore Chart	19 May 1984	We took the kids to Thrifty Drugs for ice cream cones, which they all earned this week by meeting the requirements on their chore chart. After that, we came home and had dinner.
Christmas	24 Dec 1980	The kids are all excited in anticipation of Santa Claus coming and leaving them gifts. In the evening, we read the Christmas Story from the Holy Bible. This has become an annual event.
Christmas	25 Dec 1980	Today is Christmas Day. The kids got us up at 6:30 A.M. to open their presents. As usual, they all got tons of gifts. Also during the day, I assembled Heather's table and chairs. This is the usual Christmas day frustration I go through every year trying to put together Christmas toys to impossible instructions with parts that don't always fit right. But we finally got them put together after much grunting and forcing. In the evening, we all played a game, which fit together cards with plumbing fixtures on them. It was another of the many silly games we have. We also watched a Dick Clark Special on TV called "The Good 'Ol Days." It featured many of the singing stars of the 1950s and 1960s. It was nostalgic.
Christmas	24 Dec 1982	I assembled Heather's doll buggy using instructions that were a pain in the you know what!
Christmas	24 Dec 1983	After Karen came home from work at about 7:00 P.M., she spent much of the evening wrapping presents for the kids. By the amount of presents we have under our tree, you would never guess that I have been unemployed for nearly six months with very little income coming in. We almost have as many gifts under our Christmas tree as we have had in previous years when I was gainfully employed.

Christmas	24 Dec 1984	Karen went with the Moody's red truck to pick up Atom and Marc's new Christmas bikes from the Davis' garage. After she came home, we put together Heather's new Christmas bicycle. It was another, as usual, frustrating experience for me. As usual, Karen overdid it again and got tons of gifts for the kids. You would never guess by the amount of presents she bought that our income this year is about one half that of last year.
Christmas	25 Dec 1984	Karen had prepared a delicious baked ham dinner, which we thoroughly enjoyed. After dinner, I dozed off for about a half hour. Then at 7:00 PM, we had the Illeras and Moodys over for dessert till about 8:30 PM. It was a wonderful, relaxing day for all of us. We are very thankful for all we have. We also received calls from Sister Yvonne Brockbank, my mom and dad, and Karen's mom today. It was a great day.
Clubhouse	20 Aug 1983	The kids built a clubhouse in the backyard today. It wasn't bad for the first time.
Cream Puffs	9 Sep 1980	Karen made some cream puffs today. They are delicious. I love them.
Crusader	1 Jul 1982	Karen and Atom went around the neighborhood taking around a petition for signatures opposing the construction of a trailer park at the end of the street. Karen and a bunch of other people are against a couple of thousand cars driving down the street every day. So, Karen is at it again on another project, or should I say cause.
Crusader	22 Sep 1982	In the evening, Karen and I attended a public meeting on the attempt to keep a mobile trailer park from being built adjacent to the Four Oaks housing tract. Karen has been quite involved in this activity. She and several other women really got enough of the neighborhood interested to the extend that they filled the multi-purpose room at Cedarcreek School. Atom baby-sat the two younger kids while were at the meeting.
Crusader	23 Sep 1982	Karen made the front page of the SFV (San Fernando Valley) *Daily News* today for her activities in attempting to keep the mobile home park from being built adjacent to the Four Oaks tract.

Cub Scouts	3 Jun 1981	After work, I attended Atom's Cub Pack meeting with him. He received four awards toward his Arrow of Light (the highest award that can be earned in Cub Scouting; the badge of which can be worn on the Boy Scout uniform).
Cub Scouts	21 Oct 1981	After work, our whole family went to Atom's Cub Scout Pack meeting. Atom was awarded the Arrow of Light Award and was graduated into Boy Scouting. Atom also received over a half dozen other awards, a couple of certificates, and a letter of congratulations from the scouting commissioner. We are really proud of Atom for receiving the highest award possible in Cub Scouting.
Cub Scouts	25 Apr 1984	Then, I came home and worked in my office until we had to attend the Cub Pack Meeting at 7:00 P.M. Marc received his Bobcat badge. He is so fired up about Cub Scouts.
Cub Scouts	26 Jun 1984	Marc has been attending Cub Scout Day Camp this week and has been having a good time. Atom has been serving as a Camp Counselor. He's big time.
Cub Scouts	28 Jun 1984	Marc won a medal and a blue ribbon today at his Cub Day Camp.
Dance	23 Sep 1982	Heather attended her first dance class today and had an enjoyable time. Marc and Atom attended their respective flag football practice.
Dance	11 Jun 1983	This afternoon, we attended Heather's dance recital called "Under the Big Top." It was a circus theme. It combined the Judy Hallen Dancers and the Canyon Country Majorettes. The recital had a packed attendance in the L.D.S. Stake Center Cultural Hall. Heather danced in the "Poodles" group, the "Finale of the Animals," and the "Grand Finale of the Clowns." She was so cute in her costumes and did exceptionally well on stage. We were very proud of her.

Discipline	20 May 1979	Because Atom and Marc were quite rowdy in sacrament meeting and thereafter, I had to levy some punishment (discipline) on them. Atom had a choice of having certain privileges taken away (such as not watching TV for a few days or going to bed early for several days) or receiving a spanking with the wooden spoon. He took the wooden spoon, evidently, because he valued his privileges more than a sore rear end. I then asked him how many spanks he should get, and he said five. I thought that was fair and agreed to give him five spanks when we got home. After we got home, I gave him five real hard ones, which he took pretty well. I then gave Marc one spank with the spoon since Atom influenced him to go onto the stage in the cultural hall and also to run and scream in the chapel. Our boys are really good boys. Though I hate to spank them, I know that it is necessary, for I subscribe to the principle that "If you spare the rod, you spoil the child." After I spank them, I always take them on my lap and in my arms and explain to them why I spanked them and express my love for them. They seem to respond very well to that method of discipline. After that, I gave the boys their baths, and then I laid in bed with them for about an hour. They are sleeping in the hide-a-bed in the living room (as they also did last night) because their bedroom reeks with odor from the paint that Karen is using to paint their room.
Discipline	10 Oct 1979	This morning Atom broke the clothes dryer door by putting his whole weight on it while getting some clothes. Karen was so mad about it that she took away the privilege of playing with his friends for three days and watching TV for two weeks. He also has to set up the table for two weeks and clean out the backyard garden. I also gave him four swats with the wooden spoon on the rump. All this punishment seems to be quite severe, but we levied it to make an impression on him. Karen had told him three times or so before about not putting his weight on the clothes dryer door, but, evidently, it just went in one ear and out the other. So, when he finally broke the door, Karen lowered the boom on him to teach him a good lesson. She would not have made the discipline so severe if it was only the first time he was warned about putting his weight on the door.

Doghouse	24 Jan 1981	Atom went to tryouts for baseball today. He wants to be an outfielder. After that, we built a doghouse for Princess (our dog). Atom designed it. Karen and Atom went out to buy the material. Atom and I built the doghouse, and Atom and Marc painted it.
Excursion	13 Jul 1984	Karen and the kids went with Kim Barney and her kids to tour the J. Paul Getty Museum in Santa Monica. After that, they went to the beach for a couple of hours.
Family Newsletter	16 Jun 1979	I almost forgot to mention that, in the mail, we received the second issue of the newsletter, "*What's Happening With the Uda Gang?*," from Carl and Cindy Uda of Provo, Utah. It was a very interesting issue which told of the doings of several of the Uda families. I hope we can keep up this publication as it will help in developing our family organization, genealogy, and family history.
Family Newsletter	15 Aug 1979	In the mail, we also received the third issue of "*What's Happening With the Uda Gang?*," which is our family newsletter that Carl and Cindy Uda are publishing this year.
Family Newsletter	16 Jan 1981	I spent the evening preparing for doing our family newsletter, *What's Happening With the Uda Gang?!* I am the newsletter editor this year.
Family Newsletter	19 Jan 1981	I am going to have to get with it on the January issue of our family newsletter.
Family Newsletter	21 Jan 1981	I spent the entire evening typing up the January 1981 issue (my first one as Editor) of our family newsletter called *What's Happening With the Uda Gang?*
Family Newsletter	24 Jan 1981	I also got our family newsletter reproduced and mailed today.

Father's Day	17 Jun 1984	Today is Father's Day. Karen cooked a nice omelet for me for breakfast along with bacon and toast.
		It was an extremely hot day today. For dinner, Karen cooked a nice large steak on the charcoal grill. She also cooked some squash and eggplant, which she picked from the nice garden she is growing behind our Doughboy pool. After dinner, I took a two-hour nap since I was exhausted from all that moving of large furniture yesterday.
		It was a very nice Father's Day. Karen and each of our kids gave me a Father's Day card each. Karen is still suffering from her severe migraine headache.
Flag Football	2 Oct 1982	At 8:30 this morning, we went to Marc's first flag football game. Marc's team, the Chiefs, beat the other team badly, 34 to 6. Marc made two touchdowns, two points after touchdown (PATs), and pulled off four flags.
		Then at 1:00 P.M., we attended Atom's first flag football game. His team, the Browns, beat their opponents 12 to 0. Atom pulled his first flag in a real game today. He is getting a lot better. Last year, he didn't pull a single flag. Now, I am trying to encourage him to pull two flags in the next game and improve each game thereafter.
Flag Football	9 Oct 1982	This morning I attended Marc's flag football game. His team, the Chiefs, beat their opponent 18 to 16. Marc made the winning touchdown in the waning minutes of the game. I was so thrilled that Marc broke loose and outran everyone on the field.
Flag Football	23 Oct 1982	In the afternoon at 1:00 P.M., we attended Atom's flag football game at North Oaks Park. Atom pulled two flags an almost made an interception. Atom's team, the Browns, tied the other team 8 to 8.
Flag Football	13 Nov 1982	I attended, with the family, Marc's flag football game this morning at 9:00 A.M. Marc made a touchdown and pulled four flags. His team lost, however, 24 to 19.
Folding Clothes	17 Nov 1980	Karen made a game for the kids out of folding the washed clothes. They were given monetary awards for winning or placing in several heats. The money is being saved up for our trip to Disneyland during the Thanksgiving holidays.

Friends	10 Jan 1984	Chris Moody fixed us some waffles with her new waffle iron this morning, which was great. Chris is so thoughtful about doing these little things for us. Don Moody (Chris' husband) brought over some lettuce from his garden to us last night. We are fortunate to have such good neighbors across the street. Tessie Illera, next door, is also always giving me her delicious Filipino dishes she cooks from time to time. I'm usually the one in the family who eats most of the exotic foods she gives us. The rest of the members of my family are meat and potato eaters. They are real *haoles*. That's Karen's influence on the kids, of course.
Girls Calling	12 Oct 1983	Atom has been getting phone calls by girls who like him. It is starting already, and he isn't even 13 years old yet!
Graduation	13 Jun 1981	We attended Marc's graduation from pre-school today at 10:00 A.M. All the kids looked really cute in their caps and gowns. They all received diplomas.
Haircut	3 Nov 1979	I cut Atom's and Marc's hair. Their hair was so long that they looked like girls. So, I gave them nice haircuts, and now they look like boys again.
Haircut	2 Jan 1981	We went to the barbers to get haircuts. Karen, as usual, wasn't too pleased with our short haircuts…particularly around the "fenders."
Haircut	1 Dec 1983	Karen gave Atom a haircut earlier in the evening. His hair was getting so long that he started looking like a girl. I'm glad he decided to get it cut after my coaxing.
Halloween	31 Oct 1980	After work today, I came home and took the kids out trick-or-treating as this was Halloween. Atom was dressed as a Storm Trooper, Marc as Spider Man, and Heather as a clown. I also took Eric and Jaime Illera, our two next-door neighbor boys. The kids got a good load of goodies. Darcy went to a Halloween Party.
Halloween	31 Oct 1982	This was Halloween today. Since this was the Sabbath day, our kids did not go out trick-or-treating. But Atom and Marc enjoyed handing out treats to all the kids that came to the door trick-or-treating.

Handyman **Karen**	5 Oct 1981	After coming home, I cooked myself some dinner because Karen was finishing up wallpapering and painting the kitchen and family room.
Heather	13 Aug 1979	Last night at about 10:30, Karen and I left home and headed for St. Joseph's Hospital in Orange, California. By the time we got there and got Karen settled in the labor room, it was about 11:30 P.M. I started keeping track of Karen's contractions from about 11:50 P.M. Karen was about three centimeters dilated at that time. For each contraction, Karen did the appropriate Lamaze breathing technique so that she could withstand the pains of labor. The contractions continued on for every five, then four, then three, then two minutes until around 1:15 A.M. when the nurse came in and found that Karen had dilated up to eight centimeters. They immediately started to take her to the delivery room while I changed into my sanitary outfit. Then at 1:34 A.M., Heather Ann Uda was born. She weighed 7 pounds 13 ounces and measured 19–1/2 inches long. It was an extremely exciting experience to see the actual birth of Heather Ann. Watching her come into this world was a sight to remember. I don't think I'll ever forget it. By the time I got home, it was 2:40 A.M. Because I got only about four hours of sleep, I took the day off from work today. Karen might be released from the hospital tomorrow, so I am also planning on taking tomorrow off from work. After getting up in the morning, watering the garden, and calling in to work, I left for the hospital at 8:30 A.M. to visit Karen and the new baby. I got there about 10 minutes till 9:00. Karen had just gotten through taking a shower and was prettying herself up. The baby was sleeping sweetly in the nursery. At about 9:30 or so, the nurse brought Heather in to Karen to feed her. I left for home after 11:00 A.M. to take the kids to swimming lessons.

We left the house about 12:15 P.M. for swimming lessons. Betty and I took the kids. Darcy, Jessi, Atom, and Traci went into the water. Marc must have been missing mommy very much, because he didn't want to go swimming. So, we didn't force him. After the swimming lessons, we came home and had lunch. We had left over lasagna and some macaroni and cheese among other things.

Then, after putting the two little ones down for a nap, Grandma Betty Rowland and I left at about 1:30 P.M. for the hospital to visit Karen and Heather. Karen had gotten about an hour-and-a-half of sleep since I had left her on my morning visit. During our visit, Toni Awai and her mother came to visit Karen and Heather.

Oh, I almost forgot. Prior to our going upstairs at the hospital to visit Karen and Heather, we stopped off at the hospital gift shop and bought Karen a vase with three pink roses in it. I also bought a box of suckers with "It's a Girl" written on them for the people at my office. We left the hospital at about 4:00 P.M.

I left home for my Business 413 class at CSUDH (California State University at Dominguez Hills) at about 4:50 P.M. I was so sleepy that I dozed off a couple of times during my drive to school. Fortunately, I got there safely. Having arrived there at 5:25 P.M., I took a 15-minute nap. It did me good even though I did doze off a couple of times during class. Class let out at 9:00 P.M., and I got home at 9:35 P.M.

Grandma Rowland fixed me up some reheated dinner of roast beef with potatoes and carrots. It wasn't bad at all. This ends a significant day in the Uda family.

Heather	25 Aug 1979	Heather is really getting cuter and cuter with every passing day. I have her in my arms as I write this journal entry. She will be 13 days old in about 2–1/2 hours. If Karen feels up to it, we are planning on taking Heather with us to sacrament meeting tomorrow. Atom and Marc are really good with Heather. They really love her and are good to her.
Heather	6 Sep 1979	Heather is really growing cuter and cuter with each passing day. I think she is really going to be a cutie when she grows up.

Heather	22 Oct 1979	Karen took Heather for her checkup today. Heather was weighed at 11–1/2 pounds! The doctor said that she was very big for her age according to the charts. If she continued to grow at the rate she is, she could be six feet tall by the time she is 18 years old! Dr. Yoshida gave Heather a shot, to which she is reacting. She ran a fever and was feeling miserable all evening. Heather rolled over three times today.
Heather	3 Nov 1979	While Karen was gone, Heather dumped in her diapers again as usual. It seems that whenever Karen leaves, Heather relaxes and dumps in her pants.
Heather	6 Jun 1980	Heather is getting close to walking. She stands up on her own now and takes a couple of steps before falling. She'll be 10 months old in one week. I'm sure she will be walking by the time she is 11 months old–and surely by the time she's a year old.
Heather	24 Jan 1981	Karen and Darcy went shopping down in San Fernando Valley this afternoon. While they were gone and the boys and I were on the patio painting the doghouse, Heather rolled the bolt on the sliding door and locked herself and Princess, our dog, in the house. We panicked for a while trying to get our way back into the house. But fortunately, I was able to talk Heather into rolling the bolt back on the sliding door allowing us to enter. [Heather was only 17 months old at the time.]
Heather	8 Mar 1981	We left Heather in the Nursery class for the first time. She cried for about 10 minutes but ended up having a fairly good time.
Heather	19 Jun 1982	Heather stepped in some dog doodoo (Princess') and stunk up the living room when she came inside. I scolded her about tracking in all that stink stuff. I don't think she'll do it again.
Heather	7 Oct 1982	Heather had her dance lesson and received a special sticker (the only one out of eight kids) for doing shuffles and hops and for being the only one in class not being rowdy and going out of the line.
Heather	25 Jun 1983	Earlier this evening, I did some flippies, airplane, and rocky chairs with Heather. I also told her about a half-dozen make-up stories, which she really enjoyed.

Heather	8 May 1984	Heather was tested for kindergarten today and got 90 out of 90–a perfect score. Nobody else tested as high as she did. I do believe we have a genius in the family in Heather. She is such a neat little girl. She's smart, cute, and sweet.
Heather	4 Jun 1984	This evening, we all attended Heather's pre-school graduation ceremony. It was really great, and we all had a good time. After that, we went to Thrifty Drugs for ice cream cones. After we got home, Karen, Apricot, and I went out for a walk. Then, I watched a car racing TV show starring Kenny Rogers.
Heather	6 Jun 1984	Karen went with Heather and her other pre-school classmates to Magic Mountain for the day.
Heather	26 Jun 1984	Karen and Heather both swam in the Pringles' pool today. They tell me that Heather swam the pool unassisted 10 times. It looks like Heather has learned how to swim.
Heather	3 Aug 1984	Heather passed Beginning Swimming today and received a Red Cross card and patch for her swimming suit. I am so very proud of her for this accomplishment.
Heather	27 Aug 1984	This morning, Atom watered Sister Brockbank's yard. Karen taught art at Cedarcreek School. Karen found out that Heather will be one of the four kids in the school's kindergarten who will receive awards at the school this Thursday morning.
Heather	30 Aug 1984	Heather received the Citizenship Award today in school. We are really proud of her.
Heather	11 Sep 1984	Heather is enjoying kindergarten and is already the teacher's pet.
Heather	15 Sep 1984	I attended with Karen, Marc's and Heather's soccer games. Marc's team lost 1 to 0. Heather's team won 2 to 0. Heather was really cute out there kicking the ball. Marc had a bloody nose just as the game started. I think it was due to the hot weather.
Heather	1 Oct 1984	Heather got almost all +'s on her report card. I think she is going to be the smartest of our three kids. Her teacher really is partial to her, and most of the kids in her class gravitate toward her. I think she is going to be a very popular lass as she gets older. I hope it doesn't go to her head.

Heather	27 Oct 1984	I worked in my office today off and on. At noon, I attended Heather's soccer game, which her team won. They are undefeated. I think they might win the championship crown. Heather sure hustles out there. She is so cute out there running around with all those boys.
Heather	13 Nov 1984	Heather and Karen put up pictures, certificates, etc. at Heather's class bulletin board titled Superstar of the Week. I think it is a really neat idea where one class member is honored every week with a display of whatever photos and other things they want to put on the board.
Heather	20 Nov 1984	Heather received a certificate and trophy this evening at her soccer team party. She is so thrilled about receiving her first trophy. She will be taking it to school tomorrow for show-and-tell.
Heather	1 Dec 1984	This afternoon, we attended Heather's dance recital. She was really cute in the special number and again in the finale.
Holoholo	27 Jun 1982	At about 6:30 P.M., we went *holoholo*, which means "going for a ride in the car" in Hawaiian. We had an enjoyable time for about an hour touring the back roads that we hadn't been on yet in the Santa Clarita Valley.
Karen	18 Oct 1979	Karen went to Relief Society meeting this morning. At her meeting, each of the sisters wrote something that was descriptive of all the other sisters. Karen's list of comments was as follows: (1) very outgoing, (2) super friendly and fun to be with, (3) enthusiastic and fun to be with, (4) does more than her share, (5) likes my children, (6) cheerfulness, (7) loves to give jokes, (8) a kind, knowledgeable Mormon sweetheart, (9) really friendly, and (10) wisdom.
Karen	2 Aug 1982	Karen, Atom, and Heather left for the Sniders' in Orange County this morning. They will be taking care of Ann Snider, who recently came out of the hospital from a hysterectomy, until Thursday morning. Marc is staying back with me because he has to attend school (year-round school). So, he left about 8:05 A.M. with Eric Illera and Kenny Moody for school.
Karen	2 Aug 1982	Karen and the other two kids will be home tomorrow. Hooray! Marc will really be happy. He really missed his mother, brother, and sister. At Safeway, he even bought some gifts for Atom and Heather for when they come home tomorrow.

Karen	3 May 1983	When I came home, I found Karen fixing the toilet–my wife is quite the plumber too!
Karen	12 Oct 1984	Karen is feverishly making dolls and other arts and crafts for a boutique that's coming up. She's making a lot of the money that will go towards the kids' Christmas presents.
Karen	16 Dec 1984	After dinner, Karen and I went for an appointment with Bishop Sutherland where she was called as the Canyon Country 2 Ward young women's president.
Karen	21 Dec 1984	Because I have been so busy on the SEMP, Karen did a neat thing for me. She helped me out by purchasing for me her Christmas gift, which she secretly gave me yesterday. I brought it home for Marc and Heather to wrap. They were so very excited thinking that I had bought the gift for Karen from all of us. I really appreciate what my dear wife has done for me. It really helps relieve the pressure off me by removing one more thing that I had to do before Christmas.
Karen	30 Dec 1984	After sacrament meeting, I assisted in setting Karen apart as the new ward young women's president. Her counselors, Sister Robin Davis and Bonnie Nichols were also set apart. After that, we had tithing settlement with Bishop Sutherland.
Knott's Berry Farm	7 May 1982	I took a day off from work so we all could go to Knott's Berry Farm. We spent 12 hours on this little excursion. The kids missed school today so that we all could go. I am dead tired from all that walking around all day. We had a great time going on most of the rides in that amusement park.
Landscaping	15 May 1982	Over the last week, Karen has been putting in some grass, trees, plants, and vegetables in the backyard. She also got some decorative bark and laid it around the swimming pool area.
Love Notes	23 Jul 1982	Karen did some sweet things. She left little love notes to me in the refrigerator, the medicine cabinet, my bureau, and on my desk lamp. She always does these little things, which mean so much to me. These are some of the reasons why I love her so much. She is such a thoughtful person–not only to me but also to the kids and to all of our friends.
Marc	4 Aug 1980	Karen took Marc to his swimming lesson from 10:30–11:00 A.M. Marc swam across the pool for the first time.

Marc	8 Aug 1980	Marc can now swim completely across the pool. He is progressing so fast that his instructor is advancing him to the next class.
Marc	27 Aug 1980	Marc swam completely across the pool and back in his swimming lessons today. He was declared "water safe" by his instructor today.
Marc	1 Mar 1981	Marc gave his first talk in Primary today and did an excellent job.
Marc	20 Oct 1981	After work, I went to pick up Marc from his soccer practice. He made his first goal at soccer practice today. I gave him a dollar as an incentive to make a goal at one of his real games.
Marc	25 Mar 1983	Yesterday, Marc finally really learned how to ride a bicycle. He was so thrilled about it. It seemed like it clicked with him all of a sudden.
Marc	7 May 1983	Marc ended up as the top speller in his class and will be competing at the school level. Karen has been helping him practice for the next competition.
Marc	14 Mar 1984	In the evening, I attended the talent show at the Sierra Vista School auditorium. It was for the kids at Cedarcreek School. Marc was one of the 16 acts. He played the "Indian Song" on the piano and did an excellent job.
Marc	28 Jun 1984	Marc won a medal and a blue ribbon today at his Cub Day Camp.
Marc	30 Jun 1984	Marc spent the night with Jeremy Davis. In the evening, Karen and the kids went to a pizza dinner with Marc's team. They brought me some pizza at work. Then, later in the evening, they all went to the Little League field for the closing ceremonies where Marc received a really nice trophy for playing and being on the team.
Marc	26 Aug 1984	Sister Sherryle LaBass came over this evening to visit teach Karen. I forgot to mention that Marc really enjoyed going home teaching with us. Marc also received a bronze medal in church today for being one of the four children in Primary to receive medals in the Scripture Olympics. He had to memorize over 20 scriptural passages to win that award. I am so very proud of him for that accomplishment.

Marc	1 Oct 1984	After FHE, I went back to my office to do some work. I forgot to mention that I took Marc with me this morning to visit the three seminary buildings. He must have really enjoyed himself because Karen said that he was boasting about it to his friends today. I also forgot to mention that, last week, Marc received at school the scholarship award for math. That apparently is his best subject.
Marc	13 Oct 1984	We went to Marc's soccer game, which they won. Marc really hustled in the game today, which made me proud of him. After that, we came home, and I took another shower before going to my office to work for a couple of hours.
Marc	27 Oct 1984	At 2:00 PM, we attended Marc's soccer game. They were up against Jeremy Davis' team, which was also undefeated (4 for 4). However, Marc's team beat them 3 to 0. Marc played an excellent game. I do believe that next year, he is going to be one of the stars on his team. He is improving greatly with each passing game.
Marc	1 Dec 1984	Marc played his last soccer game, but they tied 0 to 0, so they will have a playoff next week for the championship. Marc played forward for two quarters and did an excellent job.
Marc	7 Dec 1984	Marc ran for president of his class and was elected to that office today. I think Marc is going to be the politician in our family. He really likes to run for office. We are thrilled that he won. He also ran for school athletic director and class representative to the student council but lost both times. He said that the reason people voted for him for president is because they felt sorry for him for losing twice previously. He had also recently been elected as class editor.
Marc	8 Dec 1984	Karen and the kids went out to buy a Christmas tree today. Marc played his semifinal soccer game today, and his team won 7 to 0. Next week, they play for all of the marbles.
Massage	27 Jan 1980	After sacrament meeting, we came home and relaxed for the remainder of the day. I had the boys walk on my back while I was lying on the bed. This was a good form of massage, that is, until Karen decided to get into the act. After they got through with me, I was so relaxed and exhausted that I slept for the next three hours.

Mother's Day	8 May 1983	The kids and I fixed Karen breakfast in bed for Mother's Day. Since Karen was sick with female problems, I took the kids with me to Church. After church, I spent the afternoon and early evening reading the *L.A. Times*. Karen fixed some *kalua* pig (baked in the oven). It was really great.
Mother's Day	13 May 1984	Today was Mother's Day. The kids got up and cooked their mother breakfast, which she had in bed. We also gave her three cards and two corsages.
Movie	4 Jul 1979	At 2:20 P.M., we went to the Twin Cinema at the Huntington Mall to see the Walt Disney movie "The 101 Dalmatians." The kids really enjoyed the movie. It is exactly like the book–only animated. The movie lasted for an hour and twenty minutes.
Moving the Door	8 Jul 1981	Randy Lawrence came over at about 4:00 P.M. today and started work on moving the door that goes from our family room into the garage over about four feet towards the front door. This is one of Karen's ideas to make more room for our dining room set, where the family room now is located. It doesn't make much sense to me; but if it will keep Karen happy, then I am all for it.
Moving the Door	3 Sep 1981	Karen finished putting on the trimmings to the door going into the garage. She is always so busy working different projects. I am always amazed at the things she does. She is multi-talented.
Naming & Blessing Baby Heather	2 Sep 1979	During fast and testimony meeting, I blessed Heather. Brothers Lewis Mullin, Emerson Snider, and Merle Jager assisted me in the blessing. Heather was dressed up in a frilly, yellow, Sunday-best dress. She slept through the entire blessing. Heather is such a nice, calm, quiet baby. I think she is a special child and will grow to be quite a lady for some lucky returning Mormon missionary to marry when they are of age.

Near Accident	6 Jul 1983	Marc almost got hit by a car this afternoon (missed him by inches) while running across the street before stopping and looking both ways. Heavenly Father must have been watching over him. He was really lucky. He could have been dead or injured badly. Karen really spanked him and lectured him good. I think this episode will stick in his mind forever. He should have learned a good, valuable lesson. Marc cried and cried, more so because he was afraid of the possible consequences, had he been hit, than anything else. I hope he learned good because we sure love him and want him to be around, along with Atom and Heather, for the rest of our lives.
New Year	31 Dec 1980	Today is New Year's Eve....In the evening, we went to the New Year's Eve Pre-party at the Monte McKeon's home. Darcy baby-sat the kids. We came home at around 9:00 P.M. Then Kelly Kilgore came over to spend the night with Darcy. At midnight, we ushered in the new year. It was nothing exciting. Another year has come and gone. I'm looking forward to another great, eventful year.
New Year	1 Jan 1981	Happy New Year! Today is the first day of 1981....For dinner, Karen prepared spare ribs and sour kraut, which has become a traditional New Year's dinner in our family.
Non-verbal Communication	14 Jan 1980	This morning Atom came into the bathroom to talk with me while I was getting ready to go to work. In our discussions, he said that he knew when I was not pleased with him or Marc when they are talking during church services. He said that I would give them a look with my eyes (ye ol' evil eye) that told them they should not be talking or goofing off. I told him that that was nonverbal communication. He asked me what that meant, so I explained its meaning. I thought that discussion was a cute moment.
Parents' and Pearces' Visit	5 Aug 1983	My mother called earlier this evening and said that they and the Pearces will be by to visit us around the 10th or 11th. We should have a house full of people for a few days.
Parents' and Pearces' Visit	11 Aug 1983	I drove to Pomona to visit General Dynamics-Pomona again. After that, I came back home and did some typing until my mom and dad and the Pearce family arrived. We had some good discussions. I went swimming with the kids. Mom made beef-tomato for dinner, which was scrumptious.

Parents' and Pearces' Visit	12 Aug 1983	I spent the entire day typing up letters. Mom and dad, the Pearces, and Atom all went to Magic Mountain from about 10:00 A.M. till about 9:00 P.M. They said it was a very hot day out there and that they all got totally soaked on one of the water rides.
Parents' and Pearces' Visit	13 Aug 1983	The Pearces left this morning for a trip down to Tijuana, Mexico. They will be staying the night in San Diego. At around noon, we drove my parents out to Palmdale to see their land (about 4–1/2 acres) next to AF Plant 42. The prices are really depressed now. If we sold it now, we would lose out. We had lunch at McDonalds. After we came home, Grandpa Uda, the two boys, and I went swimming in our pool. Karen, Grandma Uda, and Heather drove to The Valley to buy me some newspapers for employment ads and also bought some cheap bread at a nearby place that Karen found. After they came home, we cooked teriyaki chicken and hamburgers on the charcoal grill and had a delicious dinner on the patio. After that, we went to Baskin Robbins for some ice cream.
Parents' and Pearces' Visit	14 Aug 1983	The Pearces came home at about 5:00 P.M. Karen and Marc went to Joshua Martin's baptism at 6:30 P.M. Mom Uda cooked up some dinner for us (a soft noodle dish), which was delicious. The Pearces and my parents will be going to Disneyland tomorrow. Then, on Tuesday, they will head back home to Ogden, Utah.
Parents' and Pearces' Visit	15 Aug 1983	The Pearces, my parents, and Atom went to Disneyland all day today.
Parents' and Pearces' Visit	16 Aug 1983	The Pearces and my parents left today for Las Vegas, where they will be spending the night. Tomorrow, they will be returning to Utah.
Parents Moved to Utah	12 Aug 1984	Mom and dad called this morning from Lindon, Utah, to tell us that they had moved up there in the house next to Randall and Sharon Jones. I hope we'll be able to see them this Christmas.

Phone Talk	5 Oct 1983	Karen talked to Kathy McKeon on the phone for over two hours. I wonder what they talk about. I don't think I could carry on a conversation that long with anyone on the telephone.
Piano Les-sons	27 Jun 1982	Over the past month, Atom and Marc have been taking piano lessons from Sister Robin Davis. They are learning pretty fast. Marc is a natural and seems to be picking things up quickly. Karen is also learning and practicing on the piano and teaching the kids. Even Heather seems to be picking up some things and enjoys plunking on the piano.
Pregnancy	29 May 1979	Karen hasn't been feeling too well over the past seven months. Thank goodness she has only two months to go before the baby is born. She thinks it will be another boy, and I think it will be a girl. I have guessed correctly 100 percent of the time in about a dozen guesses thus far. This may be my first wrong guess. I really don't care what sex the baby is, as long as it is healthy. That's the main thing. But, if it is a girl, I'm sure I will spoil her rotten.
Princess, the Dog	24 Nov 1980	A couple of days ago, we got two pups from the Illeras next door. We are holding one pup for the Awais. We now have a brown German Shepherd *poi* dog. It is about six weeks old. They have been whining the last couple of nights.
Princess, the Dog	30 Nov 1980	Our new puppy is called Princess. She is really a good dog. I think I am going to really like her as I am already spoiling her by letting her in the house at every moment she yelps and scratches at the back sliding door. Since Karen took the other pup to the Awais yesterday, Princess spent her first night alone in the garage. She was quite lonely, as she yelped off-and-on throughout the night. I'm sure she will be used to it after a couple of nights.
Princess, the Dog	2 Jan 1981	At noon, Atom and I went to the supermarket to buy Princess a food dish and rawhide bone....Before going home, we stopped at the meat market to buy Princess some real bones. To our surprise, the owner gave us a free bag of bones.
Princess, the Dog	2 Feb 1981	The Billimorias came over to pick up a returned pup from the Illeras next door. The pup looks more like a collie. It is about half the size of Princess, yet it came from the same litter. Princess is just a big "Baby Huey."

Princess, the Dog	26 Jun 1982	Karen took Princess to the dog pound today because she is allergic to Princess' fur. In addition, Atom really wasn't taking good care of the dog with food, water, attention, and cleaning up her excrement on a daily basis. She will be better off in a new home on someone's farm. We all will miss Princess. Karen said she really bawled when she left Princess, and Princess didn't want to go. But that's the way life is sometimes. We will probably get a small teacup poodle when Puffy dies of old age.
Princess, the Dog	27 Jun 1982	We all miss not having Princess around. Even the Illeras' dog, Captain Cool, misses Princess.
Puffy, the Dog	30 May 1979	Puffy just about chewed off one of her nails, so Karen took her to the veterinarian to have it fixed. It cost over $40 for the job. The vet gave Puffy an anesthetic shot, which has affected her all through the evening. Puffy is like a human being and just loves to be babied.
Puffy, the Dog	4 Sep 1979	Karen found a lump on one of Puffy's nipples over the weekend. So, today, she took Puffy to the veterinarian for a checkup and found that she had a mammary tumor. So, she had to leave Puffy at the animal hospital so that she could be operated on either tonight or tomorrow morning. She should be able to come home tomorrow night. The operation will be costing us $129.00. Puffy is almost 10 years old, which makes her equivalent to a human being that is about 70 years old. So, Puffy is a fairly old dog. Karen cried and was pretty upset about Puffy needing surgery.
Puffy, the Dog	5 Sep 1979	Puffy came home from the animal hospital this afternoon. She had her mammary tumor removed from one of her nipples. The vet also cleaned her teeth and removed two of her back molars, which were badly decayed. The vet also put some medicine in her eyes as she also has an eye disease. We also found that she has a slight skin disease, which explains why she stinks so bad even a few days after I give her a bath. Karen put an insect bomb in the house this morning to spray and kill all of the fleas that are in the house and carpets.
Puffy, the Dog	6 Sep 1979	Puffy is recuperating rapidly from her operation. Today, she was spunky and feeling pretty good.

Puffy, the Dog	10 Jul 1982	Today was a sad day, particularly for Karen. She took Puffy to the vet and had to put her to sleep. Karen came home bawling. Puffy was suffering from old age, blindness, and arthritis, among other thing. She lived almost 14 years, which, compared to a human life span, would put her about a century old. She has been a good dog to us over almost the full 14 years of our marriage. I know Puffy will go to heaven to live with our Heavenly Father.
Puffy, the Dog	12 Jul 1982	Karen is finally pulling through her mourning for Puffy. She said that she had cried herself out.
Quiet, the Dog	14 Jun 1980	While at Alpha Beta Supermarket, we met some kids who were giving away some two-month-old mutt puppies. Guess who ended up with one of the five that they gave away? We are naming the puppy (a female) "Quiet" because it was so passive and quiet when we got her. But I really wonder whether or not she will live up to her name after getting used to our home, our family, and Puffy.
Quiet, the Dog	13 Jul 1980	Karen and the kids came home late in the afternoon. It was good to have them all back. Karen started another migraine headache. It seems as though Quiet may be the cause of it. If it is so, we may have to give her away.
Quiet, the Dog	15 Jul 1980	We have come to the conclusion that Quiet's fur has an affect on Karen's sinus and migraine headache condition. So, Quiet has to stay outside most of the time. It was another hot day today.
Quiet, the Dog	20 Jul 1980	Karen started another one of her migraine headaches after we arrived home. So, we have come to the conclusion that it is either Quiet's fur that is bothering her or the Canyon Country weather with its high pollen count that may be the culprit.
Quiet, the Dog	26 Aug 1980	Quiet dumped on the living room carpet, and I had to clean it up. Uggh!
Quiet, the Dog	24 Nov 1980	We gave Quiet to some people a few streets away yesterday.
Rearranging Books	27 Jul 1982	Karen spent the day rearranging my books over my desk and in the closet. She put some of the books in the hall closet. She gets a big kick out of moving things around. So, I let her do it without too much opposition. If it makes her happy, why not? That's the way I look at it.

Renova-tion	3 Apr 1982	Karen has been removing the wallpaper, re-wallpapering, and painting our bedroom over the past few days. She has also been redoing our bathroom to our master bedroom. She is doing a really good job at it.
Renova-tion	5 Apr 1982	Karen finished wallpapering the top portion of our bedroom. She is now going to use a dark blue paint for the lower three feet of our bedroom wall. She almost completed laying the new flooring in our bathroom. She also plans on putting up some shelving on the bathroom wall for all the junk we normally have piled on the basin counter area.
Renova-tion	6 Apr 1982	Karen finished up the bedroom and bathroom. It looks really great. She is quite a talented woman. I'm glad I married her. She is quite a gal.
Report Card	25 Sep 1980	Atom's report card was pretty good. I had to pay him $2.00 for the good marks he got.
San Fran-cisco Weekend	25 May 1983	I just can't wait to see Karen this weekend in San Francisco. This will be a nice holiday together alone in the Travelodge Hotel at the Oakland Airport.
San Fran-cisco Weekend	27 May 1983	I got up at 5:00 A.M. and left at 6:25 A.M. for Redding, California. I drove for 11 hours 40 minutes to cover about 580 miles. It was a very hot day today. I think the temperature was around 100 degrees F. I am staying at the Travelodge in Redding tonight. Tomorrow morning I will be driving in to San Francisco to pick Karen up at SFO on the 2:08 P.M. PSA flight. We will be checking in for two days at the Travelodge at the Oakland Airport. I am really looking forward to having Karen meet me in San Francisco for two days over the Memorial Day weekend. It will be like a second honeymoon.
San Fran-cisco Weekend	28 May 1983	I drove the 230 miles this morning between Redding and Oakland. We are staying at the Travelodge near the Oakland Airport. I checked in and then went to SFO Airport to pick Karen up. We then went to the hotel for a while. After that, we went to the Fisherman's Wharf for dinner at Alioto's Restaurant. We had prawns and crab. After that, we went to the Wax Museum, Miner's Haunted House, and Old San Francisco cable car ride. Then, we came back to the hotel.

San Francisco Weekend	29 May 1983	We got up late this morning and left for Sausalito around 11:00 A.M. We went to lunch there and also went window-shopping to all of the quaint shops there. After that, we drove through Japan Town and also drove down the crookedest road on Lombard Street. Then, we went to Chinatown and went shopping on the main drag. After that, we went to Fisherman's Wharf and went through Piers 39 and 41. We also went to the old part of Fisherman's Wharf. After that, we went shopping at Safeway in San Leandro. Then, we returned to the motel and watched a TV show starring Richard Dryfus in "Who's Life is It Anyway?"
San Francisco Weekend	30 May 1983	We got up fairly late this morning, and by the time we left for the airport, it was after 11:00 A.M. We had hot dogs for lunch at a snack bar at the airport. Karen left on the 1:05 P.M. PSA flight to Burbank Airport. I then went and checked in at the Motel 6 in Sunnyvale. After that, I did my laundry, made copies of and mailed my weekly expense report to Eric Duncan, and ate dinner. I called Karen and found that she had made it home okay. We had a glorious two-day weekend in San Francisco. We should do this more often–like once every quarter. After coming back to the motel room, I started reading a book I bought at Pier 39 yesterday and dozed off for a couple of hours. I am really exhausted.
Saving Money	12 Jul 1983	We are also in July, the hottest month of the year. And Karen has decided to keep the air conditioner off to save electric money. It was only 107 degrees F outside today! It was so hot in the house that our air conditioner went on, and it was set at the highest temperature it could be at–that's about 90 degrees F! So, Karen had to shut off the entire air conditioning system just to keep the air conditioner from flicking on!
School	28 Jul 1983	Marc is doing really well in school. He is reading at the third grade level, but he is in the second grade. He is one of five or six kids in his class that are in the second grade. The rest of the kids are in the third grade. Marc has Kenny Moody and Bucky McKeon as classmates. Marc did extremely well on his spelling today.
School	3 Aug 1983	Marc brought home a neat little note from his principal today. We are saving it in his file of certificates, awards, etc.

School	16 Dec 1983	In the evening, we attended Heather's school Christmas play. Heather played the part of an angel. She had a speaking part and sang a solo song and did superbly!
Speech Contest Winner	19 Sep 1980	Atom won first place today on his speech contest at school. His speech was on Oscar Meyer hot dogs. He will be making the same speech to the entire school next week. Atom was so thrilled and hyped up. We are very proud of him.
Speech Contest Winner	22 Sep 1980	Atom gave his Oscar Meyer hot dog speech before his entire school today and received the Speaker of the Month Certificate and ribbon.
Speech Contest Winner	27 Oct 1980	Atom came in tied for first place on his speech last Friday on Missiles and the Space Shuttle.
Speech Contest Winner	26 Nov 1980	Atom came in third place on his speech in school, which was on the operation of the Polaroid camera.
Speech Contest Winner	31 Jul 1981	Atom won first place in his speech at school. He gave a speech on "Chocolate."
Speech Contest Winner	23 Oct 1981	Atom got second place for his speech in school today.
Swimming Pool	27 Apr 1981	We will be getting our Doughboy swimming pool tomorrow. It will be 18 feet in diameter.
Swimming Pool	28 Apr 1981	We got our swimming pool installed in our backyard today.
Tee Ball	20 Mar 1982	Atom and I took Marc to his first Tee Ball game today. His team, the Twins, creamed their opponents. Marc hit a home run and scored two other times.
Tee Ball	27 Mar 1982	We went to Marc's Little League opening ceremonies this morning at 8:00 A.M. After the ceremony, which was attended by thousands of people, Marc's team (the Twins) played the Pirates and lost by a score of 26 to 22. It was a very high scoring game. Marc hit a home run and scored two other times.

Tee Ball	17 Apr 1982	We went to Marc's tee ball game today, which his team, the Twins, won 23 to 15.... Marc hit a home run and scored two other times during his game today.
Tee Ball	24 Apr 1982	At 8:00 A.M., we left for Marc's tee ball game, which started at 8:30 A.M. Marc's team, the Twins, beat their opponents 24 to 18. Marc hit a homer and scored another time.
Thanksgiving Day	27 Nov 1980	Today is Thanksgiving Day. I had a holiday from work. In the morning, I bathed the three dogs. Then Darcy, Atom, and I went shopping. When we got home, the Sniders had already arrived from Orange County. We had a delicious turkey dinner that Karen had prepared. We also watched a couple of football games on television. After dinner, we played a new game called Five Straight that the Sniders had brought over for the day. The Sniders left for home at about 9:00 P.M. Atom went with them to spend a couple of days down in Orange County. On Saturday, we will be going down to Orange County to visit the Sniders and to go to Disneyland with them. All in all, it was another enjoyable Thanksgiving Day at home. We surely have a lot to be thankful for with the Gospel, the Priesthood, my good job, our good health, and being citizens of this great Country of ours.
Thanksgiving Day	24 Nov 1983	Today is Thanksgiving Day. Karen didn't go to work today because of the holiday, and Howard & Phil's was closed all day. I didn't do too much myself on the business. Atom watched football games on TV for most of the day. It rained all day today, so it was miserable from the weather standpoint. Karen prepared a delicious Thanksgiving dinner. We had roast turkey and dressing, mashed potatoes, yams, deviled eggs, rolls, corn, gravy, milk, and pumpkin pie. It wasn't as much as we usually have for Thanksgiving, but I ate enough to get myself a stomachache again. The Pringles came over from 7:00–11:00 P.M. for dessert and conversation. We had an enjoyable time meeting with them. Heather and Ashley had a good time playing together. I forgot to mention earlier that Heather had helped mommy prepare and bake the pumpkin pie. She looked so cute dressed in her little apron just like mommy's.

Unusual Breakfast	3 Nov 1979	Karen made an unusual dish for breakfast, which was sort of like a huge pancake (made of Bisquick) in a dish with cheese on it (and in it) and bacon bits on top–all baked in the oven. It was a unique breakfast for sure!
Vacation	18 Jul 1980	I took a vacation day off from work today. However, since Karen said she was not going to be ready to leave until sometime between 10:30 and 11:00 A.M., I decided to go in to work for a couple of hours. After coming home at about 10:30 A.M., we did not leave finally until 11:45 A.M. We drove to the Tanners' cabin, which we rented for two days at $30 per day, in Crestline by Lake Gregory. After missing the turnoff and going 20 miles out of the way, we returned and finally got there at 3:00 P.M. I took a nap for an hour because I was drowsy from taking a couple of hay fever pills (as I was suffering from hay fever). At about 4:00 P.M., we went for a drive around the lake, stopped off at the Arcade for a while, stopped at an antique shop, and went for another swing around Lake Gregory. We got back to the cabin at about 6:00 P.M. Karen then fixed us hamburgers for dinner. We spent the rest of the evening watching television.

Vacation	19 Jul 1980	We got up fairly late in the morning, took our showers, had breakfast, and then went to town at about 10:15 A.M. We went to an arts and crafts shop and then to an antique shop. Karen bought an old horseshoe and a calf wiener. It'll be a nice conversation piece. After that, we went to the north shore of Lake Gregory. We had to pay $.75 each for Atom, Karen, and me to get into the beach park. Marc and Heather were allowed in free. We spent over two hours at the lake. Karen and I got sunburns. The water was quite cold. But that didn't phase Atom and Marc. They dove in the cold water anyway. We also rented a surfboard for a half-hour for $.50. We had a good time riding on the board. After leaving, we drove around the lake again and then went back to the cabin at about 1:30 P.M. for lunch. Before we got back, however, we went to the grocery store to buy some groceries. Karen fixed us some sandwiches for lunch. I took about an hour nap. We spent the afternoon watching TV. At 4:30 P.M., I watched the Sugar Ray Leonard-Roberto Duran fight on TV. It was a good boxing match where Duran won the welterweight title from Leonard. After that, Karen fixed us some hot dogs for dinner. Then we went to the store to buy Heather some disposable diapers. We also stopped at the Arcade to play a round of miniature golf. We also took a couple of pictures in the photo booth at the Arcade. They didn't come out too good. After coming home, we spent the rest of the evening watching television.
Vacation	20 Jul 1980	We got up at about 8:00 A.M. After we all took our showers, had breakfast, and watched cartoons on TV, Karen cleaned up the cabin. We left for home at 11:20 A.M. and arrived home at 1:45 P.M.
Valentine	14 Feb 1979	Today is Valentine's Day. I got Karen a Valentine's card and two white carnations. Karen gave me a card also.
Valentine	13 Feb 1982	In the evening, we went to Alpha Beta to buy Karen a large Valentine's card (about 2'X4'), a corsage, and a decorative plate suitable for hanging on the wall.
Video Game	10 Apr 1982	I spent about six hours today playing Pac Man on our Atari video game. I got so involved in it that I got muscle aches from being so tensed up for hours.

Wallpaper	20 May 1979	Karen is still not finished with putting wallpaper on one of the walls. She has already put on two strips of the wallpaper. It was Atom's selection, which is a Star Wars decor. I really don't think it looks that great, but Atom is thrilled with it. So, I tolerate it realizing that *this too will pass.* Fortunately, the wall-paper can be easily removed and replaced with more conservative ones as Atom grows older. If Marc had his way, we would have another wall papered with the Muppets characters, e.g., Ernie and Bert, et al. Already, Marc has Muppet slippers, shoes, sheets, and pillowcase. Atom has Star Wars dolls, Imperial Fighter, X-Wing Fighter, robots, picture cards, etc., etc. I wonder whatever happened to the Disney characters, et al. *Things have really changed.*
Water Fight	11 Jun 1979	Karen bought a child's swimming pool for the kids. They had a ball playing in the pool. The atmospheric temperature today must have been over 100 degrees F. In the evening, I watered the garden again. It ended with the whole family involved in a water fight. Karen and I were soaked to the skin. The kids really had a good time. Atom, especially, had a blast soaking his dad. Karen, who volunteered to finish watering the garden, while I went in to take a shower, deviously turned the water hose on me.
Wedding Anniversary	8 Jun 1979	Karen had prepared a beautiful candlelight dinner for us in commemoration of our 11th wedding anniversary today. We had teriyaki steaks, which I cooked on the charcoal grill; rice; corn-on-the-cob; bean sprouts; a salad of cottage cheese, lettuce, and tomatoes; rolls and margarine; and milk. It was a fantastic meal.
Wedding Anniversary	7 Jun 1980	In the afternoon, I went to get a haircut and bought a tabletop ironing board for Karen as a 12th wedding anniversary gift. Normally, she irons my shirts on the carpet floor. Hopefully, now it will be a little more decent ironing on a real ironing board.
Wedding Anniversary	28 Aug 1981	This was our sixth anniversary since being sealed in the Washington Temple. Karen and I had a date. We went to see "An Eye for an Eye" at the Mann 6 Theater. It was an action-filled karate movie starring Chuck Norris. Julie Kolman baby-sat the kids for us.

Wedding Anniversary	8 Jun 1982	This day is also Karen and my 14th wedding anniversary. It's been 14 grand years, and it's getting better. Karen made a delicious dinner tonight. We broiled steaks on the charcoal stove on the patio. We also had tossed salad, corn, rice, French-fried potatoes, and milk. It was a great meal.
Wedding Anniversary	11 Jun 1984	It just dawned on me this evening while driving to San Diego that I had forgotten our 16th wedding anniversary, which passed us by this Friday, June 8th. I cannot believe it! And to top it off, Karen also forgot about it! I guess our lives have become so busy that we forget about the important things. I called Karen as soon as I arrived at the Travelodge, where Don Knapp and I are staying. We will all go out to dinner when I return home. This is unbelievable.
Wedding Anniversary	29 Jun 1984	After I got home, we had dinner. Then, Karen and I went to see "Indiana Jones and the Temple of Doom" at the Mann 10 Theater in celebration of our belated 16th Anniversary of our wedding. After the movie, I went to my office to do some work.
Wedding Anniversary	28 Aug 1984	Today is Karen and my 9th temple sealing anniversary. I bought her some carnations. Since I am in the panic mode on my GDC work again, we are postponing going out together to celebrate till this Saturday night. So, Instead, Karen took the kids and Kenny Moody and Chris Nichols to the movies.
Work	11 Jun 1983	Atom did an excellent job this morning mowing and trimming the front lawn. He also pulled the weeds and grass growing out of the cracks and crevices on the driveway.
Work	12 May 1984	The kids cleaned their rooms, folded clothes, and cleaned the patio and back yard.
Zoo	6 Jul 1981	Today was another holiday from work. Our entire family went to the Los Angeles Zoo today. After that, we had a picnic lunch in Griffith Park. After lunch, we went for a ride on the merry-go-round in the park. Then we got some snow cones. After that, we headed home and arrived home at about 2:30 P.M.

15

Health Things

*H*ealth problems have been pervasive in our family. We all had our share, but Karen has had the most difficulty with health challenges. The kids had their usual childhood diseases and illnesses. I had ulcers and severe hay fever but have seemed to have overcome both.

Karen has suffered for many years with migraine headaches and allergies. She has had female problems and continues to suffer from debilitating irritable bowel syndrome (IBS) or some form of it. She has endured pain and continues to endure pain throughout our entire 37 years of married life. However, she never lets the pain get the better of her. She's a real trouper.

Allergies	4 Sep 1981	Karen found that she was allergic to tumbleweed, dust, and the dogs.
Bicycle Accident	11 Oct 1983	Marc crashed his bike and got an abrasion on his knee today. It almost seems like he is accident-prone.
Blindness	14 Feb 1979	I went to the optometrist today to have an eye examination and to get a new prescription for glasses. This time, instead of plastic lenses and bifocals, I will be getting monofocals and "glass" lenses. My eyesight has been deteriorating these past five years. I hope I don't go blind. My left eye could just about be classified as legally blind.

Blindness	25 Jul 1980	This morning I went to the Department of Motor Vehicles to get my driver's license renewed. I could have gotten a perfect score on the written exam, except I changed one answer from right to wrong at the last minute. My eyesight has deteriorated so badly that, this time, they are putting a restriction on my license. I will now have to wear glasses when I drive.
Bladder Infection	17 Dec 1979	Karen has come down with a bladder disease similar to the one she had when we first arrived in Florida in 1974.
Broken Nose	8 Oct 1979	Karen tells me that while she was at the supermarket, the metal gate on the grocery card fell down on Marc's nose. She said that it really bled and that he screamed up a storm. She is afraid that his nose might be broken.
Broken Toe	2 Oct 1979	Karen dropped a shutter (which she had sitting on the windowsill in the kitchen) on the second toe of her left foot and broke the toe. She has been limping around all day.
Bronchitis	22 Feb 1982	Heather is down with a bad bronchial condition. Karen took her to see Dr. Mysko today. Even Dr. Mysko was down with the flu, but he was still seeing patients.
Calories	8 Aug 1979	Tonight, Winnie (Karen's sister) made some onion dip, which we had with potato chips. Karen also baked up some cinnamon rolls. I think I gained back twice as many calories as I lost jogging earlier tonight.
Chicken Pox	27 May 1979	Marc is down with chicken pox. It started breaking out on Friday and was verified yesterday. Today, he is covered with eruptions on his skin. We have been applying Calamine lotion to soothe the pain. This morning, I got up to go to priesthood meeting. Marc had a rough night. Karen stayed up most of the night taking care of him. Marc got me up at 6:30 A.M., and I was unable to sleep till 7:30 as I had planned. Atom and I returned to the chapel about noon for Sunday school. After Sunday school, we returned home for some cake that Karen had just made per Marc's request....Karen stayed home with Marc during Sunday school. Then, for sacrament meeting, I stayed home with Marc, while Karen and Atom attended it.

Chicken Pox	28 May 1979	Marc's chicken pox is getting better; however, he has some outbreaks inside of his mouth, which has been quite painful. In the evening, we held family home evening. We made some banana splits for dessert.
Chicken Pox	29 May 1979	I gave Marc a bath tonight and was very careful to wash him ever so softly so that I wouldn't irritate his chicken pox sores. He seems to be healing well. In a couple more days, the sores should be dried up. Poor guy, he surely has had his share of illness in the short three years he has been with us.
Chicken Pox	30 May 1979	Marc is recuperating well from his chicken pox.
Chicken Pox	1 Jun 1979	Marc has almost fully recovered from his chicken pox, and Puffy is well on her way to recovery from her foot ailment.
Chicken Pox	6 Jun 1979	Atom wasn't feeling too well tonight. He didn't eat any dinner because he said that he had a stomachache. I hope he isn't coming down with the chicken pox.
Chicken Pox	8 Jun 1979	Well, Atom did come down with the chicken pox last night. So, he didn't go to school today and will probably miss the last week of school for the year. That's too bad because he may miss the school party on the last day, next Friday. We hope he will pull through before next Friday so that he can go to school the last day. His class all made individual get-well cards for him, which he really appreciated.
Chicken Pox	9 Jun 1979	Atom is still down with the chicken pox and has broken out with a bunch of skin ruptures over his body. He is really itching badly and is finding it quite difficult to refrain from scratching.
Chicken Pox	10 Jun 1979	Since Atom is still down with the chicken pox, I stayed home with him while Karen and Marc went off to Sunday school.
Chicken Pox	3 Oct 1981	Heather is down with the chicken pox.
Chicken Pox	4 Oct 1981	Heather really has very bad chicken pox. She has broken out all over her body with red spots. Karen is putting calamine lotion on the spots to reduce the itching.
Chicken Pox	6 Oct 1981	Heather is still suffering from the chicken pox.

Chicken Pox	7 Oct 1981	Heather is finally starting to get over her chicken pox. She has scabs all over her body. Poor thing.
Chicken Pox	9 Oct 1981	Heather's chicken pox scabs are drying up and falling off. We think she will have a big scar (hole) on her face above the side of her mouth, where one of the poxes got pretty bad because she scraped the scab off a couple of times when she rubbed it against her blanket.
Chicken Pox	11 Oct 1981	The boys and I attended our Sunday meetings today. Karen stayed home with Heather, who is still recuperating from chicken pox. Atom bore his testimony in Fast and Testimony Meeting today and did a good job.
Cold	11 Nov 1981	Karen is down with a cold or maybe the flu. She has a cold blister on her lip.
Cold	26 Jun 1984	Karen is down with the cold again. It seems like she forever is sick with something or another. I think she really needs to improve her bowel movement regularity. I'm sure it is contributing to her migraine headaches, colds, overweightness, poor complexion, and her many other maladies, aches, and pains. She has got to improve her diet, exercise, and regularity. Karen definitely has premenstrual syndrome (PMS). She also has TMJ, allergies, and poor menstrual cycles. She feels she might even need to have a hysterectomy. That might solve her female problems. But I really think most of her problems stem from her irregularity. She goes for 3–4 days at a time between bowel movements. I get a headache and ill if I went for a day without a bowel movement. In fact, I move my bowels two to four times a day. Nothing stays inside of me very long. I guess that is why I don't get sick very often.
Concussion	22 Sep 1981	When I got home, I found that Marc had fallen off a human tree formed by Chris Wood, Atom, and himself about five minutes before. Marc had a big bump and strawberry over his right eye. He was no doubt suffering from a concussion because he started to throw up later in the evening. Brother Dave Fretz came over, and we administered to Marc....Marc missed his soccer practice today because of his mishap.
Concussion	23 Sep 1981	Karen took Marc to the doctor today after an almost sleepless night watching over Marc. It was diagnosed that Marc really had a concussion. He is resting up and is recuperating fast.

Croup	31 Oct 1982	I failed to mention that Karen stayed up with Heather for most of the night last night. In the early morning, she took Heather to Henry Mayo Newhall Memorial Hospital for some tests and found that Heather had croup.
Croup	23 Oct 1983	Heather got sick last night with the croup, and so Karen stayed home with her today.
D&C	8 Nov 1984	I took Karen to the hospital this morning for douche and clean (D&C) surgery. It went well. I took her in at 11:00 AM and picked her up at 3:00 PM. Karen needs to be in bed for 24 hours, and she needs to take it easy for four days.
D&C	9 Nov 1984	Karen is recovering today. She can't keep herself in bed as the doctor ordered. She is always doing something, e.g., cooking, washing clothes, talking on the phone, washing dishes, etc. Then, she gets a little pain and has to lie down. I don't know what I'm going to do with her.
D&C	12 Nov 1984	Karen is bleeding where she had her D&C surgery. I tell her to call the doctor, but she says she'll wait and see for a day or so first.
D&C	20 Nov 1984	Karen has been recovering pretty well from her D&C surgery. She is now in the process of making some Christmas arts and crafts stuff.
Dental Work	22 Apr 1980	I went to the dentist today to have a temporary cap put on my upper left front tooth. Three weeks from now, I will be going back for the permanent crown.
Dental Work	15 May 1980	I went to see Dr. Carter today who put on a permanent crown on my upper left front tooth. I rather regret getting a crown put on. It was just fine when I just had a filling in it before. At least I could bite down in apples, etc. Now, I am afraid to do that in fear of the crown coming loose.

Exercise	15 Feb 1979	Atom and I started jogging tonight. We ran around the block. It is about one-third of a mile, I think. Lately, I have been feeling tired and sluggish. I think my body was telling me that I had better start exercising and getting into shape before I have a heart attack. For the last 10 years, I really haven't been getting much exercise. My body feels like it is atrophying away. So, tonight I bought myself a $17 pair of jogging shoes and wool socks. I hope I will be able to keep up on a sustained running program indefinitely. I know if I can get into the habit I will start to feel better and even may enjoy running. Atom says that he will run with me every day.
Exercise	23 Feb 1979	Well, I had better get some sleep since it is already midnight. In the morning, at about 8:00 A.M., I plan on going down to the track at Golden West College to clock myself at running the (I think) 1–1/2-mile run. Tim Greaves, our ward welfare chairman, will be clocking the times of all of those members of the ward who show up between 8:00 and 10:00 A.M. He will do this once every three months to measure the progress of each participating member in our ward-jogging program. I think he is doing a great job on this program.
Exercise	24 Feb 1979	I got up at 8:00 this morning and went with Atom to the Golden West College track to jog with Tim Greaves. Atom did about three laps, and I did five. My five laps came to a total of 1.25 miles since the track is 440 yards around. I did the five laps in 12 minutes, which is fairly poor. But, because of the bad physical condition I'm in, I consider it pretty good. I was able to make the five laps without stopping or walking. Tim will be clocking us every three months to see how we improve. I plan on keeping up with a sustained jogging program.
Exercise	22 Jan 1981	During the day, Karen played racquetball with some of the Relief Society sisters for two hours. She was sore all over. I told her, "Wait till tomorrow." She will get up with nothing but aches and pains.
Exercise	28 Jan 1981	I tried on the new sweat suit that Karen had bought me in hopes that I would start jogging to get in better physical shape. Boy, do I need the exercise.

Exercise	8 Mar 1981	After we got home, I played with the kids for a while giving them flippies, horsy back, etc. It was good exercise for me.
Exercise	21 Mar 1981	Karen and I went to play racket-ball from 4:00–5:00 P.M. in Valencia....It was my first time playing racket-ball, and Karen beat me all three games. I am so badly out of shape that my whole body aches now, and I have blisters all under my toes.... I bet I will get up in the morning stiff as a board. Karen is a pretty good racket-ball player.
Exercise	27 Dec 1982	We got up this morning about 8:00, and all five of us plus Apricot went jogging around the block. Before that, however, Atom led all of us in calisthenics. After our jog, Karen fixed us breakfast. She made me an omelet with ham, cheese, and mushrooms. It was good.
Eye Infection	18 Dec 1983	Karen's eye looked pretty bad with infection today. But, by the evening time, it started to improve.
Fever	1 Sep 1983	Heather was sick today with fever that went up to 104.5 degrees F. Bro. Sam Davis dropped by, and we administered to Heather.
Fever	2 Sep 1983	Heather was sick all night and all day today. She is still not out of the woods tonight....Atom stayed at home to baby-sit Heather while we were gone. We had a very enjoyable evening at the McKeons' home.
Fever	3 Sep 1983	Heather was still sick all day today. She still ran a fever. Looks like Karen will have to stay home from Church to watch her tomorrow.
Fever	4 Sep 1983	Heather and Marc were sick today, and so Karen stayed home from Church to watch them.
Fever	5 Sep 1983	Heather is still sick and has run a fever for four days now. This is the worst sickness she has had in her short four years on this earth thus far. I think she will be well by tomorrow.
Fever	6 Sep 1983	Heather is still sick but seems to be getting better this evening.
Fever	7 Sep 1983	Heather is pulling out of her illness. Her fever is gone. Now, Atom and I have come down with a slight touch of the flu. Karen is the only one thus far that has come out unscathed.

Flu	26 Dec 1979	Heather has the flu today. She is running a 102-degree fever. Karen took her to the doctor for an examination. Heather has vomited several times and has had diarrhea. Looks like Atom may be coming down with the flu too. Tonight, he threw up. I spent much of the day and evening reading. I also spent a lot of time holding Heather today. It seem as though Heather is less fussy when we are holding her close to us. I sure hope I don't come down with the flu also. I simply cannot afford to get sick. Maybe if I think positive enough, I won't come down with it.
Flu	28 Dec 1979	Tonight we went to visit the Billimorias in Culver City....I thought Heather was doing so well all day. However, at the Billimorias', she barfed a couple of times. Therefore, it seems like Karen will have another rough night watching Heather. For the past couple of nights, Karen slept in a sleeping bag on the floor in Heather's room.
Flu	20 Jul 1982	Karen was really sick with the flu, so I gave her a blessing.
Flu	21 Jul 1982	Karen is feeling better today. She just rested a lot today. The neighbor kids did something real nice for Karen. They all chipped in to buy Karen a dozen carnations. It cost them around $15.00. To my understanding, it was an original idea of little Don Moody. He got his brother, Kenny, Marc, and the Illera kids to chip in. Little Don Moody and Eric Illera also helped Karen out today by vacuuming out the swimming pool. That was very nice of them.
Flu	5 Aug 1982	Karen, Atom, and Heather got home about 10:00 A.M. Heather had a 106-degree F fever, as she was down with a flu virus. Karen took her to the doctor. Her fever had come down to the 100–103-degree level.
Flu	6 Aug 1982	Heather is getting well. Her fever is gone, and she has been running around today like she had not been sick at all.
Flu	29 Oct 1984	Today, I fought off the flu along with a terrible headache and diarrhea–the runs.
Foot Problems	6 Nov 1981	After dinner tonight, I took the kids shopping at K-Mart and Save-On Drug. I went to buy some vitamins and to fill a prescription for Karen. Karen has some problems with her arches now.

Hand, Foot, and Mouth Disease	26 Jun 1979	Marc came down with hand, foot, and mouth disease. I wonder what else he will be coming down with in the future.
Hand, Foot, and Mouth Disease	27 Jun 1979	Marc is still suffering from his hand, foot, and mouth disease. He is also coughing, which means he might also be coming down with the cold.
Hand, Foot, and Mouth Disease	28 Jun 1979	Atom also came down with the hand, foot, and mouth disease. I really hope Karen and I don't catch it. It is quite contagious, so we are told by the doctor.
Hand, Foot, and Mouth Disease	29 Jun 1979	Marc is recuperating rapidly from his case of the hand, foot, and mouth disease. However, Atom is still suffering from it.
Hand, Foot, and Mouth Disease	30 Jun 1979	Marc has just about fully recuperated from the hand, foot, and mouth disease, but Atom is still suffering from it.
Hand, Foot, and Mouth Disease	1 Jul 1979	Since the boys still had the hand, foot, and mouth disease, I stayed home to baby-sit them while Karen went to fast and testimony meeting and Sunday school. Marc is beginning to eat well and play well too. He is definitely well on his way to recovery. Atom is feeling better also. He ate something today, which is a marked improvement over the past two days.
Hand, Foot, and Mouth Disease	2 Jul 1979	Marc is just about totally recuperated, and Atom is getting better with the hand, foot, and mouth disease.
Hand, Foot, and Mouth Disease	3 Jul 1979	Marc is totally well from the hand, foot, and mouth disease, and Atom is well on his way to recovery. Karen's getting closer to delivering the baby–only four weeks left to go!
Hand Injury	26 May 1984	Karen went to work today and fell down and hurt her hand.
Hay Fever	16 Apr 1979	My nose ran like a water faucet again today. This hay fever of mine is really bad. One of these days I may have to go see an allergist to see what can be done about alleviating this annoyance.

Hay Fever	18 May 1980	This morning our entire family attended the morning general session of the Southern California Area Conference at the Pasadena Rose Bowl. It was an enjoyable meeting even though the sun was very hot, and I was suffering from another hay fever attack. I sneezed, my eyes watered and itched, my nose ran like a faucet, and I'm sure I was running a temperature. I had three handkerchiefs, which were sopping wet from my running nose. I took a hay fever pill but to no avail. It just made me feel tired and sleepy. After the session was over at noon, we went back to our car, sat under a shady tree, and ate a baked chicken lunch (picnic) that Karen had prepared. Then we went home. I slept the hour on the way home. Then I went directly to bed and slept for six more hours till 8:00 P.M.
Hay Fever	31 Aug 1980	I suffered all day with a bad hay fever attack. It came on when I powdered Heather while changing her diaper. I must be allergic to Johnson's baby powder.
Hay Fever	24 Sep 1980	I have been suffering from hay fever all week with running nose, sneezing, itchy eyes…the whole works. Today, I had a splitting headache all day. I finally was able to get rid of it by taking an Excedrin tablet. Prior to that, I took two Tylenol tablets but to no avail. But the Excedrin really did it for me.
Hay Fever	5 Oct 1980	I went to bed early because I had taken a couple of hay fever pills during the day, which made me drowsy and sleepy.
Hay Fever	12 Oct 1980	My nose ran like a water faucet all day. The smog in Southern California has been extremely bad over the past two weeks. And I have been suffering from hay fever constantly over that period of time.
Hay Fever	19 Sep 1981	I had a bad hay fever attack again today.
Hay Fever	2 May 1982	I have a terrible hay fever attack today. My nose is running like a water faucet.
Hay Fever	23 May 1982	I had another bad hay fever attack today. My nose ran like a water faucet, and I sneezed like crazy. My eyes watered and itched. The smog and pollen counts were pretty bad this weekend.

Headache	18 Aug 1980	We didn't have FHE (Family Home Evening) tonight because Karen was suffering from another of her bad sinus headaches.
Headache	13 Oct 1980	Karen went to see Dr. Mysko today because of the bad migraine headaches she has been having over the past couple of weeks. She has also been running a fever and has had a couple of cold blisters on her lips. Dr. Mysko prescribed some pills for her to take. If things don't get better, she might have to get some surgery done to correct the situation. Right now, she has some infected sinuses. This bad smog we have been having the last couple of weeks has really been taking its toll on us. My hay fever has really been acting up over the past couple of weeks.
Headache	22 May 1981	Karen is suffering from a bad headache tonight. She is trying to stay off headache pills and is finding it quite difficult.
Headache	11 Jun 1981	Karen is suffering from another migraine headache.
Headache	13 Jun 1981	Karen had another migraine headache again today. At Atom's baseball game, the wind really blew and kicked up a lot of dust. I think that had something to do with bringing on Karen's migraine headache.
Headache	5 Jul 1981	Karen is suffering from another one of her migraine headaches today.
Headache	15 Aug 1981	Karen went to the hospital to get some tests done to determine what is causing her severe migraine headaches.
Headache	26 Aug 1981	I had a splitting headache this evening. It was so bad, I hit the sack from 9:00 P.M. until this time (10:50 P.M.). But it finally went away, and I now feel decent again.
Headache	26 Jan 1982	Karen has been down today with a severe migraine headache, which started at about 10:00 this morning.
Headache	20 Mar 1982	Karen and I attended an adult dinner-dance at the Stake Center tonight. We paid $20 for our tickets. The dinner was Greek food, which was interesting. We only danced a couple of times before we left for home about 10:00 P.M. Karen had a severe migraine headache all day today. It got worse after our first dance, which was a fast one.

Headache	21 Mar 1982	Karen is feeling a lot better today. Her migraine headache has diminished to a regular headache.
Headache	4 Jun 1982	Karen has a bad migraine headache from going out to Edwards AFB yesterday. It was quite windy up there, and the tumbleweed, ragweed, etc. were really in the air. That caused her allergies to really react last night.
Headache	9 Jul 1982	Karen went to a specialist to find out what causes her daily headaches. It seems that her jawbones are out of whack, and she has arthritis in her jaws. So, she will be going on a soft diet over the next few weeks so she doesn't chew hard food. She will also receive treatments to alleviate the arthritis.
Headache	11 Jul 1982	The kids and I attended our three Sunday meetings. Karen stayed at home because she had a severe migraine headache caused by being emotionally upset because Puffy had to be put to sleep yesterday. Karen has taken Puffy's passing quite hard.
Headache	13 Aug 1982	This morning between 9:30–11:30, I went to Karen's doctor's office where I met her (Karen) for lessons on physical therapy for her headaches. I was taught the various methods of massaging her neck, shoulders, and back. We also learned some neck exercises.
Headache	16 Nov 1982	Karen is on her fourth day of severe headaches.
Headache	8 Aug 1983	I've had a splitting headache today. I think the lack of exercise, crouching over this typewriter all day, the hot weather, and these tight pants all contribute to the stress on my neck, head, and brains. I'll live through it. It can never be as bad as those migraine headaches that Karen has almost every day, 24-hours a day.
Headache	4 Sep 1983	Karen has had another of her bad migraine headaches all day today. She has been popping a lot of aspirin, but it has been to no avail.
Headache	30 Mar 1984	Marc came home from school early today because he had a bad headache. He seems to get frequent headaches. He reminds me of myself when I was a boy. I used to get frequent headaches too.
Headache	15 Jun 1984	Karen has been suffering from a severe migraine headache again today.

Headache	12 Jul 1984	Karen went to a Relief Society Board meeting tonight. She is still suffering from a severe migraine headache. I am going to have to get her out of this valley.
Headache	13 Jul 1984	Karen is suffering from her continuous migraine headache again today. She said that when she went to the beach, it went away. I guess I am going to have to move her to the beach.
Headache	28 Aug 1984	I forgot to mention yesterday that Karen started therapy on her headaches. The therapist massages her head, neck, and shoulder areas. She really was in pain after the session. She will be going to the therapist on a weekly basis.
Headache	29 Aug 1984	Karen went to the therapist again today and had her muscles worked over. She stubbed her toe on a door today and nearly took her large toenail off. She is in real pain now. It seems like she is always so illness and accident-prone. If it isn't one thing, it's another. Sometimes she is such a klutz. I do believe she will always be experiencing some kind of pain or another. She thinks she is another biblical "Job." Poor, Karen.
Headache	4 Oct 1984	Karen went to her physical therapist today. She has been suffering from a migraine headache so severe that she didn't attend her Stake Welfare meetings tonight.
Hiking	7 Mar 1981	I went on a seven-mile hike with Atom and his Webelos den. Emerson and David Snider came up from Orange County to go along with us so David could meet his Father-and-Son hike requirement too. It was the best exercise I had in years. Boy, am I exhausted! I'm sure I will feel the muscular aches and pains on Monday morning.
Hysterectomy	4 Apr 1982	At 12:30 P.M., Karen and I went over to the McKeon's home, where the bishop and I administered to her. I did the anointing, and Bishop McKeon gave the blessing. Karen received from her doctor a preliminary test result, which indicated that she may have uterine cancer. She will be going in for a biopsy this coming Thursday to determine whether it is benign or malignant and whether or not she will have to have a hysterectomy.
Hysterectomy	14 Apr 1982	Karen will be going in for her tests tomorrow. She has been worrying so much about it all day that she worked up a headache.

Hysterec-tomy	27 Nov 1984	Karen went to the doctor for an examination today and found that her female organs are all messed up. She may need a hysterectomy within two years. I hope that solves the out-bursts she has every so often. Something has got to change with her health so we can get back to living normal, happy lives. It's a good thing I am calm, cool, and collected. Ha! Ha!
Illness	16 Aug 1982	Karen is down with some kind of illness again. She has been running a high fever all day. She either has strep throat or mononucleosis. She went to the doctor today and had a throat culture taken. She won't know for a couple of days as to exactly what she has.
Illness	8 Oct 1984	Heather is really sick again. She's beginning to be like her mom–always sick. I think part of her problem is she always kicks her blanket off at night and, consequently, gets cold in the morning hours. Plus that, she eats like a tweety bird. I really don't think she gets enough vitamins and minerals by the little amount of food she intakes every day. She is tiny and skinny as a rail. She has got to start eating more good food.
Jamie Illera	28 Jan 1981	By the time I got home, it was 5:45 P.M. The entire family was not home. I found out later that they had taken Jamie Illera (the little boy next door) to the hospital because he practically cut his finger off when he slammed it in his door.
Karen Falls III	1 Apr 1981	Karen fell ill today and is now in the hospital. Apparently, she either has a uterine infection, a tumor, or a ruptured cist on her uterus. They (the doctors) will be doing some tests on her in the morning to find out exactly what is wrong. I am taking care of the kids tonight. Tomorrow, they (the kids) will be staying with Chris Moody, across the street, while I go to work for about six hours. We will have a team visiting from Japan tomorrow. That's why I have to go in to work. If not, I would stay home and watch the kids as I probably will on Friday.

Karen Falls III	2 Apr 1981	Because we had a team from the Shinko Electric Company (of Japan) visit us today, I had to go into work for about six hours. I dropped some things off at Henry Mayo Hospital for Karen this morning at 9:00 A.M. before going in to work. I left the three kids with Chris Moody across the street. I got home at about 3:45 P.M. to pick the kids up from the Moodys. At about 4:30 P.M., I took the kids with me to visit Karen at the hospital. After that, we went shopping for groceries at Von's Supermarket. Then I came home and cooked dinner. Karen had some tests done on her today. The verdict is that she tore some muscles in her abdomen playing racket-ball or doing aerobic dancing, which resulted in a blood clot. Karen should be able to come home tomorrow. I'll be staying home from work tomorrow to watch the kids. It has really been a hassle taking care of the kids while Karen has been in the hospital. Thank goodness Atom has been such a help to me. Without his assistance, I would really be in a frenzy.
Karen Falls III	3 Apr 1981	I didn't go in to work today because I had to take care of the kids. In the morning, I fed the kids breakfast, cleaned the house, washed the dishes, washed some clothes, bathed and dressed Heather, and got ready to pick Karen up at the hospital. Atom did most of the dishwashing, vacuuming, and cleaning up. Marc helped with some vacuuming. Atom and Marc fixed their beds. Atom fixed our bed also. At about 11:40 A.M., I dropped the kids off at the Billimorias and then proceeded to the hospital to pick Karen up. We got home at about 12:30 P.M. After that, we had the casserole that Sister Nena LaBass had brought over. Later in the evening, Sister Robin Davis brought over a German chocolate cake for dessert. I spent the entire evening loading and unloading the washer and dryer. I also did some reading and studying.

Karen Falls III	4 Apr 1981	I got up at about 9:00 this morning. I was busy all day washing clothes, cooking, etc. Atom washed Princess with Eric III-era. He also went to Eric's baseball game today. Brother Roland LaBass came over, and we administered to Karen. In the afternoon, the boys and I went shopping at Safeway for more groceries. I spent $13.00. I spent some time doing some homework in preparation for class on Monday. The Billimorias brought over spaghetti sauce for dinner tonight. Atom is a big help. He cooked up the spaghetti tonight. He also washed and put away the dishes. He stacked up the newspapers in the garage, cleaned up Princess' dump in the backyard, and even cooked some eggs for breakfast. I gave Heather a bath, and Karen dressed Heather. Karen also folded up the tons of clothes we washed today. Because I had to stay home and take care of Karen and the kids, I missed going to the telecast General Conference Priesthood Meeting at the Stake Center. I may also miss the sessions being shown on television at the Stake Center tomorrow.
Karen Falls III	5 Apr 1981	I rolled out of bed about 9:00 this morning. We watched the General Conference on television from 9:00–11:00 A.M. Don Moody, from across the street, brought over a fruit tree, which we planted in the corner of our backyard. In the afternoon, we went for a ride up through Agua Dulce. It is really nice out there. I wouldn't mind moving out there. The Gratrixes dropped over for a visit in the later afternoon. Sister Ann Damon (later became Wallace) brought over a complete roast beef dinner, which we enjoyed thoroughly. In the early evening, Nena LaBass dropped over for a visit. Karen seems to be recuperating in fine fashion. I will be going to work tomorrow, so I put Atom in charge of taking care of his mother.
Karen Falls III	7 Apr 1981	Karen is getting better.
Karen Falls III	12 Apr 1981	I came home to pick up the boys to return for our Sunday meetings. Karen and Heather stayed home because Karen is still recuperating from her hematoma.
Laryngitis	25 Mar 1982	Karen is sick again and probably has laryngitis. She has a frog voice.

Laryngitis	26 Mar 1982	Another enjoyable thing is that Karen still has her laryngitis. Everyone is teasing her because she can't talk as loud and as much as she usually does. Even though, she does pretty well for someone who supposedly can't talk.
Lice	10 Jan 1983	We also found out that some of the Snider kids had lice when they came over to visit us this past Saturday. So, Karen gave each of us a scalp treatment with some medicine she bought from the drug store. She also gave Apricot (our dog) a treatment.
Lice	24 Jan 1984	Marc was sick today and stayed home from school. He had also picked up three lice in his hair from someone at school. Karen washed his and Heather's hair out with lice shampoo and also washed all of his bedding. I think we got it all before it multiplied.
Miraculous Recovery	20 Sep 1980	We got a call from our baby sitter who said that Marc was sick and crying. After we got home, Karen gave Marc some aspirin, and he went to sleep. By about 10:00 P.M., Marc seemed to have made a miraculous recovery as he was running around as if he wasn't sick a couple of hours earlier.
Miraculous Recovery	8 Mar 1981	During the sacrament meeting, however, Marc started to run a fever again, so I took him home. I gave him a couple of baby aspirins, put an ice rag on his forehead, and put him down for a nap. By the time the rest of the family came home, Marc's fever had subsided sufficiently that he started running around and playing again.
Mumps	2 Jul 1980	The illness Karen has been experiencing the past couple of days has turned out to be the mumps!
Mumps	5 Jul 1980	Karen is just about over with the mumps. Heather looks like she now has it.
Mumps	6 Jul 1980	Karen and Heather stayed home because of their mumps.
Nose Bleed	4 Jun 1981	Heather and Marc were jumping on the bed, and Heather hit her nose on the wall causing her nose to bleed. Fortunately, I don't think she broke her nose.
Overeating	15 Aug 1979	I overate at dinner earlier tonight and am presently suffering from an upset stomach. That should teach me to be more sparing at mealtimes.

Pigging Out	29 Jun 1979	I headed for the La Fiesta Restaurant in Hawthorne where many of the people in our department were attending a luncheon birthday party for John Ellison. It was a Mexican restaurant with delicious Mexican food. I really enjoyed it, but oh am I suffering tonight! I seem to be reacting from the hot peppers in the food. My stomach is aching. That's what I get for making such a pig of myself.
PMS	16 Oct 1984	I worked in my office all day today preparing for my visit to GDC-San Diego tomorrow. Karen was really sweet today and typed up 43 Form B's for me to turn in tomorrow. She also went to the doctor for a checkup on her female organs. The doctor thinks she has premenstrual syndrome (PMS). I could have told him a long time ago that that is what she has. All the symptoms point to it. He will be giving her some prescription drugs to counteract it. I hope it works because every month, just before her period, she turns into a wild woman and throws everything at me including the kitchen sink. This PMS also probably is contributing to her severe migraine headaches. I hope this is the solution. Heavens knows, she has tried every doctor and every treatment you could think of to get rid of her migraines. We'll keep hoping and praying that we will find the cure some day soon.
Pneumonia	3 Nov 1982	Heather has pneumonia. She is still running a fever off and on.
Pneumonia	4 Nov 1982	Heather is still recuperating from pneumonia.
Pneumonia	6 Nov 1982	The way Heather has been so mischievous today, I do believe she has overcome her pneumonia.
Pneumonia	7 Nov 1982	I gave Marc a blessing this evening for his flu. Heather is just about fully recovered from her pneumonia.
Pneumonia	8 Nov 1982	Marc and Heather are well on to recovery from their illnesses.
Pneumonia	9 Nov 1982	Marc is pulling through his illness. Heather is totally well.

Sinus Infec-tion	18 Jun 1982	Karen is down with a sinus infection. It seems like if it isn't one thing (she is sick with), it is another. I hope, some day, she gets fully well. We sure seem to keep the doctors in this town in the money.
Smashed Finger	10 Oct 1983	Marc smashed his finger in a folding chair today and ran in the house crying. Karen fixed it up pretty well. For a while there, it looked like Marc may be losing a fingernail. Time will tell.
Stitches for Heather	12 Apr 1982	Heather fell off the toilet and hit her chin on the corner of the basin counter. She received three stitches for that mishap.
Stitches for Heather	17 Apr 1982	Heather's cut chin is healing well. Her three stitches should be removed in the next few days.
Stress	8 Jul 1979	Trying to raise a family, working on a pressing job, going to school two nights a week and studying whenever I can on an MBA degree, and getting the Young Men Program organized as young men president has really put me under great stress lately. Plus that, with a new baby arriving in three to four weeks, this will add even more stress to a presently stressful situation. I think if I can make it through the next few months, I will have been able to survive the test that the Lord has placed me in to grow.
Stress	16 Jan 1984	I spent the entire day and evening working in my office typing letters and working on the SBA proposal. I don't know if I am going to finish this one on time. I am so exhausted. My back is starting to ache me. It must be the stress.
Sun Stroke	30 May 1981	Karen and the kids worked in the yard all morning while I was gone to the Church peach farm. Marc must have gotten sun-stroke. He has been sick all day and evening with a fever. He has also thrown up and has been complaining about being chilled. I hope he gets well by tomorrow.
Tetanus Shot	3 May 1984	Karen is still running her severe migraine headaches. Marc had a tetanus shot yesterday, which he is suffering the effects of all day. The day before, he had cut himself with a rusty saw blade. Therefore, to preclude lockjaw, we took him to the doctor for a tetanus shot.
TMJ	27 Aug 1982	Karen went to her orthodontist today and got some splints for her teeth to help alleviate her TMJ condition.

Torn Foot Ligaments	15 May 1982	After breakfast, we went to Marc's game. Marc's team won by a score of 19 to 13. At the game, Karen tripped in a hole in the ground and tore some ligaments in her foot. She is now limping around. If it's not one thing, it's another.
Ulcers	10 Apr 1980	I'm writing in this journal for Robert to tell of the last six days. On Thursday, April 3, he came home and passed out and was bleeding from his nose, mouth, and rectum. He (I took him) went to the emergency room at the hospital (Henry Mayo Newhall Memorial in Valencia). They said that he had a bleeding ulcer. He was going to come home on Sunday, April 6, (Easter) for four hours, but when we went to pick him up, he passed out in the bathroom and chipped his front tooth. Needless to say, he didn't come home. They hooked him up to the IV and gave him a blood transfusion in the middle of the night. Fortunately, he does not need surgery. He came home on Wednesday, April 9, and has to rest for one week before he goes back to the doctor to be checked. After that, he may go to work in another week. When he is a little better, he can write more of the details and his feelings about it all. I know I was really scared but am thankful he is all right. (by his wife, Karen)

| **Ulcers** | 16 Apr 1980 | It has been a week now since I left the hospital. Today, I went to see Dr. Mysko to get a checkup to see when I could return to work. I am recuperating well, and he tells me that I can return to work next Wednesday (April 23, 1980). |

We picked up the exercycle Karen bought for me so I can get some exercise and work off the stress after I come home from work. I feel pretty good and can't wait to go back to work. However, Dr. Mysko feels that I should rest for two weeks after getting out of the hospital before going back. I am getting a lot of rest, watching a lot of TV shows, and catching up on a lot of reading.

So far, I haven't been called to a position in Church yet. Thank goodness; with the stress of my new job and my present illness, it would have been too much.

Traveling 140 miles per day for four months between Westminster and Valencia for 3 to 3.5 hours a day in heavy traffic really took its toll on me. In addition, I was carrying nine semester hours in graduate school at the California State University at Northridge added to the pressures. Since we moved to Canyon Country on March 1, 1980, the traveling pressures went away. Now, since my collapse from bleeding peptic ulcers, I have dropped completely out of school.

My new job (of which I have been holding for the past 5–1/2 months) as program manager of about a half dozen Boeing programs is extremely challenging and enjoyable. However, it is a really high-pressure, high-stress job. The customer pounds us on the head and shoulders every day with panics. We are past due on a lot of hardware deliveries, which has caused them to press us for critical hardware that is holding up the rollout of airplanes.

All I have to do is to learn how to deal with the stress and not keep it all inside, where it starts to eat up my stomach. I am now on a bland diet and taking Tagamet, Mylanta, and iron tablets. In a couple of days, I will be starting on an exercise program using my exercycle and perhaps jogging and calisthenics.

Ulcers	17 Apr 1980	I went to the dentist today to fix my chipped front tooth. When I was in the hospital, the doctor gave me permission to come home for four hours on Easter Sunday. While I was getting ready to come home, as I was urinating in the restroom, I passed out because I was still weak from loss of blood. I guess I must have hit my teeth on the toilet bowl as I was falling to the floor. Needless to say, I was not allowed to come home that day. Once before, I had a cavity filled on my front tooth. I really think part of that filling was knocked loose and fell out. We were going to put a crown on the tooth, but we didn't get an okay from the insurance company to get it done. So, we just had it filled. However, by the afternoon, we were informed that the insurance company would pay for the crown job. So, we will be scheduling it for next week some time.
Ulcers	30 Dec 1981	Bob had to go to the doctor for his bleeding ulcer. He's very weak and has to go to the hospital the next day for tests. (By Karen Uda)
Ulcers	31 Dec 1981	Bob went to the hospital for tests, and it showed his ulcer was bleeding. He was admitted because his blood count was down to 8.9. (By Karen Uda)
Ulcers	1 Jan 1982	Bob was very sick today. His blood count was down to 7.9. The doctor said it was serious, and they gave him a blood transfusion. (By Karen Uda)
Ulcers	2 Jan 1982	Bob is doing better today. His blood count is up to 9.3. The doctors feel he might be able to go home on Sunday. He's very grumpy. He must be getting better. (By Karen Uda)
Ulcers	3 Jan 1982	I went to the hospital today, and they said Bob could come home today. He was really happy about that. The Dale Sutherlands (Bonnie), the Jack Gratrixes (Sharon), Bill Hatch, Caroline Weaver and her son Brad (all from the Church) came to see Bob today. Also, the Wallaces (Jim and Ann) came to visit. On Friday the 1st, the Bishop (Monte McKeon and Kathy) and his wife came to visit. On Saturday, Brother Jack Gratrix, Brother John Houck and his son John, and their Native American Indian son, Ambrose, visited Bob. On Thursday and Friday, Bob's good friend, Billy Billimoria, came to visit him and spent several hours with him on Friday. (By Karen Uda)

Ulcers	4 Jan 1982	I did not go to work today because I am recuperating at home from my bleeding ulcer condition. I am getting better and hope to go back to work next week. Karen has been feeding me a bland diet. It's not that bad, since Karen prepares pretty good meals. I am spending my days taking notes for my thesis project and watching television. I spent the entire morning sleeping…till noon.
Ulcers	5 Jan 1982	It was another day of R&R from work. I worked on my thesis research for most of the day. Roger Pascoe called, and we had a nice chat. I called Willadean Bryant in the late after-noon to find out what was going on at work and to give her some instructions. Pat Teigland dropped off my work mail at our house after she came home from work. I spent some time in the evening catching up on reading all of my mail. I am feeling fine and am well on my way to recovery.
Ulcers	6 Jan 1982	I went to see Dr. Mysko today. My blood pressure was normal at 108/80, and my blood count had risen to 11.2! He told me that I could return to work on Monday. Sister Bradford brought over a delicious chicken dinner for us tonight. The gravy on the chicken and the potato with cheese and sour cream were absolutely scrumptious. I spent the entire day and evening working on my thesis research. I also had a call from my secretary, Willadean Bry-ant, and spoke also to Roger Pascoe.
Ulcers	7 Jan 1982	I spent the entire day and evening today working on my thesis research and doing my Social Science Research final exam. In the afternoon, Willadean Bryant called to inform me about my mail and about what went on at work today.
Ulcers	8 Jan 1982	I spent the entire day reading and working on my Economics final exam.
Ulcers	9 Jan 1982	I spent the entire day working on my Economics final exam. Tomorrow is our ward conference. I will be giving about a 5–7-minute talk on the 1981 accomplishments and 1982 goals of the High Priests Group.
Ulcers	10 Jan 1982	I will be returning to work tomorrow. Thank goodness. This laying around being sick is the pits.

Ulcers	27 Jan 1982	At the end of the day, I took off from work at 3:50 P.M. to make a 4:15 P.M. doctor's appointment for a checkup on my ulcer condition. I'm healing well. In about two weeks, I will have another blood test to see how much my blood count has improved. My weight is now back up to 159 pounds. My blood pressure is normal.
Ulcers	11 Feb 1982	I went to Miller Laboratory at 9:00 A.M. to have some blood taken from my arm for a blood test to determine my blood count.
Ulcers	4 Mar 1982	I went to Henry Mayo Hospital to take the stomach probe test to see if my ulcer was healed. It was! Dr. Nelson conducted the test after administering ether (anesthesia) to me.
Ulcers	16 Nov 1983	I spent the evening working in my office. My stomach is beginning to ache. I hope my ulcers are not acting up again. I have been under a lot of stress and strain lately.
Ulcers	6 Dec 1983	My ulcers have been acting up lately. I have been feeling pain and have been taking a lot of Mylanta tablets. I think all the stress is beginning to take its toll on my stomach. I have got to start relaxing. If I would win a contract soon, that will relieve a lot of the pressure.
Uterine Condition	20 May 1982	Karen had surgery today to treat her uterine condition.
Uterine Condition	25 May 1982	Sister Kathy McKeon had brought over dinner because Karen had started bleeding again. Every time she feels a little better, Karen does some work and gets worse. I don't know if she'll ever learn. She bled on Saturday also.
Vision	13 Nov 1984	I'm going blind. My eyesight is really going blurry. I hope I do not go totally blind. I cannot drive anymore without my glasses on.
Vitamins	4 Mar 1981	Atom and Marc are down with colds. Karen seems to be pulling through on her cold. I'm thankful that I have been healthy. I think that my taking vitamins every day has something to do with it.
Wisdom Tooth Removal	6 Aug 1982	I stayed home this morning to watch the kids while Karen went to the oral surgeon to pull her last wisdom tooth. She is really in pain now.

16

Miscellany

This is my catch-all chapter. All of those journal gems that did not fit neatly within any of the previous seven chapters are included in this chapter. Note that this book covers only the first decade of my three decades of journal writing. My next two sequel books will cover the next two decades. Life is great!

Air Condi-tioning	8 Apr 1983	It was another miserably hot day today. Karen set the thermostat at 85 degrees F. It gets so hot in this house that when the air conditioner kicks on and cools the house down to 80 degrees F it feels pretty comfortable!
Artist	11 Jun 1979	Marc is really becoming quite an artist. Already, at three years of age, he can draw pictures of dinosaurs.
Award for Karen	1 Jun 1979	Karen received a DeMille School Certificate of Recognition (Volunteer Award) for unselfish dedication in helping the children of DeMille during this past school year. She served as a room mother and went in every Friday to assist the teacher in teaching the children. The certificate was signed by Principal Hodge Hill.
Baby Sitting	25 Oct 1979	Tonight, while Karen attended the Primary in-service meeting, Todd Blan baby-sat Atom and Marc. This was his first time ever at baby-sitting. Karen paid him $2.00 for the two hours he baby-sat the boys. The boys liked him. Karen said that Todd told her that if all kids are like Atom and Marc, he would be glad to baby sit often. I'm glad this was a good first experience for him.

Billy Billimo-ria	26 Sep 1979	Billy Billimoria called me at work today. He told me of a new girlfriend he met a few weeks ago. Her name is Denise Miller. She is a divorcee with an eight-year old daughter. For these two facts, Billy appeared apprehensive about a possible binding relationship. But I told him that these things shouldn't hold him back if they are compatible in all other respects.
		Billy is concerned about what his parents and relatives would think and say because divorce is looked upon unfavorably in India. I told him that they won't have to live with her, but only he will. And if they get along well, then it is okay. From the way Billy spoke about her, I think he is crazy about her and vice versa. I think this girl might be the one to haul him to the alter. I told him that I would talk to Karen about setting up a date when we could have Billy, Denise, and her daughter over for dinner with us.
Billy Billimo-ria	7 Oct 1979	Billy Billimoria, his girlfriend Denise Miller, and her daughter Angie surprised us at about 12:00 noon today. They had come down here planning on surprising us at church today. But, because of General Conference and since we didn't have Sunday school today, they were surprised instead. When they got to the chapel, to their surprise, nobody was there. So, they came over to our home and surprised us there. We were all dressed casually since sacrament meeting was not till 6:00 P.M. We had an enjoyable afternoon meeting with them.
		Angie is eight years old and got along really well with Atom and Marc. I think Denise is the one for Billy. She is a pretty, blond woman, 28 years old. We made a dinner date to have them here on Saturday, 27 October 1979, at 6:00 P.M. Karen cooked up a spaghetti lunch, which we all enjoyed. After they left about 4:00 P.M., we started getting ready for sacrament meeting.
Billy Billimo-ria	19 Oct 1979	Billy Billimoria called me at work at about 4:45 P.M. today. It seems as though everything is going real fine with him and Denise Miller. It seems like they are going to get married before the year is up. I think they will make a really fine couple.

Billy Billimo-ria	10 Dec 1979	I left for home at 6:15 because Billy Billimoria, Denise Miller, her daughter Angie, and her mom were going to be over for a visit. We had a good visit with them until 10:30 P.M. We discussed the plans for their wedding, which will take place this coming Friday. Karen baked some cookies, candy, and gingerbread.
Billy Billimo-ria	14 Dec 1979	Because I was to serve as best man at Billy Billimoria and Denise Miller's wedding, I left work for home at 2:30 P.M. After arriving home at 3:55 P.M., I took a shower and dressed in my blue, three-piece suit. At about 4:30 P.M., we headed for Billy's apartment in Culver City. We arrived there at about 5:20 P.M. Then, Billy and I went to pick up the flowers and Angie, who was at Lee Ann's apartment where the reception took place. The wedding was held at a local Methodist church. Atom and Angie served as ring bearers. Karen sang a duet with another lady. Billy was so nervous the entire evening. Only after the reception did he begin to calm down. Mike Hadley flew in all the way from Florida to attend the wedding. I was able to meet a lot of Billy's coworkers at Hughes and Denise's friends. By the time we left for home, it was about 10:45 P.M. Angie came home with us to spend the weekend until Billy and Denise returned next Monday evening from their honeymoon at Lake Tahoe.
Billy Billimo-ria	24 Dec 1979	Because we were having the Billimorias over for dinner tonight and Puffy, our dog, was really beginning to smell, I gave her a bath this afternoon. Karen bought two hamsters for Angie's Christmas present. The Billimorias arrived at about 6:15 P.M. and stayed till 10:00 P.M. We ate a delicious dinner that Karen had pre-pared. The main course was some chicken rolls, which had boned chicken wrapped in a roll mix and baked in the oven. The Billimorias brought gifts for all the kids and a magazine rack for Karen and me. Billy was going to show us the mov-ies of their wedding, but he misplaced the cord, so we won't be able to see it until the next time we go and visit them (which may be New Year's Eve). We spend part of the evening playing with our electronic game on our TV. It was a most enjoyable evening. I must have been quite exhausted because as soon as they left, I hit the sack and was quickly sound asleep.

Birthday	1 Aug 1982	Today was my 40th birthday. I can hardly believe that I am four decades old, two score years old!
Book Gift	3 Sep 1984	Sister Brockbank came back from Utah today and gave us a really neat book on the writings of the Prophet Joseph Smith.
Boutique	7 Nov 1981	Karen was at her boutique all day today, so I baby-sat the kids. Karen did really well at the boutique, which was held at a school in Newhall. Karen's booth grossed over $1,200. She personally grossed over $500. Toni Awai made about $500. And Chris Moody made over $200. I'm glad it was a success. Karen sold everything except a couple of items.
Choates	3 Jun 1982	I left work at about 2:00 P.M. today to go home to pick up the family to drive to Edwards AFB (Air Force Base) to visit the Choates, who are visiting California on TDY (temporary duty). John Choate is attending a seminar at Edwards AFB for three days. Gretchen (his wife) and their four children (Mark, Molly, Beth, and Amy) are also here. We visited with them from about 4:30 P.M.–7:15 P.M. I hadn't seen the Choates for about eight or nine years. John and I attended the University of Oklahoma (OU) together. I used to live at his house, where I rented a basement room during 3–1/2 of my 5–1/2 years at OU.
Cleaning	8 Aug 1983	Karen cleaned out all of her drawers in the kitchen. The garage looks decent now since Karen and Atom cleaned it, and the mounds of dirty clothes are finally being washed and put away (Karen says one of her greatest downfalls is doing the laundry such that she gets ahead of the game). And all this is being done because my parents and the Pearces are coming from Utah to visit. We should have houseguests more often!
Earning Money	9 Jul 1979	Atom watered the garden this morning and again this evening. I gave him a quarter for each time he watered it.
Earning Money	10 Dec 1983	Atom mowed the Hatches' lawn today and made $6.00 for two hours of work. They really overpaid him. They will spoil him if they continue to pay him so well.

Electric Razor	7 Jan 1980	Karen's dad, Glen Rowland, came in to LAX (Los Angeles International Airport) today. Karen went to pick him up at about noon. Grandpa Rowland will be visiting with us for about two weeks. He brought a whole bunch of gifts for everyone in the family. I received an electric razor, which is really neat. Now I can shave while driving to work!
Entrepreneur	11 Jun 1979	Atom has decided to become an entrepreneur. He is planning on holding "Atom Uda's Garage Sale" from 9:00 A.M. to 2:00 P.M. on Saturday, June 30, 1979. He prepared a flyer to be handed out to his friends. He will be selling his old toys, books, cookies, and Kool-Aid.
Entrepreneur	12 Jul 1979	Atom distributed some of his fliers to advertise his upcoming garage sale this Saturday. Karen said that Johnnie Cutrell was really impressed when she found out that Atom is putting on this sale all by himself. It shows the kid has business sense.
Entrepreneur	14 Jul 1979	Atom held his garage sale. He sold his old toys and books. He also sold some balloons, cookies, and punch. All in all, he made a total of $4.59.
Entrepreneur	1 Oct 1983	Marc and Kenny Moody made a refreshment stand in our front yard and sold Kool-Aid and candy. They made about $1.50.
Friends	15 May 1984	In the evening, Karen and I were treated by the Pringles to a Chinese dinner in China Town–L.A. It was really great. After the dinner, we went to Marie Calendars in Valencia and bought a chocolate pie. We brought it to our house, had it as dessert, and enjoyed about an hour of conversation. The Pringles are a great couple to have as good friends. We sure appreciate and enjoy their friendship. Atom baby-sat Heather and Marc while we were away.
Fussing	24 Aug 1979	Karen just got up and turned on the TV. She is up with Heather, who had been fussing. This is not normal, for Heather is usually a quiet baby. Well, she has got to have her moments sometimes.

Grandma Wallace	6 Jul 1982	In the evening, between 7:30 and 8:30 P.M., the whole family went to Sister Wallace's 79th birthday party. I hope I am as "young" as Shirley Wallace when I get to be 79 years old. She is such a delightful, energetic lady. Everyone calls her grandma Wallace. I really admire her and hope that she stays with us for a long, long time.
Grand-mother Passes Away	28 Mar 1984	Karen went to work but came home early in the evening because she was suffering from a migraine, which was no doubt brought on from hearing the news this morning of her grandmother passing away.
Howard & Phil's	12 Oct 1983	I worked in my office all day today. Karen went for a job interview at Howard & Phil's and felt pretty good about it. She thinks they will offer her the job, which pays only $3.90 per hour. But it will provide some food on the table.
Howard & Phil's	15 Oct 1983	Karen found out today that she got the job at Howard & Phil's.
Howard & Phil's	17 Oct 1983	Karen was offered another job by Candy Felt to work in the Granada Hills store of Howard & Phil's. So, she quit the Canyon Country Howard & Phil's job before even starting.
Howard & Phil's	20 Oct 1983	Karen went to work her first day at Howard & Phil's in The Valley. She said that she was really exhausted and had a splitting headache from working so hard. She also said that she now has a special appreciation for those who have to work all day for a living. Looks like she learned something valuable today. I had a splitting headache today too from driving for over six hours in the car.
Howard & Phil's	10 Dec 1983	Karen went to work today and sold over $2,000 worth of goods. She is now about 60 percent towards her monthly goal before she starts receiving a bonus. She found out today that last month she was the most productive worker when comparing sales generated per hour of work. She did about $105 per hour. Today, she did about $200 per hour!
Howard & Phil's	31 Dec 1983	This was New Year's Eve. Karen worked from 9:00 A.M.–7:00 P.M. She sold about $1,400 worth of goods today. Her total for the month over her goal was about $8,200. She did exceptionally well this month on commissions.

Howard & Phil's	6 Jan 1984	Karen went to work today. This evening, she received an offer from Dave Fretz to work for him up in this Canyon Country store when he takes over as manager. He offered to increase her wage from $3.35/hr to $3.75/hr. I told her she should take it.
Howard & Phil's	16 Mar 1984	Karen went to work today and sold $681 worth of goods. We found that she was the top salesman for the month of February. Karen really is an excellent salesperson.
Howard & Phil's	6 Apr 1984	Karen went to work, and they were "ripped off" by a couple of men. They came into the store, stole some jackets, and ran off. However, Karen and the other women got their car license number, so I imagine the police will apprehend them.
Howard & Phil's	7 Apr 1984	Karen worked all day today. This was her last day at the Howard & Phil's store in Mission Hills. On Monday, she starts at the Canyon Country store. It will be a lot better. She will be closer to home. The drive to and from work will be only five minutes one-way instead of 25 minutes. There will be a much lesser gasoline bill and less wear and tear on her car. There are many pluses in her coming to the store up here. She found out tonight that she was the top salesman in the company for March. That made it two months in a row! I really think retail sales may be Karen's vocational calling.
Howard & Phil's	9 Apr 1984	Karen went to work for the first day at the Canyon Country branch of Howard and Phil's, and she sold $219 worth of goods. She said the total store took in only about $450 the entire day! She said that April and May are usually bad months for the total company.
Howard & Phil's	1 Jun 1984	Karen worked this evening from 5:00–9:00. Their store came in #1 of all the Howard & Phil's Stores for the month of May. That was the first time that has ever happened in the time they moved to that location. Karen had a lot to do with that happening.
Neighbor, Great	9 Mar 1984	Chris Moody brought over a triple-decker chocolate and white layered cake. It is so huge; I don't think we will be able to eat all of it. She always does nice things for us. She is a great neighbor. I wish there were a way for us to baptize their entire family. They sure would be good Mormons.

Neighbor, True	12 Mar 1984	Chris Moody gave us a delicious rice casserole and Jell-O salad for dinner tonight. She is a really neat, thoughtful neighbor–a true neighbor.
Nighthawk	5 Jun 1979	Atom and Marc watched "The Six-Million-Dollar Man" on TV. After the movie was over (which was at 8:00 P.M.), I had nighttime prayer with the boys and then put them down to bed. Atom usually goes to sleep within five minutes. But Marc is a nighthawk like me. He usually lingers for about an hour before falling asleep.
Peanut Butter Cookies	19 Aug 1979	Atom got a recipe from Sis. Smith, his Sunday school teacher, on how to make peanut butter cookies. All the batter consisted of was 1-cup peanut butter, 1-cup sugar, and 1 egg baked at 350 degrees F for 8 minutes. They weren't bad! And I thought you needed to put flour in the batter to bake any kind of cookies. I learned something for today.
Pillow	25 Dec 1979	For Christmas, I received a copy of the new *Holy Bible* published by the Church of Jesus Christ of Latter-day Saints, three pairs of socks, and a pillow. I tried sleeping with the new pillow, but found it difficult to get used to. So, in the middle of the night, I switched back to my old reliable, soft pillow. I guess it's going to take a while before I can be weaned from my old pillow.
Potty	21 Jul 1979	As usual, I went to bed about midnight. But before doing so, I usually take Marc to the potty. He normally can't make it through the night without wetting the bed. Plus that, he is still too young to get up in the middle of the night by himself and go to the bathroom.
Records	23 Dec 1979	I spent the time between the end of Sunday school and the beginning of sacrament meeting separating, organizing, and categorizing the personal letters we have received from people over the last five years, which I have been accumulating. I feel these letters will come in handy for historical purposes.
Relatives, Visiting	6 Mar 1984	We took Karen and Heather to LAX for an 11:05 P.M. United Airlines flight to Cleveland, Ohio. Marc cried and even Atom's eyes started to tear. Karen and Heather will be visiting her dying grandmother, her family, and friends over the next eight days. I think this trip will be a little tough on Marc. We arrived home from LAX at about 11:45 P.M. I hope they have a safe and enjoyable visit with friends and family.

Relatives, Visiting	7 Mar 1984	Karen and Heather made it okay to Ohio. They are staying at her sister's (Winnie Rausch) home. Tomorrow, they will be visiting her mom and grandmother in Circleville.
Relatives, Visiting	9 Mar 1984	Apricot is really missing Karen and Heather. She feels so lonely. Well, Karen and Heather have been away for three whole days now, and we all sure do miss them. Mark especially misses his mother.
Relatives, Visiting	11 Mar 1984	Karen called in the morning while I was at the chapel. She talked to the boys for a few minutes. Fortunately, it is only three more days before we will see her and Heather. We sure do miss them a lot. It will be really nice having them home on Wednesday evening.
Relatives, Visiting	13 Mar 1984	Karen and Heather will be home tomorrow. Yeaaaaah!
Relatives, Visiting	14 Mar 1984	We found out that Karen and Heather's flight out of Cleveland was delayed because of fog. Instead of TWA flight #137 coming into LAX at 11:41 P.M. tonight, it will be arriving at 1:35 A.M. tomorrow. The ticket desk clerk said that they couldn't and wouldn't tell us whether or not Karen and Heather were on that flight. We will find out after we get there, and only when and if they step out of the plane. Sounds like a really raunchy system to me. I put the boys down for a two-hour nap at 10:00 P.M. We will leave for LAX around 12:00 midnight.
Relatives, Visiting	15 Mar 1984	I have been sleepy all day today because by the time Karen and Heather came in last night, it was 1:30 A.M. We got home at about 2:45 A.M. By the time we went to sleep, it was around 3:15 A.M. I got up at 8:15 A.M. to get ready to go to Santa Fe Springs.
Scalped	4 May 1984	I got a haircut today. In other words, the barber scalped me today! My hair is quite short.

Thanksgiving	22 Nov 1984	Today was Thanksgiving Day. We Udas certainly have a lot to be thankful for to our Heavenly Father for bringing us through the past year and four months. I am much indebted to Heavenly Father for helping me build our company. I know, with His continued help, we will grow a lot more next year. We spent the day with the Sniders and Jagers in Orange County. The feast that was prepared by Ann Snider, Shannon Jager, and Karen was great. All 17 of us gorged ourselves. We left there around 9:30 PM and arrived home around 11:00 PM. Apricot was really happy to see us as usual whenever we return home from going anywhere.
The Real World	18 Apr 1984	Karen took the kids swimming today. She also went to work and got to the point of almost quitting because the assistant manager got mad at her and used foul language to her. She is finally finding out what the "real world" in business is all about.
Uncle Kelton Uda	24 Dec 1979	In the mail, the three kids received $10.00 each for Christmas from Uncle Kelton Uda. I got the two boys to write thank you letters, and I wrote one for Heather since she is only 4–1/2 months old.
Weeding for Dollars	17 Jun 1980	In the evening, the boys weeded the back yard for a penny a weed. They picked over a thousand weeds. Atom and David earned $4.00 each and Marc earned $2.50.
Who's Who	13 Nov 1984	Today, I received an invitation to be listed in *Who's Who in Frontiers in Science and Technology*, 2nd Edition. It was only last week that I was invited for listing in *Who's Who in Finance and Industry*, 24th Edition.

About the Author

Robert Takeo (Bob) Uda was born in Hawaii and raised there for the first 20 years of his life. He is the third of seven children of Masao and Irene Kuualoha Uda (both deceased). In the 43 years since leaving Hawaii, he has lived in Oklahoma, Ohio, Florida, Connecticut, and California with short stints in Utah, Alabama, Massachusetts, Texas, and Washington. He has traveled in 46 of our 50 states as well as in Canada and Mexico.

Bob has earned BS degrees in aerospace engineering from the University of Oklahoma and in general business from Regents College of the University of the State of New York (now called Excelsior College). Furthermore, he earned an MS degree in astronautics from the Air Force Institute of Technology and an MBA degree from the University of La Verne located in La Verne, California.

Bob currently serves as president and principal consultant of Bob Uda and Associates (BU&A), a San Marcos, California, consulting firm in proposal development, counterterrorism R&D, and career coaching. He is also owner of Buda Books Publishing (a subsidary of BU&A), a firm that writes and publishes non-fiction books. Further, he serves as director and vice president of the International Technology Institute (ITI).

Bob has over 30 publications including eight books. As an adjunct faculty lecturer, he teaches "Career Development" in the College of Business Administration (CoBA) at the California State University at San Marcos (CSUSM). He taught "Writing and Publishing" as an instructor in the Osher Lifelong Learning Institute (OLLI) Program at Cal State San Marcos Office of Extended Studies. Furthermore, he taught logistics graduate students as an adjunct faculty member of National University.

He is a fellow in the British Interplanetary Society, associate fellow in the American Institute of Aeronautics and Astronautics, Certified Manager with the Institute of Certified Professional Managers, and a founding charter member of the Association of Proposal Management Professionals.

He is listed in 46 Who's Who-type publications including *Who's Who in the World, Who's Who in America, Who's Who in Science and Engineering,* and *Who's Who in Finance and Industry.*

In his church, The Church of Jesus Christ of Latter-day Saints, he has served on the stake level as stake executive secretary, stake clerk, stake high councilor (4 times), stake mission president, 1st counselor stake mission presidency, stake young men (YM) president, and stake employment specialist.

On the ward level, he has served as bishop (2 times), 1st counselor bishopric (2 times), 2nd counselor bishopric (2 times), ward executive secretary (3 times), high priests group leader (3 times), 1st assistant in the high priests group leadership, 1st counselor elders quorum presidency, ward YM president (4 times), and 2nd counselor YM presidency. He also served as 2nd assistant Sunday school superintendent, ward activities committee chairman, gospel doctrine instructor, ward scout committee chairman, and ward employment specialist. Bob currently serves as bishop of the Palomar Ward (young single adults) in the Escondido California South Stake.

An avid journalist, Bob has prepared 32 journal volumes covering the past 30 years and over 6,500 handwritten pages. He is over half way through with volume 33. Of those 30 years, he has written daily in his journal for the past 26 years. He knows journaling; he loves journaling; he has a passion for journaling; and he has a strong testimony of journaling.

Bob and his wife, the former Karen Elizabeth Rowland of Circleville, Ohio, have sired two sons, a daughter, and four grandchildren. You may contact Bob Uda by e-mail at <u>bobuda@adelphia.net</u>.

Index

978-0-595-37118-1
0-595-37118-3